Educational Philosophy of Madan Mohan Malaviya

Dr. Sunita Singh
Assistant Professor
Department of Education
University of Delhi

ATLANTIC
PUBLISHERS & DISTRIBUTORS (P) LTD

Published by

ATLANTIC

PUBLISHERS & DISTRIBUTORS (P) LTD

7/22, Ansari Road, Darya Ganj, New Delhi-110002
Phones: +91-11-40775252, 40775214, 23273880, 23275880
Fax: +91-11-23285873
Web: www.atlanticbooks.com
E-mail: orders@atlanticbooks.com

Printed & bound in India by Atlantic Print Services

Foreword

The work of Dr Sunita Singh is based on the thesis submitted for the degree of doctor of philosophy of Banaras Hindu University. It studies the educational philosophy of Mahamana Pt. Madan Mohan Malaviya who was a great patriot, nation lover in his right—Philosopher, advocate, teacher, educationist, politician, and moderate leader of incomparable lucidity. Malaviya was a man of multifaceted activity; and his thought and character left a profound effect on the generations. The value of Dr Singh's work lies in the fact that she deals comprehensively with the educational philosophy of Malaviya and its social and philosophical foundations; the concept, aims, and objectives of education; Malaviya's ideas about social, political, economic, and religious education; and the role of education in promoting communal unity and nation understanding. The work also attempts to compare Malaviya's education philosophy mainly with M.K. Gandhi, R.N Tagore, and Sir Syed Ahmad Khan; and finds it not only compared in-depth with originality and systematic way but writing also reflects contradiction approach. Indeed, no philosophy has been above criticism of all kinds.

The philosophy of education is a branch of philosophy that deals with the nature of man and his culture; and the totality of humanity's achievement is called culture which consists in the development of the powers residing in man to a farm expressing the density of man. Whatever education means, it is at least cultivation of the power to think in an orderly and comprehensive way in the continuous pursuit of a given theme to a meaningful end. To make a knowledge-based society it is important to go through techniques of science and technology and, at the same time, there is a need to add quality wisdom which adds flavour, order, and measure to knowledge and makes itself manifest in the application of knowledge to human needs. We are told that we are living in a period of crisis unequalled in history and, to my mind, it is the symptom of our failure in the present age, to achieve unity and balance of knowledge which is filled with wisdom. A philosophy of education should answer the question: How can we hope to obtain wisdom, the wisdom which is meaningful in our own time and how the two great branches of human knowledge the sciences and humanities can be blended in the minds of individual man and woman so that they can discover a community of thought which can lead them out of the darkness and the confusions oppressing all mankind?

I am glad to recommend this work to students and teachers of education, as well as to teachers in general and members of the learning community.

Justice Giridhar Malaviya
(Retd.)

Acknowledgements

This book is an outcome of the cooperative efforts, directly or indirectly, of different people who showed immense faith in me. As a learner, I feel highly obliged to all of them.

With a sense of deep gratitude in my heart to an omnipotent, omnipresent, and omniscient Lord Krishna, whose blessings and grace made me what I am today, I desire to thank that Almighty wherever He is. I am highly grateful to Indian Council of Philosophical Research (ICPR), New Delhi, for providing the required funds and administrative support for the publication of this book.

I wish to place, on record, my extreme thankfulness and profound regards to my supervisor, Prof. Parmanand Singh Yadav, for his scholarly guidance, constant suggestions, and valuable opinion which helped me in a great deal to bring perfection in this research work which has been expressed in the form of a book. His image of a great motivator and a positive attitude towards all aspects of life will always remain a source of inspiration to me.

I am highly grateful to Prof. H.C.S. Rathore, Head and Dean, Faculty of Education, BHU, for providing motivation and all helpful resources related to this research work. I would like to thank my co-supervisor, Dr. Ajit Rai, for his valuable suggestions when I was in phase of completion of this book.

I am thankful to Prof. G.C. Bhattacharya, for his help of varied nature. At this juncture, I would like to put on record my special heartfelt and grateful thanks to Prof. Harikesh Singh, Prof. B.D. Singh, Prof. R.P. Shukla, Prof. S.K. Swain, Dr. Sunil Kumar Singh, Dr. Anjali Vajpai, Dr. Minakshi Singh, Dr. Seema

Singh, Dr. Ajay Kumar Singh, and all other faculty members who helped in completion of this work.

I am thankful to Prof. Ram Pratap Singh, Officer on Special Duty, Rajiv Gandhi South Campus, BHU, who motivated me for completion of this research work. I consider it to be my misfortunate that he is no more to see the publication of this book. I express my gratitude to all other teachers and staff members, students of Rajiv Gandhi South Campus and Faculty of Education for their cooperation. My thanks also extended to the staff of Department of Education library, University of Delhi, for providing me required library facilities.

I gratefully acknowledge my sincere thanks to all research scholars at Faculty of Education, BHU. Lastly, I would like to thank all those whose names have not been mentioned here but helped me at various stage directly or indirectly in this task. My thanks are also due to Former ICPR director, Prof. R.P. Shinha and Programme Coordinator, Prof. Shashim Dubey, and present Programme Coordinator, Dr. Saroj Kanta Kar, who have not only allowed me to publish this work but also have extended their assistance in various ways for arranging its publication. I am also thankful to Prof. R.P. Singh and Prof. Pankaj Arora who have taken personal interest in the publication of the book and shared their experience of publication. I am also thankful to Justice Giridhar Malaviya who has been kind enough to write the foreword for this book in spite of heavy engagements.

I owe my sincere gratitude to my parents and my dear Scholars Rashmi Pal and Kajal whose support in completion of the work and their expectations always worked as an enduring source of inspiration to me.

It gives me immense pleasure in putting on record the cooperation, inspiration, and encouragement which I received from my husband Dr. M.B. Singh, son Suyash Vasudev Singh, and daughter Sudhiksha Vasudev Singh, without whose support this work would not have been possible.

Sunita Singh

Preface

The present work is a modest attempt to study the education philosophy of Pt. Madan Mohan Malaviya. Malaviya has made rich contribution to different aspects of the education and society, and has profoundly influenced modern higher education. The solemn words may be used for Malaviya that he is the person who had progressive ideas and a great love for the cultural heritage of India. He is a matchless public figure in the records of the modern India. His multidisciplinary selfless personality established excellence in various professions like teaching, journalism, law, politics, social, cultural, religious, and educational, with self-guiding and self-controlling manner in the pursuance of humanity. The author of this book without any claim for the scholarship and incentive felt the requirement for studying such a versatile thinker like Malaviya and has tried to critically examine the main aspects of his education philosophy. It is a critical research work in comparative perspective. In this book researcher delineates the foundation of Malaviya's education thoughts and compare them with the doctrines of some of the contemporary educational thinkers who were the visionaries of higher education in India.

This is a golden opportunity to delve into Malaviyan literature once again and to find out concretely his educational ideas, which he cherished throughout his life and to whom he gave a positive shape in the form of a great center of learning/ institutions, i.e., Banaras Hindu University, which stands today as a beacon of light and an inspiration to coming generations.

There is an abundance of literature on Madan Mohan Malaviya, dealing with many aspects of his multifaceted personality written by eminent scholars. However, there are only few books which entirely reveal his educational views.

The book includes six chapters—(1) Introduction, (2) Malaviya and His Time, (3) Philosophical Thoughts of Madan Mohan Malaviya, (4) Educational Philosophy of Madan Mohan Malaviya, (5) An Evaluation of Madan Mohan Malaviya's Educational Philosophy in Contemporary Comparative Setting, and (6) Critique and Conclusions. A critical estimate along with conclusion drawn from the discussion of the chapter has been given at the end of each chapter. The book tries to review Malaviya's philosophy of life, his educational thoughts, and the various enduring experiences he had, especially in shaping his ideals in the form of educational institutions which are ever growing and full of vitality even approx. sixty years after his death. The aim of the present book is, therefore, to focus on Malaviya's achievements and to judge how far his educational thoughts and ideas have filtered invisibly into our present-day educational system and are the part of it.

By critical comparative analysis, the author has tried to focus on the key thoughts of the contemporary visionaries of higher education, such as Tagore, Gandhi, Malaviya, and Sir Syed Ahmad Khan, who were the product of the same Indian culture and tradition, but have divergent views on the same problems of the country. The author has tried to explore the similarities and differences in these visionaries which might be because of their different upbringing, home environment, and working in different conditions. By critical analysis, these philosophers have been compared considering several aspects, such as originality, principles, aims, medium of learning, way of distribution of knowledge, and harmonization of national views.

Sunita Singh

Contents

1
Introduction

1.1 Introduction

Education is an indispensable factor in the qualitative development of life. It can be defined as the 'training of human resources in pursuing truth and practice of virtues'. Philosophy has always endeavored to find the solution of right learning and right education. The treasures of philosophy are contributed by the galaxy of philosophers, educationists and thinkers, who always thought of the building of the nation. There is a need to develop an education system based on some philosophical perspective because education and philosophy are the two sides of the same coin. The more fundamental question that needs to be asked today is about the deeper meaning of education. What is the purpose of education? What kind of human being do we wish to create in schooling? How does an educated person relate to society and the world? The predominant thrust of the modern educational system seems to be the promotion of "technocratic-meritocratic" world-view and creation of a class of people who accept rather than question, agree rather than inquiry. It is no wonder that an environment is created where docility abounds while the strength of spirit and courage of conviction falter, discipline is valued and spontaneity is resented. In a current age of globalization and consumerism, the education system has been communized. It has become a tool for a better lifestyle, power, and status. It has become market oriented with the focus of creating funds and profit. In the race of economic and technological advancement, Indian culture, values, and ethos have been cornered in the educational process, resulting in the vast erosion of human values in the current generation. There is a lopsided development of our society, which has disintegrated and turned men into robots. In these grim situations, radical change is required in the education system. In order to find the solution to the ethical crisis in the world, there is a need to go back to the philosophies of great visionaries.

No doubt philosophies are understood in one important sense as "right thinking" must precede the solution of any problem, especially moral and intellectual that affects social and economic conditions of the society. A philosophically sensitive nation can't be communalistic. It can't be consumerist or individualist or worshiper of false gods like market and money and lust for power or greed. In India, in 19th century many visionaries such as Gandhi, Aurobindo, Swami Vivekanand, Tagore, J. Krishnamurti, Madan Mohan Malaviya deeply thought on radical potential of education, who were not followers of British Education System, which imposed to create a class who may be interpreters between the British and whom they govern. Malaviya was undoubtedly one of the major stars of the galaxy of philosophers whose philosophy of education is dynamic. It mirrors every aspect of life, and problems of the society. He conceptualized harmonious, social order in such a way that the interest of self and society are not in conflict. Malaviya as a philosopher, leader, teacher, advocate, journalist, and educationist, spent his energies and life on the cause of education. Religion and ethics are the integral part of his educational philosophy. Madan Mohan Malaviya was basically an educationist whose major focus was to reform education for social change and development of Indian Society. His realistic attention was keen to grasp the idea of an appropriate educational system which can meet the urgent social and economic needs of the poor country. Malaviya wanted to make education "Universal and better". Malaviya's philosophy of education is coordinated with his conception of social welfare. Banaras Hindu University is a glorious epitome of Malaviya's idealism and realism. He combined religion and education to develop the national spirit. Religion and Science are the integral part of his educational philosophy. Malaviya was a constructive idealist with a passionate love and vision for the country. He did not believe in mere materialistic advancement that had no roots in a moral solidarity of man. Like other philosophers, Malaviya could not resist himself being influenced by the social events of his times. He was born just after four years of Indian mutiny 1857, in the year 1861, in Allahabad, which played an important role in shaping Malaviya's spiritual and academic life.

1.1.1 *Status of Education during Malaviyan Era*

Higher education achieved noticeable growth during the period between the years 1857 and 1882. The missionary raised a campaign in opposition to Indian educational policy. They wanted to have a complete hold over the educational institutions. In the year 1882, Hunter Commission was appointed and in the same year, Punjab University was established. The Allahabad University came in to existence in 1887.[1]

The beginning of the 19th century was remarkable in the history of Indian Education. It was when a sound wave of national awakening overwhelmed the country. An enthusiastic awareness and love for their culture, civilization, and literature had been encouraged in the hearts of the people. The awakening positively influenced the educational system of the country as well. The people realized that their education should have a national character. Under these situations, Lord Curzon came to India in 1899 as the Viceroy of the country. Soon after his coming, Lord Curzon planned certain one-sided reforms due to which Indian people became suspicious about his vision. It was supposed about Lord Curzon that,

> "By temperament he was a benevolent autocrat, and by training a diehard imperialistic with implicit faith in a strong rule" as mentioned by Rai (1986).

The period from 1897 to 1902 was the most dormant in the records of Indian education. During this period, two severe famines and an extensive epidemic of plague as a natural disaster influenced the economy and manpower of India. In September 1901, Lord Curzon organized a meeting to discuss the problems ranging from primary education to that of higher education, but

1. Rawat, P.L., *History of Indian Education,* Agra: Ram Prasad and Sons, 1994, p. 195.

no Indian was called at this conference. National consciousness gathered intensive momentum in Indian masses.

In 1902, the Indian University Commission was appointed by Lord Curzon. Due to the educational policy of Lord Curzon Indians were not satisfied and the sequel of the warfare between Russia and Japan had obviously proved that Asiatic civilization still commanded some position in the world.[2] It also gave much motivation to the national sentiments of the Indian people.

The Indian youth with revolutionary sentiments agitated to carry educational reforms in the country. Anti-dividing movement of Bengal had been rampant in Bengal. All this movement burst out as the Swadeshi movement in the country. The basic principle of this movement was the complete boycott of the foreign goods. Using the Swadeshi goods in place of foreign goods diverted the attention of the people towards industrial education, consequently public leaders of the country visualized plans for the spread of national education. This movement led to the establishment of an organization known as, "*The National Council of Education*".[3] The famous leaders of this movement were Sir Gurudas Banerjee, Rash Behari Ghosh, and Rabindra Nath Tagore. Next Viceroy Lord Minto-Morley tried to implant the seeds of communal discord between the two communities, i.e. Hindus and Muslims.[4]

The spread of Minto-Morley reforms occurred in 1909, which, along with legal changes in the political and social conditions, influenced the educational system of the country. A rising tide of educational reform had overwhelmed the entire country. *Gurukulas* were established for the sake of regenerating and reviving ancient Indian culture and civilization. Arya Samaj group was fully active to bring about mental and ethical revitalization in the country. The Vedic hymns chanted by the pupils in the *Gurukulas* at Vrindavan and Haridwar sent forward the message of ancient glory of India.[5] The Dayanand Anglo Vedic College was established in Lahore. National College was

2. *Ibid.*, p. 202.
3. *Ibid.*, p. 210.
4. *Ibid.*, p. 211.
5. *Ibid.*, p. 210.

founded in Calcutta, Sri Aurobindo was its first principal.[6] Shri Gopal Krishna Gokhale invited the attention of the government and public towards primary education and demanded for the free and compulsory education in 1910. Another important event was the establishment of the Muslim league in 1906.[7] Certain convinced, wealthy and educated Mohammedans with a view of safeguarding the political and economic interest of the Muslims founded this League.

So, the Muslim leaders raised campaign for the reservation of seats in the electorate at political platform, and for the establishment of separate schools and universities. Therefore, the educational atmosphere was being vitiated by communalism, which ultimately proved to be a great nuisance.

The people of both the communities understood they could not improve their generation without raising the proportion of literacy and education. Political awakening was found among the masses. The government of India increased the grant-in-aid from ₹ 40 Lakh in 1905 to 75 Lakh of rupees, and besides that they promised to pay an annual recurring grant of 35 Lakh of rupees. Therefore, the number of primary schools between 1902 and 1912 was doubled.[8] In Baroda state in 1906, compulsory primary education was introduced by the Baroda king.[9] In relation to higher education after the formation of the University Act, much improvement was to be seen in the financial position of the college of this period. Punjab University received ₹ 30,000 for the faculty of oriental learning.[10] Malaviya, a well-known politician of Indian National Congress, journalist, and popular Hindu leader worried for the sake of Hindu religion and for the country. So, he analyzed and criticized the policies made by the British Government.

Mahamana Pt. Madan Mohan Malaviya ji realized education as a single tool by which a nation attains prosperity. As in a

6. *Ibid.*, p. 210.
7. *Ibid.*
8. *Ibid.*, p. 211.
9. *Ibid.*, p. 212.
10. *Ibid.*, p. 218.

speech on financial statements in April 1904 in Allahabad, he said,

> It is now well understood that in all the countries, the happiness of the poor depends in a great measure on their education. It is by means of it alone that they can acquire those habits of prudence and self-respect from which all other good qualities spring: and if ever there was a country such habits are required. It is this.[11]

He thought education enlightens the total behavior of the individual and finally helps in the realization of self and supreme. Education enables the human mind to enjoy the contemplation of supreme Truth, Goodness and Beauty. He considered that education should have a spiritual base.

As Malaviya ji was not satisfied with the scheme of higher education so he exhorted

> Life's best lessons are not learnt in the school room. Education has done and can still do much for India but it is hopeless to expect from it alone the higher type of character. I agree with those who think that education should from the beginning be combined with religious instruction.[12]

He also contended,

> Where the true religious spirit is inculcated, there must be an elevated feeling of humility and where there is love of God there will be greater love and less hatred of man.[13]

He brought attention to the necessity of education, as it seems by his lecture during the financial statement 1904 (April in Allahabad) he said,

> We have all often heard of the ills of early marriages and overflowing population; of the savings of a life

11. Panday, R., *The Making of Malaviya*, India: Kishore Vidya Niketan, 1956, p. 122.
12. Malaviya first speech on BHU Bill. Oct. 1915.
13. Viswnath Pandey (2017). BHU, Asia's largest residential university, celebrates centenary retrieved dated 26/02/2022 https://www.thehindu.com

> squandered on some occasion of festivity; of the helplessness of the riots, which renders them a prey of money-lender; of their indifference to good clothes of houses, which have been urged on some occasions as an argument against lowering the public demands on them; and finally of the vanity of all laws to protect them, when no individual can be found who has courage enough to talk advantage of those educated in their favour; there is but one remedy for all this which is education. He wanted it by legislative support because he understood that it is more essential to provide statutory provision for adequate funds of education.[14]

So, continuously he had focused his locus of control for cause of Education and left all his earning sources such as advocacy at Allahabad High Court and started discussion with academicians, social reformers such as Annie Besant regarding establishment of Higher Education University in India which fulfill the need of Indian National Education and since 1906 to till 1916 he had worked hard for the manifestation of BHU.

After the decision of 1913, the Act of 1915 brought the Banaras Hindu University into existence and it functioned by 1917. Next to it, other universities were established in different places, viz. the Mysore University (1919), the Patna University (1917), the Osmania University, Hyderabad University with Urdu as medium of instruction (1918), and the Dacca, Aligarh and the Lucknow University (1920). Thus, the number of universities rose from 5 in 1916 to 12 in 1921. By 1937, the number of universities became 15. In Delhi (1922), Nagpur (1923), Andhra (1926), Agra (1927) universities were established. Other institutions as Bose Research Institute of Calcutta (1917), The Harcourt Butler Technological Institute Kanpur (1921), Imperial Agriculture Research Institute, New Pusa, New Delhi, Indian Institute of Science, Bangalore (1911), Indian Institute of Mines, Dhanbad (1926), Indian Women University, Bombay (1916), Vishwa Bharti (1929), and Serampore College (1918), these

14. Dar, S.L. and Somaskandan, S. (1966). *History of the Banaras Hindu University*. Varanasi: Banaras Hindu University Press, p. 381.

colleges, universities gave the education in science, vocation and industry.[15]

The Constitution of 1935 laid the foundation for independent rule in India. In 1937, a system of government known as Provincial Autonomy came into action. Literacy movement or adult education movement, education of women, rights of untouchables, and a number of other similar projects of mass education were spread with great vitality and passion.

In 1937, Mahatma Gandhi launched the scheme of basic education in Wardha.[16] In the meantime, because of the outbreak of World War II, and objection of the Indians against the government policy of interest in India to take part in the war, many Congress ministers resigned in 1939. Thus, the increasing tide of educational expansion was for the time being slow due to these situations. Afterward in 1942, the Quit India Movement burst in the country.

During the decade of 1937-47 alongside Primary and Secondary Education, other important fields of education, such as engineering and technical education, expanded. Women's education status was not as good as male education and the progress was far slower. Girls received general education and on the whole there were 41 girls' colleges in 1937, which became 91 in 1947.[17] During these dark days of political domination and adversity created by War, under Gandhi's leadership people of India started agitating for complete freedom and got freedom on August 15, 1947.

1.1.2 *Challenges of Education in Post Malaviyan Era*

The present educational system of India has been continually facing a model of change from the Ancient Aryan era to the existing Scientific era. After independence, substantial changes occurred in the political, social, and economic sphere of the country, throwing many responsibilities and challenges before the universities to provide leadership, guidance, and qualified persons in various fields of job for nation building. These

15. *Ibid.*, p. 225.
16. *Ibid.*, p. 248.
17. *Ibid.*, p. 321.

aspirations and objectives of higher education led to speedy growth of universities in the country.

In 1947, there were 27 universities, 500 colleges, with hardly 200,000 students and 15,000 faculties.[18] During the seven decades of independence of the country, now celebrating 75 years of independence and also acknowledging it as 'Azadi ka Amrit Mahotsav' and Twelve Five-Year plans were implemented to boost the process of development of the country. Many commissions and committees were established by the government as University Education Commission (1948-1949), National Education Commission (1964-1966), National Policy Education (1986), Program of Action (1986), CABE (Central Advisory Board of Education), National Knowledge Commission (2005), Yashpal Committee (2006), etc. New agencies like the UGC (1956), NAAC (1994), Indian Council of Social Science Research (ICSSR), Indian Council of Philosophical Research (ICPR), Indian Council of Historical Research (ICHR), All India Council of Technical Education (AICTE), etc. also were recognized for specific purposes like maintaining standards and quality in higher education.

In AISHE 2018-19, 944 Universities, 36,308 Colleges and 8,354 Stand-alone Institutions have uploaded the form on the portal. Out of 944 there are 46 Central University, 1 Central Open University, 127 Institutions of National Importance, 371 State Public Universities, 5 Institutions Under State Legislature Act, 14 State Open Universities, 304 State Private Universities, 1 State Private Open University, 34 Deemed University-Government, 10 Deemed University-Government Aided, 80 Deemed University-Private. Institutes of National Importance which include AIIMS, IIMs, IIITs, IISERs, IITs and NITs in India.[19] In 2016, Govt. of India initiated the planning of Draft New Education Policy to meet the changing dynamics of the population requirement with regard to quality education,

---

18. Prakash, V. (2012), Universities need to become knowledge power houses. *University News*, 50 (23), 19.
19. AISHE Report 2018-19. Retrieved from https://www.education.gov.in/sites/upload_files/mhrd/files/statistics-new/AISHE%20Final%20Report%202018-19.pdf

innovation and research aiming to make India a knowledge superpower by equipping its students with necessary skills and knowledge to eliminate the shortage of manpower in Science, Technology, Academia and Industry. The five pillars proposed in NEP (2020) are accessibility, equity, quality, accountability and affordability. This vision of NEP 2020 was a reflection of Mahaman's Views as he wanted the youth of India to benefit from an integrated education that incorporated modern scientific knowledge, practical training, ethical standards and the study of arts. His vision was to impart the meaningful education for rural students regardless of caste, creed, region and religion to those for whom it had earlier been a mere dream.

From the last decade there has been extraordinary growth seen in higher education, which has inspired growth of private entrepreneurship and private bodies will cheerfully establish the institutions needed. Conversely, it will be quite difficult to manage the growth of private universities. Experiences and observations of higher evaluating bodies show that many private bodies establishing institutions for higher education in the country are just money minded, business minded. People who are keen to harvest more income by investing small money with no promising quality education or to fulfill the national goals. So, the first challenge will be to keep out such fewer quality educators from the educational system. Another challenge in front of higher education will be to select qualified faculties and administrators. Another challenge will be corruption during the affiliation of private colleges, business in appointment of teachers, administrators, and other faculties in the universities.

According to Suma (Education road map article 2013),

> At present 70% of the graduates from the technical stream and 85% from the general stream are unemployed. Scores of positions in industry, in government and other sectors of employment lie vacant for want of suitably qualified personnel. So, by this data, there is a serious mismatch between what educational institutions produce and what the market needs. Higher education becomes an industry to produce degree to graduates by

> which they cannot fulfill the market or society needs and become rejected because the quality of their education is not as par the market needs.[20]

It is a common fact that with the growth of institutions of higher education, although enrollment has increased in the country, the overall quality of higher education has fallen down. Today, cognitive skills and the ability to think independently and creatively are not sufficiently developed by the degree courses provided in higher education institutes. As a result, degrees and diplomas are only certification, not the meaning of practical knowledge. Thus, while Indian higher education tries to run with worldwide society, even the best institutions such as the IITS, IIMs are not equivalent to world class. Not a single university of India has made its place on the list of the top 200 universities across the globe.[21] Therefore, today's great challenge is to know why the general standard has been declining so rigorously, and how it can be lifted out. In India, although the Right to Education Act came in status from 2009, the condition of secondary and primary education is not so excellent, so there is a need to give proper shape to the backbone of higher education, i.e. secondary and primary education. Therefore, it would be in the center of attention of policy makers that quality school education is accountable for raising the quality of higher education.

Today people face chaos in culture segments, lack of completeness in professional degree courses to fulfill the market needs, alarming growth of social evils, degradation of human values, fragmented humanity and a missing link between Indian culture and scientific and technological advancement. Indians behave like middle-class families that are running behind the Western culture and education hastily trying to become modern while forgetting or ignoring age/old/rich/Indian human values, which has caused enormous varieties of problems hindering the individual development and of the society as well. The commoditization of education has occurred in the present age of

20. Chitnis, Suma, "Bharat: Bhavisya ki Shiksha Mahasakti", Yojana, Sept.2013, p. 7.
21. QS World University ranking report

globalization. It is increasingly being realized that the defects of the present educational system will be removed. It is not related to the ideals and actions of an educated person. It is alien to life and creates more problems in the metaphysical domain than solving problems of the materialistic world. The problems related to violence, corruption, crime, and unrest are increasing by leaps and bounds. The modern man has failed to face the meaning and purpose of life. Values are being preferred over virtues. Man has become self-centered, narrow minded and greedy; education is dividing the people and society more rather than uniting them. The modern paradigm is based on reductionist and mechanistic principles; it promotes a fragmented and limited world view.

It was felt by the author that there is a missing link in the present educational system due to blind race towards material prosperity. In order to find the causes of missing links in education, the author studied the educational philosophy of Pt. Mahamana Madan Mohan Malaviya in a contemporary comparative setting. The educational philosophy of Tagore, Gandhi, and Sir Syed was chosen for comparative critical study. In order to know the relevance of Mahamana's Educo-philosophical thoughts for higher education and social welfare, this book entitled, *Educational Philosophy of Madan Mohan Malaviya* was chosen for the extensive and detailed discussions.

This is not only a book which only offers Malaviya's perspective on education or his educational philosophy but a large number of studies has been completed such as Rai (1986), Krishnadatta (1989) sadly Markandey and Krishnadatta did not take full account of Malaviya's educational work but their research reveals sociological importance of Mahamana thoughts. Shrivastav (1992)[22] finding states Malaviya and Bhagwan Das's social thoughts in a comparative setting. Panday

22. Srivastava, A., "Mahamana Malaviya Evam Dr. Bhagwan Das ke Samaj Darsan ka Adhyayan", Ph.D. Thesis Depart. of Philosophy and Religion BHU, Varanasi (1992).

(1992)[23], Tripathi (1996)[24], Chandra (2002)[25], Sneha (2007)[26], Singh (1992)[27], Abhudaya (2007)[28] have studied the educational, philosophical views of Malaviya ji on Hindu Dharma Hindi, politics and higher education, respectively. Besides above research, other philosophical works of Malaviya ji reviewed to know the trend of his philosophical thoughts such as Raghavan J.A. (1984)[29], study was followed by analytical exposition and critical appraisal of Sri Aurobindo's educational philosophy and outlined the practical steps that needed to be adopted in the present context. In Paul, R.'s (1976)[30] study, the ideas of Tagore were critically analyzed, organized and evaluated regarding art as a medium of education. Along with this Abhyankar (1987)[31], Panday (1985)[32], have studied the educational thoughts/ contributions/philosophy of Swami Vivekanand, philosophy

23. Panday, J.B., "A Comparative Study of Educational Philosophy in Gita and Koran", Ph.D. Edu., Kum. Uni. (1985).
24. Tripathi, U., "Madan Mohan Malaviya Kai Shakashik bicharo ka adhayan Va Unki adunik kall mai upadaiyta", Ph.D. Thesis Sampurnanand University, Varanasi (1996).
25. Chandra, S., "Mahamana Pt. Madan Mohan Malaviya aur Hindu Dharma", Ph.D. Thesis, Depart. of Philosophy and Religion BHU Varanasi (2000).
26. Sneha, "Politics of Language and Identity in Higher Education: Pandit Madan Mohan Malaviya and the establishment of BHU", Ph.D. Thesis School of Social Science, JNU, New Delhi (2007).
27. Singh, K., "Pt. Mahamana Ka Hindi Mai Yogdan", Ph.D. Thesis Department of Hindi, BHU, Varanasi (1992).
28. Abhudaya, Premchand, "Ek Mahan Siksha Sastri ke rup mai Madan Mohan Malaviya ke vicharo ka Adaayan", Dissertation study BHU (2007).
29. Raghavan, J., "A Critical Study of Sri Aurobindo's Contribution to Building of Modern Indian Philosophy of Education", Ram Manohar Lohia Avadh University (1984).
30. Paul, R., "Art as a Medium of Education" in Tagore, Ph.D. Phil., Osm. University (1976).
31. Abhyankar, S.V., "A Comprehensive, In-depth and Critical Analysis of Swami Vivekananda's Educational Thought and its Philosophical Foundations with Special Focus on Value Education in the Context of Nuclear and Space Age 'Global Value Crisis' and the Need for Value Education in India Today", Ph.D. Edu., Poona Uni. (1987).
32. Panday, J.B., "A Comparative Study of Educational Philosophy in Gita and Koran", Ph.D. Edu., Kum. Uni. (1985)

of Gita and Quran, respectively. Some of the contemporary research work and books related to Mahamana Madan Mohan Malaviya such as Singh (2017)[33], Tiwari (2009)[34], Gajrani and Ram (2009)[35], Prasad (2013)[36], Jyoti (2014)[37], Mishra (2015)[38], Kumar (2018), etc. discussed contribution of Mahamana Madan Mohan Malaviya in education. Some authors such as Tiwari (2009) wrote more books on Mahamana's biography and inspiring episodes on Mahamana. Some books such as Dar and Somaskandan (2007) book on *History of Banaras Hindu University* and Parmanand (1991) *Mahamana Madan Mohan Malaviya: An Historical Biography* created more interest in author because those books give insight about primary resource collection related to Mahamana.

The above-mentioned researchers have used different methods such as historical, library research, descriptive, logical, comparative, and content analysis. An exhaustive survey of related literature reveals that there are many studies carried out on Madan Mohan Malaviya's Educational Philosophy, but there is not a single study where comparative and critical analysis of Malaviya's educational thoughts are done with other contemporary educational visionaries such as Gandhi, Tagore and Sir Syed Ahmad Khan who contributed practically in higher education. This book incorporates this view of different Visionaries of higher education in relation to their idea of praxis

---

33. Singh, S.K., "Life, Vision and Contemporary Significance of the Great Educator Mahamana Madan Mohan Malaviya", University News, a weekly journal of Higher Education, New Delhi, Association of Indian Universities, 55 (52), (2017).
34. Tiwari, U.D., "Mahamana Pandit Madan Mohan Malviya (Sankshipt Jeevan-Parichaya)", Varanasi: Mahamana Malviya Foundation, 48 (2009).
35. Gajrani, S. and Ram, S., "Pandit Madan Mohan Malaviya". New Delhi: Commonwealth Publishers (2009).
36. Prasad, M., "Malviya Ji's Contribution to Education, International Journal of Education and Applied Research" (2013).
37. Jyoti, "Madan Mohan Malviya and His Visions Towards Education: A Study". GLOBUS Journal of Progressive Education, A Refereed Research Journal, 4(1) (2014).
38. Mishra, V., "Madan Mohan Malaviya's vision on agriculture education and research". Current Science, 108 (2017).

including Mahamana Madan Mohan Malaviya philosophy of education. Besides this, the principal reason for writing this book is to provide a rational and logical philosophical understanding to all the educators and readers about Malaviya's educational work which is not confined or limited towards the establishment of Banaras Hindu University but he did abundant work in education, religion, politics, and economics. He was keenly interested in education. His abiding interest in the field was not merely academic, he was rather deeply involved in the application of his ideas. Though his educational activities were overshadowed by his activities in other diverse fields nevertheless they were more than sufficient to demonstrate that Malaviya was an outstanding Eastern thinker who have not only propounded ideas at abstract levels but also brought them down to the practical levels which he had attempted by in establishment of BHU and many other educational institutes. So, in this work the author creates a debate through various discussions that Malaviya is the visionary of higher education including comparative critical analysis of Malaviya's thought with other Indian philosophers.

The book has several aims. First, it attempts to fully inform about Making of Mahamana Madan Mohan Malaviya through his brief life sketch, social background including his writing and speeches. Second, it attempts to provide the philosophical thoughts of Madan Mohan Malaviya in the frame of his social, political, economic, religious thoughts. This work seeks to extend Malaviya as a person of multiple causes. Third, it attempts to discuss the educational philosophy of Madan Mohan Malaviya. Here an effort has been made to critically examine his thoughts on education, teaching, training and curriculum, and in relation to aims of education, teacher-students relationship, views on discipline and educational environment. Fourth it attempts to critically evaluate the educational thoughts of Malaviya with other Indian philosophers. The author of this book offered that the educational thoughts of Madan Mohan Malaviya will be relevant in the present social context and they may be enlightening the educators to seek solutions to the present educational crises. Author was very fortunate that she had the experience of working as Assistant Professor in BHU, RGSC Campus at a time when her thesis work was going on in the Department of Education at BHU and the 150th birth anniversary was celebrated in BHU. I have also been influenced by the various Professor articles such as Prof. B.N. Dwivedi Department of Applied Physics, Institute of Technology, Banaras Hindu University wrote an article in 2010 on "Malaviya's Vision on Science and Technology: Celebrating his 150th Birth Anniversary" in current science. Like him many authors as K. Chandramouli, Dr. S.K. Mani, Dr. Vishwanath Pandey wrote a book on *Visionary of Modern India Madan Mohan Malaviya* in 2011. Working as a teacher and researcher since 2010 author have got many opportunity to attend the national, international seminar and presented my views and publish a edited book after financial approval from BHU on 150 Years of Mahamana's Service to Humanity. The author believes that Mahamana showed sustained consonance between God, Goodness and Morality including modern scientific vision, which made him an institution itself. Mahamana put emphasis on integrated and complementary continuum of science and technology, medical, culture, religion and indigionuos manufacturing the same idea was visualized in contemporary New Education Policy 2020 in relation to Higher Education pursuit.

During writing this book, the primary sources such as books, letters, magazines, newspapers, articles written by Madan Mohan Malaviya and secondary sources including literature on Madan Mohan Malaviya written by other authors were carefully consulted. The investigator has tried to trace and identify the primary resources together with secondary sources as well to realize the aim of the book. The present work has been delimited towards educational and philosophical thoughts of Malaviya. His educational philosophy has been compared with the educational thoughts of Rabindranath Tagore, Mahatma Gandhi, and Sir Syed Ahmad Khan only. In accordance with the objectives of the study, historical and chronological approaches were used. Based on documentary evidence, juxtapositional analysis has been done to identify the similar and dissimilar components between different visionaries as Malaviya and

Tagore, Malaviya and Gandhi, Malaviya and Sir Syed Ahmad Khan. Another set of important issues raised by this book is the relevance of Malaviya's vision of Higher Education with reference to implementation of NEP 2020.

The structure of the book is as follows. This chapter has sought to provide the backdrop to the history of higher education in India during Malaviya and Post Malviyan Era and briefly examine some of the recent reforms contemporary NEP 2020 in relation to integration of visionaries who were practically associated with higher education in India. This chapter creates a rationale about a book that shows how Malaviya's Philosophy of Education manifestate and is applicable in contemporary scenarios of higher education. This chapter also discusses the inclination of Malaviya's in previous philosophical research. It helps to create a knowledge base and to trace the knowledge gap in relation to establish the rationale behind choosing the area for writing the book including needs and significance of this research work. This chapter also delineates several aims of the book, using research methodology, identifying the primary resources together with secondary sources to realize the aim of the book including delimitation of this research work. Chapter 2 examines Malaviya and his times through a detailed social background brief life sketch of Malviya including his writings and speeches. Chapter 3 offers a philosophical viewpoint of Malaviya and focuses on his social, economic, political and religious thoughts. In Chapter 4, reference is made to about educational philosophy of Madan Mohan Malaviya where the genesis and foundation of Malaviya's educational philosophy along with Malaviya's educational activities, Malaviya's approach to education and aim of education, his view on different levels of education discussed. In this chapter of the book the author critically concentrated on his views in relation to religion, women and deprived class education, scientific and vocational education including curriculum, teacher, teaching method, teacher-students relationship, educational administration, school environment, etc.

Chapter 5 offers a critical evaluation of Madan Mohan Malaviya's educational philosophy in contemporary comparative setting. In this chapter, educational thoughts of Malaviya are analytically compared with contemporary visionaries such as Rabindranath Tagore, Mahatma Gandhi and Sir Syed Ahmad Khan conclusions of the study are described along with its relevance. Finally, the relevance of Malaviya's thought in contemporary educational settings is detailed in the last Chapter 6. A critical estimate, along with conclusions drawn from the discussion of the chapter, has been given at the end of each chapter.

2
Malaviya and His Time

2.1 Introduction

In this chapter, Malaviya's social background has been described. Researcher has tried to analyze the socio-economic and political forces which were accountable for shaping the life philosophy of Madan Mohan Malaviya. A brief life sketch of Madan Mohan Malaviya, his writings and speeches has also been described. Related literature has been collected from the available sources. In the last phase of this chapter, those persons who had influenced his personality and by whom he was motivated, during his life time has been identified.

2.2 Malaviya's Social Background

Before describing the social background of Madan Mohan Malaviya, it is important to discuss the existing socio-political, literary, religious and educational conditions of the society. During the period of growth of the Indic-civilization roughly 1300-700 B.C. the great philosophic-religious Vedic literature was born in India. So, the ancient culture and social ethnicity were much religious, in mythical traditions, in educational contribution, and in and other factors. Although a definite cultural unity had existed in ancient India but it had never been united into political whole. There was no programme of state education however a type of formal education was designed to develop moral character through the study of the Vedic literature and other religious writing. In the time of Buddha, democratizing influence is found on society, as evidenced by example all castes were accepted into Buddhist centre of learning. The Muslims began their vigorous invasions in India in the 10th century A.D., but not until the end of the 17th century the sword of Islam succeed in uniting briefly the entire subcontinent under one ruler. Hindu and Muslim, community were different and separate, however they exerted a great deal of influence on each other. Hindi a common Indian vernacular combined with some Arabic formed Urdu which became a kind of lingua franca among the Muslims. During the later Muslim period, especially, during the Mughal empire (1526-1707), India became once again a centre of scholarship and literary creativity. Neither Hindu nor Muslim rulers had established a state educational system, both groups considered the support of education as a religious obligation.

But after the attack of different foreign invaders like Dutch, French, Britishers, etc. religious heterodoxy and the powerful secular force of rationalism in the form of difference between sects were established by European culture. Thus, Indian culture became altered and gradually influenced by the Western culture and civilization. Indian people felt suffocation by such attitude of foreign invaders who directly attacked their religion, tradition, culture and social norms. Thus at contemporary time to Malaviya near the end of Indian mutiny till independence movement Indians faced different situations in social, political, economic and educational sectors which awakened the social consciousness in the people and shaped their mindset to think the solution of all problems in their own way.

The socio-political problems were looked by Indians and described by E. Blunt (1939)[1] as, the first socio-political problem was concerned with the survival of united India including 561 princely states, not been under British control, but somewhat had been ruled in an authoritarian manner by inborn princes, and the princes fought among themselves and the benefit of their fight was taken by the Britishers. So Britishers took advantage of the Indian rulers who were batting with each other for the sake of their own state and absence of felling of wholeness. The Britishers made numerous attempts and far reaching policies to manage the internal affairs of these rulers and gradually all of them were under the control of colonial administration.

1. Blunt, E., *Social Service in India*, U.K.: H.M. Stationery Office, 1939, p. 169.

Consequently, some of the princely states remained unexpectedly backward and practically cut off from the change taking place in India during the colonial period.

Second problem was the lack of national language. English was a well-known language of those educated elite class, who were engaged in high government and profitable positions. But it was almost unfamiliar in the midst of the masses where the local vernaculars remained strong. *Third problem* was the cleavage in the Indian society which had economic and social dimensions. Caste delayed mobility of work, forced usually offspring to take up the profession of the parents. This situation had unfortunate implication for both dying skills, and oversupply of unskilled labour and shortage of new occupations. Although financial and other rewards assisted in later time in removing the economic defects of the cast and society but the inherent social evils remained. Therefore a society developed where Untouchability exists as a social evil. Although some of the social reforms like abolition of Sati at the time of Lord William Bentinck further converted Hindus mind set from illogical, inhuman to more logical, civilized and gentle. *Fourth problem* was related with the political growth. The policy of the British East India Company initially did not allow to Indian rulers to rule out widely and their vision was to develop India, as a source for raw resources and as bazaar for the English rising business economy.[2] *Fifth problem* was related to the process of association between Hindu and Muslim communities. The Muslim minority, long uneasy about the prospect of Hindu majority rule, took steps through its own political party, formed the Muslim league to form a separate nation. According to Adams,

> The Indian Muslims felt themselves to be Muslims before they were Indians.[3]

Thus, Britishers by providing the facility of separate electorate which was first introduced among the Muslims, and then spread out to other minorities, tried to create political camps organized against each other and taught men to think as partisans and not

2. *Ibid.*, p. 394.
3. *Ibid.*, p. 109. Also quoted in Wallbank, *A Short History of India and Pakistan*, p. 169.

as citizens. They encouraged separatist tendency and prevented the growth of national unity. By giving the ideals of equality they created a new vested interest in reactionary mind and diverted attention from real economic problems of the country which were common to all.[4]

During the time of Malaviya the *socio-economic problems* faced by Indians, were inability in the agriculture sector to provide sufficient food for the population, lack of industrialization, imposition of British land revenue and tenancy system which act as a great burden on the peasant community. Due to the lack of adequate irrigation facility and high rises in the price of food grains further aggravated the problem of poverty and famine in the country. Since 1866 India faced twenty-two famines and it has been estimated that nearly 29 millions of the lives have been lost.[5] The enormous mortality more than 82 lakhs caused during the great famine of 1876-78.[6] So the famine commission was constituted by the Britishers. In spite of the repeated recommendations of the famine commission of 1880 and 1901-03[7] people of India faced irrigation problems. The attention of Britishers was much on the Railways than the irrigation, though irrigation yield was five times more than the railways. Tariff policy of the colonial government and the country veiling excise duty on Indian goods had destroyed the indigenous art, handicraft and industries. The educated middle class felt reforms. It was given by the Britishers under the act of 1892 which were not being planned for the best interests of the people of the country they found level of taxation in the country was much higher.[8] The expenditure on the military purpose was far beyond the capacity of the country to bear and it was growing year after year. The activities which would directly benefit the people, such as promotion of general

4. Nehru, J., *The Discovery of India*. New York: John Day, 946, p. 355.
5. *Ibid.*, p. 170.
6. *Ibid.*
7. *Ibid.*
8. *Ibid.*

scientific, agriculture, industrial, and technical education and the provision of medical relief and sanitation were ignored.

Nearly fifty-five lakh people lost from the plague.[9]

The socio-economical condition of the country was connected with the poverty, misery, deficient or ill-nutritious food and overcrowding. By industrial growth after coming of railways to India, Indian natural economic development was arrested and consequently masses of India were desperately poor and growing poorer.

The socio-educational problems faced by the Indians, before appearance of Malaviya were the Anglicization of education system. By the middle of the eighteenth century, the Britishers tried to modify the social structure of the Indian society which was basically completing the need of an efficient administrative system. So, this goal eventually prompted the establishment of an educational system which used English as a language of instruction and followed the curriculum of British schools. The motive of transplanting English schools in India was to produce clerks and other government servants who had the language skills and character traits necessary to operate the British Government offices. During the eighteenth century the Bible and other Christian texts were translated into Indian vernaculars, and by end of this century the missionaries' school started by the Britishers to expend Western culture, language, religion, etc. By the early part of the 19th century controversial issue in relation to education was basically related to whether the basic objectives in India be prompting oriental learning, or the introduction of western languages and culture? So, in 1813 there was an issue created between Orientalist and Anglicizes over ₹ 10,0000 to be used up yearly for the progress of literature of Indian languages as Sanskrit or Arabic literature or English literature. In 1834, Thomas Babington Macaulay, as president of the general public committee of public instruction came to India. He composed his famous "Minutes on Education." Macaulay was totally unaware of Sanskrit and Arabic literature, so he easily dismissed the literature of Sanskrit and Arabic

9. *Ibid.*

language and argued that they are insignificant in comparison to Western education.

In 1854,

> Wood dispatch called Magna Carta of Indian education system was passed.[10]

By this dispatch education was filtrated to the masses from the elite educated class. Thus, the third stream of education that entered in India was in some respects similar to other two: it had its own special language, its special concern with the education of one class, and its highly literary character. It differed to others in its secular outlook and it concerned with science and Western thoughts. After establishing three universities on the basis of London University the objective of Britishers was not to expand higher education according to the need of India but its aim was to establish pure English education. Students after matriculation were found to unable to understand lectures in English. When they join college, many students pass through the entire university course without acquiring approach to a command of the language and proceed to a degree without even learning to write a letter correctly and idiomatically.[11] So, the results were more discouraging. The purpose of Englishmen was to create new class in India, i.e. English educated class, which lived in world of its own, cut off from the mass of the population, and looked always even when protesting, toward their rulers.[12]

2.2.1 Reforms and other Movements among Hindus and Muslims

To overcome these problems, a new social-consciousness was arising. Society needed such Western educated Indians who understood the awful policies of Britishers and found the right solution of such problems. Thus, political reformation started under the banner of Indian National Congress. Much of the

10. Rawat, P.L., *History of Indian Education.* Agra: Ram Prasad and Sons, 1994, p. 154.
11. *Ibid.*
12. Dar, S.L. and Somaskandan, S., *History of the Banaras Hindu University.* Varanasi: Banaras Hindu University Press, 1966, p. 43.

middle class western educated Indians gathered and started their revolt by establishing Congress sessions in whole part of India and awakened the people against the British policies which ruins Indian culture, heritage, religion, language and economy of the country. Although English statesmen tried to create elite group of Indians who in taste and loyalty would be oriented toward England, but from these elite class most ardent nationalist came. Indians reacted against for the unkind British governance and imposed western education. Indian National Congress became gradually the center of organization for nationalism. The Nationalism fused with religion and led to the revival in Hindu and Muslim society. Although the leaders of Indian National Congress such as Malaviya, Gandhi, Annie Besant, Aurobindo, etc. were educated in English medium colleges, they were the men who also had deep appreciation for Mother India. Certain Hindu Leaders although influenced by the Western culture such as Rajaram Mohan Rai was taking innovative attempts to prevent malpractices made by the Hindus mind set such as worshipping the imageless God, in order to prove that Hindus also have the custom of worshiping the imageless God parallel to Islam and Christianity.

The awakening of Indian was two folded: on one side they looked towards the west and at the same time they looked at their own past. At the end of the 19th century a lot of Social reformers through their new discourses, like Raja Ram Mohan Rai (1776-1835) through Brahma Samaj, Swami Dayanand (1824-83) by Arya Samaj gave slogan as Back to Vedas, Keshab Chandra Sen (1838-84) by Prarthana Samaj, Annie Besant by theosophical society urged their countrymen to introspect, in order to determine the origin of the evils and weaknesses in their spirit. In society, there was a reaction towards the influence of Islam and Christianity. It was a crusading and reforming movement from within, as well as a defensive organization for protection against external attacks. It introduced proselytization into Hinduism and thus tended to come into conflict with other proselytizing religions.[13] Swami Ramkrishna Paramhansa

13. Nehru, J., *The Discovery of India*. New York: John Day, 1946, p. 412.

(1835-86) and his celebrated student Swami Vivekanand (1863-93) began Ramkrishna Mission to enrich the traditional Indian philosophy in new and dynamic terms and introduced a fresh breath of life into the indigenous Vedantic values that were dying under the burden of superstition and blind faith. These discourses provided new direction, new sense to Hindus and inspired local Hindus to be united at national level for the welfare of Hindus. Vivekanand was a man who again and again laid stress on the necessity of liberty and equality and raising the masses for a thought that liberty of thought and action is only the condition of life of growth and well-being. Progressively Vivekanand in his outlook became international and wanted to combine western progress with Indian spiritual background.

Likewise Tagore by establishing Shantiniketan tried and broadened the basis of Indian Nationalism. The year 1905 was an eventful year in the history of modern India. This year witnessed the birth of great cultural, economic and political movements. Gokhale, preached the gospel of service to motherland, and proclaimed himself as the first and foremost servant of India. East Bengal reverberated with the cry of Vandemateram, Bengal division and Aurobindo Ghose ignited the Swadeshi movement. With the thought of Swadeshi the dream of Swaraj came into action. The spirit of nationality was awakened by songs and lyrics, by slogans and speeches of the visionaries.

Much of this was common to the Muslim masses also, which were well acquainted with these traditions. But it began to be felt, especially by the Muslim upper classes, that it was not quite proper for them to associate themselves with these semi-religious traditions that any encouragement of them would be against the spirit of Islam. They searched for their national roots elsewhere. Although those periods were common for Hindus and Muslims and the sense of foreign invasion for Muslims had disappeared from Hindu minds. All classes of people, including many Muslims joined, but the Muslim League kept aloof.

> This search for cultural roots led Indian Muslims (that is, some of them of the middle class) to Islamic history, and to the periods when Islam was a conquering and creative force in Baghdad, Spain, Constantinople, central

> Asia, and elsewhere. There had always been interest in this history and some contacts with neighboring Islamic countries. But all such contacts were limited and superficial and did not really affect the general outlook of Indian Muslims, which was confined to India.[14]

Sir Syed was an ardent reformer and he wanted to reconcile modern scientific thoughts with Islam. He pointed out the basic similarities between Islam and Christianity. The beginning of the national movement frightened him, for he thought that any opposition to the British authorities would deprive him of their help in his educational program. So he tried to tone down anti-British sentiments among the Muslims and to turn them away from the National Congress which was taking shape then.

> One of the declared objects of the Aligarh College which he founded was 'to make the Muslims of India worthy and useful subjects of the British crown.'[15]

He was not opposed to the National Congress because he considered it predominantly a Hindu organization; he opposed it because he thought that it was politically too aggressive (though it was mild enough in those days), and he wanted British help and co-operation. He tried to show that Muslims as a whole had not rebelled during the Mutiny and that many had remained loyal to the British power. He was in no way anti-Hindu or communally separatist. Repeatedly he emphasized that religious differences should have no political or national significance.

So among all such awakening people, three men as Mahatma Gandhi, Madan Mohan Malaviya, and Rabindranath Tagore who were usually different in their views but acted as representatives of India. All three were born approximately near the same year after 1860, and they wanted not only freedom of India from Britishers but also freedom from poverty, growing Muslim-Hindu conflict, the caste system, and the other social and religious as well as political restrains. Tagore and Gandhi bring us to our present age. But Malaviya was the person who was considering importance of earlier period and produced

14. *Ibid.,* p. 336.
15. *Ibid.,* p. 344.

effect on the people, especially on the Hindus by laying stress, like Vivekananda, on the greatness of the past of India and her pride. Malaviya himself was careful to warn his people not to dwell too much on the past, but look to the future also. This tendency of looking back to the past and finding comfort and nourishment there was due to his depth study of ancient literature and history which made him unique than Gandhi and Tagore. Malaviya was more modern in his approach to deal with life's problem and acted as a bridge between past of India and her present.

In 1902, Indian University commission was formed under the chairmanship of Sir Thomas Raleigh, which was further modified by Lord Curzon who declared that there was scarcity of funds for education and therefore the people were required to raise funds for their own education. After this declaration, most of the visionaries started to think that only education is a single tool by which they may gain their own status again in respect to their own culture, tradition and national development. Muslim leader Sir Syed Ahmad Khan tried to upgrade his Anglo oriental college to Muslim university for the welfare and education of Muslims. Tagore established a college at Shantiniketan devoted to the revival of Indian culture refocused on establishment of such educational institutions which fulfils the National needs. Other leaders also felt the pain of the India's poverty and pauperization under British rule.

So in the whole country there was an environment obtained which reflected educational renaissance. Like others Malaviya also could not resist himself by the social educational events of his time. So, he felt eagerly the pain of Indians and Hindu community ascribed the factors responsible for low economic and educational growth. Due to his moderate view and negotiating tendency, rationality and genuine interest for all common men, Kings, Hindus, Muslims, Sikhs, leaders, and Britishers approached him and joined hands with him. His interest in dealing with the social, economic, political problems from the political platforms and his keen tendency to frame his propounded abstract ideas into practical shape facilitated him to think in relation to welfare of the society.

Along with the socio-political, economical condition of the country, Malaviya's family background also played a major role to shape his social background. He had his deep faith in Sanatan Dharma because of listening to Bhagwat Katha from his father since childhood. He always realized that the condition of Hindu religion was not as good as it was in ancient time, Sanatan Dharma was eternal dharma which preached in the immanence of God. When all such reforms ran in country, Malaviya felt comfort when he analyzed and looked back to the past ancient literature and history, riches of Vedic literature.

Thus along with the crisis, problems of society which discussed above, all the racial memories, home environment, dream actions which he listened by his teachers, father, mother and relatives in infancy, from childhood and onwards, religious training given in his traditional schools, journey of Kumbh Mela from his childhood, religious discourses, interest in reciting Bhagvat, religious meetings attended by him from his childhood, love of Sanatan Dharma, deep understanding about Hinduism and deteriorating condition of Hindu religion at that time, hopes of Hindu community from Malaviya, and his eagerness to attain the knowledge of English, Hindi, Sanskrit, Urdu language were accountable for evolution of Malaviya's social background. No doubt railway industries, evolution of big cities, roads, transport facilities, modern means of communication were responsible factors given by Britishers for social changes but at the cost of loss of Indian cultural heritage, Malaviya didn't want to welcome it.

Man's action is never divorced from his thought and the same thing was found in Malaviya's action and thoughts. So, his social background forced him to build up the respect for ancient custom and culture over the educated classes of the country. Thus, Malaviya tried to develop such higher education system in India which is educationally superior, philosophically perfect, culturally and materially rich and not the imitator of London education system. Malaviya made efforts for establishing Hindu University by uniting the Hindu Leaders, kings for the common welfare of the Hindu community and tried to bring harmony between the ideals of the east and the west. So, the social, political, economic, and educational background as which discussed above are accountable to get ready Malaviya as social reformer, political leader, religious man and great patriot of the motherland.

2.3 A Brief Life Sketch of Madan Mohan Malaviya (1861-1946)

2.3.1 *Birth, childhood and family background*

Madan Mohan Malaviya was born to an orthodox Brahmin family, belonged to Chaturvedi branch, Bharadwaj Gotra. He felt pride that he was from the same Gotra as the great scholar-warrior Dronacharya.[16] Nearly four hundred years ago his ancestors migrated from Malwa to Allahabad. His father Pandit Braj Nath was one of the best scholars of Sanskrit literature and scripture such as Veda, Bhagvat, Geeta etc. As a Vyas, he narrated and presented the sacred text and popular exposition of the *Srimad Bhagvat* and other *Puranas* for which he was much appreciated by all.

> He had deep devotion in Lord Krishna. Princes like late Maharajah of Darbhanga and the late Maharajah of Benaras were among those who paid respect to him and regarded him as almost a *guru* for his learning and goodness.[17]

He wrote many religious works as *Siddhant Darpan*[18] in Sanskrit which was later published by his dutiful son. Malaviya was always fond of studying the manuscripts and collection of books which was saved by his father and he got much knowledge from these books and this was accepted by Malaviya.[19] The family was never rich and very small income was earned by Pandit Braj Nath, thus he hardly could educate his children.

> His mother Moona Devi was from Shazadpur in Allahabad District. Madan Mohan Malaviya was the

16. *Ibid.*, p. 345.
17. Tripathi, R.N., *Pujay Malaviya ji key Saath Tees Din,* p. 210.
18. Tandon, D.P., *Speech at Introduction of Malaviya's Portrait in Parliament House*, p. 11.
19. Pandey, S.R., *Contribution to the Malaviya Commemoration,* Vol. 2, p. 108.

> third son of his father. He was born at 6.54 p.m. on Wednesday, Pausha Krishna, the 25th December 1861 in Allahabad.[20]

The part of the town where Madan Mohan Malaviya was born is located on the bank of a *nala* running to the Yamuna. The House was rebuilt in *pacca* brick by Malaviya during his brief active career at the Bar.

2.3.2 *Early Education and student's life*

Malaviya received his education first in Sanskrit Pathshalas.

> At the age of eight years, he was sent to a remarkable institution run by Hardevji Pundit of Mathura named as the *Dharma Jnanopadesh Pathshala* providing religious knowledge.[21]

At the age of eight years, Madan Mohan was invested with the scared thread with customary ceremony. His father initiated him in chanting the Gayatri mantra.

> In his childhood age, he liked to play *Gulli danda, Kabaddi* and certain local shopkeeper gave him the nickname 'Masta.'[22]

Next Pathshala was the *Vidya Dharma Vardhini Sabha* run by Devakinandan, and later he was sent to an English medium school. He passed his high school entrance examination from Allahabad Zilla School (1878 at the age of sixteen) and then joined Muir Central College (1879).[23] As a student, he began to take a warm interest in literary subjects, public questions, religion and distinguished himself in handwriting, spelling, and pronunciations. Malaviya passed the college life in five years from 1879 to 1883 (from 12th to B.A.). He passed the intermediate exam in 1880. He was one of the two candidates sent up by the college for the B.A. exam of the Calcutta university in Arts in December 1883, and the only one passed that year

---

20. Tripathi, *Raton Ki Jholi*, p. 217.
21. Parmanand, *Mahamana Madan Mohan Malaviya: An Historical Biography.* Varanasi: Malaviya Adhyayan Sansthan, BHU Press, 1967, p. 6.
22. *Ibid.*, p. 15.
23. Tripathi, op. cit., p. 7.

in which Malaviya was placed in second division.[24] Due to his busyness in the literary and social pursuits, he was not paying any attention to studies. So, he failed in the previous year exam of Muir Central College.[25] Malaviya got admitted to M.A. class. His responsibility for his family did not allow him to further continue his studies, so he left his M.A. classes after a short period of three months.

2.3.3 *Malaviya's Family Life*

In 1881, Madan Mohan got married to Kundan Devi. She was the daughter of Pt. Nand Ram who belonged to Mirzapur. He was then eighteen years of age and was an undergraduate at Muir Central College, Allahabad. Malaviya had twelve children out of whom four sons and three daughters attained maturity.

2.3.4 *Malaviya as a Teacher*

In July 1885, Malaviya accepted the appointment as an English teacher in the district Government High School in Allahabad on the salary of Rs. 40 per month which he had left as a student six years ago. His salary became exceptionally good and rose to Rs. 60 per month.[26] Due to his firm character, learning and sympathetic behavior towards his pupils, Malaviya soon won their love, admiration and respect. The key of Malaviya's success as a teacher was that he always went to his class fully prepared. He himself records

> During my regular preparation at home I tried to know the origin and meaning of all important English words. For this purpose I thoroughly studied "Biography of English Words" and "English past and present" that enabled me to know the origin, meaning and history of the English words. I used to learn from books and imparted that knowledge to my students. That period of the teaching was very happy phase of my life.[27]

In June 1887, he renounced his teaching career forever.

---

24. *Ibid.*, p. 19.
25. *Calcutta University Minutes*, Feb. 4, 1884.
26. *Ibid.*, Feb. 19, 1883.
27. Parmanand, *op. cit.*, 1967, p. 25.

2.3.5 *Malaviya's (Seminal Years during 1877 to 1886)*

Malaviya's guru, Aditya Ram Bhattacharya initiated Malaviya to participate in many social activities, as starting the *Hindi Uddharini Sabha* around 1877; participation in social activities in *Hindu Samaj* (1880); turning to *Swadeshi* (1881); inspiring his friends to start a *Deshi Trading Company* (1883); writing articles in Pradeep on public issues (1880-84); starting a literary debating institute in 1884 for regular discussions on literature; organizing a farewell to viceroy Lord Ripon in 1884; participating in the Madhya Hindu Samaj in 1885 (Whose objectives were social reforms and promoting education); giving lectures on religious ideals on almost all the available platforms; and assisting his teacher in writing editorials for the Indian Union (1885-86). These formative years shaped Malaviya who was to become the champion of social reforms and educational cause.

2.3.6 *Malaviya's turning point of life (1886)*

Second Indian National Congress sessions had been chaired by Dadabhai Naoroji. On the fourth day of the Congress session, a young man of 25 years, said

> May I speak, asked Madan Mohan, his preceptor—Pt. Aditya Ram Bhattacharya said 'speak, speak'. After being advised by the Guru, Madan Mohan sent a chit to the president, and made a maiden speech in support of the resolution demanding extension of popular representation in the legislative Councils (Second Indian National Congress session).

Mr. Hume was deeply impressed by his speech and wrote high appreciation for him in Report as

> But perhaps the speech that was most enthusiastically received was one made by Pandit Madan Mohan Malaviya, a high caste Brahmin, whose fair complexion and delicately chiselled features, instinct with intellectuality, at once impressed every eye, and who suddenly jumping upon a chair beside the president poured forth a manifestly impromptu speech with an

> energy and eloquence that carried everything before them.[28]

From that day Malaviya's life begins to shine as a sun in political field, and all through 86 years of his life it kept on shining.

2.3.7 *Malaviya's career as a Journalist*

During the Indian National Congress session 1886, Malaviya came in contact with Raja Rampal Singh of Kala-Kankar, who was the owner of the *Hindustan* paper, wanted to offer him the editorship of his paper. He left the job of teaching and joined his paper. His Professional career as a whole time journalist started in July 1887. He believed in the power of press which was also expressed by him in October 1929 in his own edited newspaper Leader in the following words

> I do not know any institution, neither school, nor college nor university—which supplies such daily instruction to the public as large as newspaper.[29]

He was the editor of the *Hindustan* in 1889 and his salary being of ₹ 200 per month.[30] He continued his work as a journalist in the *Indian Union*, along with Baldeo Ram Dev from 1889 to 1892.[31] Madan Mohan's interest in journalism and faith in the Press acted as a dominant factor in the formation of powerful public opinion and influenced the manner of administration of the Britishers also. After some years he was shocked at the administration of Britishers and evils of the communities and understood bitterly the importance of paper and press for progress of the country, and then he started the weekly Hindi paper the *Abhyudaya* (1907)[32] and labored hard to make it

28. Tiwari, U.D., *A Short Biography Mahamana Malaviya*. Varanasi: Mahamana Malaviya Foundation, 2007, p. 13.
29. *Ibid*., p. 64.
30. The leader, October 23, 1929, speech reprinted in the magazine section of the leader, January 7, 1962.
31. Chaturvedi, S.R., *Builder of Modern India Madan Mohan Malaviya*. New Delhi: Ministry of information and broadcasting government 1995, p. 22.
32. Dave, R., oral speech cited in BHU pragya (Young Brother of Sir Sundar Lal an advocate of the Allahabad High Court).

informing and instructive by contributing numerous articles to its columns. The *Abhyudaya* had made an excellent progress and had done a great deal of public service, but its owner had been out of pocket for the substantial time and money. So, it was planned to extend it by issuing it twice a week, and it was to be hoped that the biweekly *Abhyudaya* may present news in skilled form. Malaviya felt keenly the need of an *English Daily* in Allahabad to voice the opinions and ventilate the grievances of the people of the Provinces, so he worked hard to bring other newspapers *Leader* (24 October 1909) into existence.[33] The two previously running newspapers *Indian People* and *Indian Opinion* merged in the *Leader*.[34] He also started *Maryada* in 1910 as a Hindi monthly, which was later replaced by *Bharat*. In 1921 a *Kisaan,* a Hindi monthly was started. To convey the spirit of Sanatan Dharma, Malaviya patronized Ganesh Guru Dutt of Punjab who started *Sanatan Dharma* weekly in 1933. He organized the first All India Editor's Conference in 1908 to fight for freedom of the press when the press act of 1908 was passed. He also offered financial help to fight the case of the Muslim editor of *Swaraj*, an Urdu daily.[35] Malaviyan ethics of journalism were seen by the example when he wrote a letter to the editor for writing an objectionable editorial on widow marriage. He wrote,

> The previous night I had a dream in which I saw that the *Abhyudaya* (press) was on the fire. The sadness I felt after reading today's *Abhyudaya* is more than the scene of the press burning in the dream. It is not right, even while I am alive to publish such an article which makes me feel like a culprit in the society and put me to shame.[36]

Thus, Malaviya by the power of press wanted to do critical analysis of slow governmental reforms and spread awareness in Indian youth on social, political, religious, issues.

---

33. Tripathi, R.N., *Pujay Malaviya ji kay Saath Tees Din*, p. 56.
34. Keene, H.G., *Science and Sights of Allahabad,* 1946, p. 603 traced the origin of *Leader.*
35. Parmanand, op. cit., p. 46.
36. Maine, S.K., et al., *Visionary of Modern India: Madan Mohan Malaviya*. New Delhi: Commonwealth Publication, p. 30.

2.3.8 *Malaviya's career as a Lawyer*

Many well-wishers like A.O. Hume, Gopal Krishna Gokhale, Pandit Ayodhya Nath, Sir Sundar Lal persuaded him to study Law. As he left the Hindustan, Raja Rampal Singh offered to pay him to study for the Bachelor of Laws degree and offered to pay him ₹ 100 per month.[37] Malaviya was awarded a second class L.L.B. degree in 1891 and joined the Allahabad High Court in 1893. His mastery of juristic principle and his firm grasp of statutory laws were sufficiently revealed by his manner to handle the cases. It would be completely wrong to conclude from the class of his degree that his study of Law had been surface based.[38] Malaviya's mind and attitude was always ready for civic work mainly in the fields of religion and education. Money-making process as such had no attraction for him. Pandit Ayodhya Nath on one occasion complained to Mr. Hume that as he had taken interest to study Law, so his interest in Congress work was rather slackened. "Quite right", said the old man with fatherly solicitude, "He must concentrate all his attention on law." And turning to Madan Mohan, Mr. Hume spoke to some extent as follows—

> Madan Mohan, God has gifted you with plenty of brains. Slave at the profession for ten years and you are bound to get to the top. Then your public usefulness will increase greatly owing to the position you will attain, and you can do much for the country.[39]

Though he had got high respect in the legal profession and was recognized as a skilled and successful advocate, tasted all joys of wealth but lastly he discarded all of them. On 1 January 1906, Malaviya declared to leave his practices however he actually retired in 1913 for the building of higher education where Hindu culture might be conserved i.e. Banaras Hindu University. Gokhale characterized it as

---

37. *Ibid.*, p. 30.
38. Chaturvedi, S., op. cit., p. 42.
39. Katju, *Days I Remember*, pp. 3-5.

> Malaviya did the real sacrifice. He came from a poor family, earned well, tasted the riches and sacrificed for the sake of the country.[40]

On 7 February 1922, during Chauri-Chaura case Malaviya again decided to appear in this case, mainly for the justice and rescue the innocent accused from the repressive actions of the British Government. 151 people were freed from the death punishment due to Malaviya's arguments.[41]

2.3.9 *Malaviya's life action in his home town Allahabad*

Malaviya took an active interest in the public affairs from his student life. He started his social work from Allahabad. Allahabad Literary Institute served today due to his efforts. He was the trustee of the Bharati Bhavan Library.[42] He was a member with Bhattacharya in Hindu *Samaj* which was established in 1880 as the political organization in Allahabad primarily concerned with the social reform and upliftment of the Hindu community. After a serious communal riot between Hindus and Muslims, this *Samaj* was reoriented as a provincial organization under the title of *Madhya Hindu Samaj*. This organization acted as an active political body whose members were elected in the annual session of Indian National Congress.

At the session 1886 held in Calcutta Malaviya was a representative from Allahabad out of total 74 delegates from Uttar Pradesh. Malaviya had the deepest interest in the benefits of the student population who came in large numbers from their native places to this district for their education, and faced difficulty in finding suitable quarters in Allahabad therefore he met Sir Antony MacDonnell for the purpose of establishing the Hindu Boarding House. Madan Mohan, with all his efforts, tried to raise funds for the Boarding House and he had the satisfaction of seeing it in a flourishing condition and serving the purpose for which it was intended. Although Malaviya's work was criticized by Gandhi by saying

40. Parmanand, *Mahamana Madan Mohan Malaviya: An Historical Biography*. Varanasi: Malaviya Adhyayan Sansthan, BHU Press, 1967, p. 54.
41. *Ibid*., p. 59.
42. Maine, op. cit., p. 34.

> How can students after living in these palatial building, provided with electricity and other modern amenities, reconcile themselves to village life on return from here? You spoil their habits.

Malaviya spoke

> You are perfectly right I do it deliberately so that students returning from these hostels may erect comparable houses in their villages which may thus be filled with palaces.[43]

Before the establishment of this Hindu Boarding House, a Musalmaan Boarding House had already been constructed on the ground of the Muir Central College for the residence of Muslim students. Its foundation was laid by Sir Auckland Colvin in March 1892.[44] Malaviya termed the establishment of Hindu Boarding House, as the first stone towards foundation of the Hindu University to his friend.[45] Malaviya had not the friends of the approximately same age, he felt comfort with old aged and experienced people and always interacted with them. Bishambhar Nath was appointed as representative of Allahabad Municipal Board. Malaviya always helped him, and after his death on October 16, 1900, Malaviya became a member of the Allahabad Municipal Board and re-elected in 1904, 1906, and in 1908.

He was deeply paying attention to social and humanitarian work and was much happier when relieving human's unhappiness. As under his chairmanship of Municipal Board at the time of plague in Mauaima about 15 miles away from Allahabad across the Ganga, people show unwillingness to vacate the houses and go to the plague camps. Malaviya encouraged the people to go into camps and got the best possible solution to prevent this disease. Malaviya's work as a chairman of municipal board was appreciated by officers. On daily paid basis he visited there and sent those persons to the camp for treatment, who

43. *Ibid.*, p. 78.
44. Padamkant, *Malaviyaji: Jeevan Jhalkiyan*, National Publishing House, New Delhi, pp. 61-62.
45. Parmanand, op. cit., p. 114.

were ill.[46] Malaviya personally superintended the disinfection of a dark lane in a *mandi* where it had broken out and where deaths had occurred in almost every house. In the following year the health camp became so popular that at one time nearly 3000 persons were living there with perfect safety.[47] So, it was Malaviya who knew how to co-operate with the government, when co-operation was beneficial and how to oppose when the country's interests demanded opposition.[48] He was elected as fellow of the University fifteen years ago and succeeded Pt. Bishambhar Nath as a member of the Legislative Council in 1902, when the latter retired owing to increasing age. In 1911, Malaviya moved in the Legislative Council of India. Malaviya had comprehensive understanding of the varied economical problems of India which have mostly engaged his attention and on any platform he frankly discussed it with rationales, therefore he would have become a member of the Imperial Legislative Council. In the same year Malaviya attended the Coronation Darbar of George Vat Delhi proceeded there on Hindu University Business.[49] In March 19, 1912 Malaviya had powerfully supported the Gokhale Bill providing for the free and compulsory education.[50]

2.3.10 *Malaviya's progressive and preservative actions for the sake of Hindi Language*

During the days of Muslim rule, and later the British rule, Persian and Urdu continued to be the court language in many parts of India. Thus, other regional language and cultural language such as Hindi and Sanskrit declined. Thus, Malaviya fought for the improvement of the mother tongue along with Bharatendu, Purshottam Das Tandon. A society was established at Prayag in 1884 called "*Hindi Uddharni Pratinidhi Madhya Sabha* as the cultural counterpart of the *Madhya Hindu Samaj*.[51] Malaviya was very enthusiastic worker of this Sabha, at that

46. Das, S.G., in C.C.V.P., p. 188.
47. *Ibid*., p. 119.
48. Tripathi, op. cit., p. 95.
49. Parmanand, op. cit., p. 118.
50. *Ibid*., p. 186.
51. *Malaviya Centenary Commemoration*, Vol. 1, p. 2.

time he was only 23 years old. The aim of this Sabha was the preservation of Hindi Language and Devanagri script. Gradually Banaras became the center of the Hindi renaissance due to the efforts of Raja Shiv Prasad as well as Bhartendu along with the motivation of Malaviya. In 1892 by the effort of Shyam Sundar Das "Kashi Nagri Pracharni Sabha" was established. Malaviya was a Chief Patron and supporter of this organization.[52] Malaviya presided over the inaugural session of the Hindi Sahitya Sammelan at Banaras. Local societies emerged to strengthen the Hindi language.[53] Next effort was made by Malaviya to commit Sir Antony MacDonnell for the substitution of Hindi in the *Devanagri* script then Urdu in the Persian script to use in the law courts and revenue records. He took great pains in collecting statistical data to prove the futility of continuing Persian script and Urdu and the necessity of introducing Hindi language and *Devanagri* script in the law and courts. He made the committee of seventeen members and as a leader of this movement, almost, stopped his legal practices for three years and prepared a 100 pages report with great firmness. This report was signed by 60 thousand people of the provincial government on March 2, 1898. On April 15, 1900 the petition was accepted by Sir Antony MacDonnell. An order of the government was issued for acceptance of Hindi written in *Devanagri* script for Official and court work[54] (Proceedings of the U.P. Legislative Council cited in Malaviya's Magnum opus: The Hindi Memorandum). All Official records revealed that how much this task was difficult, as it was expressed by Sachchidanand Sinha as,

> It was an immensely difficult task to have obtained such an order thirty years back and none but Malaviya could have successfully achieved this purpose.[55]

52. Parmanand, op. cit., p. 98.
53. *Ibid.*
54. Prashad, R., *Autobiography*, pp. 76-77.
55. *Ibid.*, p. 103.

2.3.11 *Malaviya's life action for the sake of Hindu Sanatan Dharma*

From the school age to the end of his life, Madan Mohan made efforts for the sake of the Hindu religion. It is well-defined faith in his mind that religion is the foundation of all greatness and goodness, and that without an enduring religious faith no man can do well. During his life he followed rituals and practices of orthodox Brahmins and hopefully made Hindu Organization for revival of Sanatan Hindu Religion in India. He was the originator of the Sanatan Dharma Mahasabha held in Allahabad in January 1906. In the same year, Malaviya organized an impressive assembly in the support of *Sanatan Dharma* on the occasion of fair at Prayag. The book *Sanatan Dharma Sangrah* was brought in focus during this conference.[56] Malaviya on, 12 March 1906, issued the first prospectus of the Hindu University in Sanatan Dharma Mahasabha. In 1907, Malaviya's scheme and other scheme of Annie Besant establishing University of India met their hands and formed revised plan.[57] From July 1911 to 1916 and till his life Malaviya continued the collection campaign to give concreteness to his abstract idea. The Sanatan Dharma Sabha became the All India Sanatan Dharma Mahasabha in 1911.[58] In order to lead Hindus, Malaviya decided to form an All-India Hindu Mahasabha headquarter in Allahabad.

On this Occasion Nehru was offended with Malaviya, and Motilal Nehru also did not like the unity of Hindu-Muslim Conference dated 6 January 1911.[59] He wrote,

> Another new feature has been obtained in the Congress that, it has given the birth of an all-India Hindu Mahasabha which in my opinion will not only minimize the chance of the Hindu-Muslim unity but sap the foundation of the Congress itself.[60]

---

56. *Malaviya Commemoration,* Vol. 1, p. 101.
57. Chaturvedi, R.S., op. cit., p. 33.
58. *Ibid.*, p. 196.
59. *Ibid.*, p. 43.
60. *Ibid.*, p. 45.

But Malaviya was supported by Abul Kalam Azad during a special session of Congress in 1923. He said,

> Hindu-Muslim unity must be the foundation of any political structure in the country; without it, freedom of India will remain in dream.[61]

The first session of the new All-India Hindu Mahasabha was held in Varanasi under the president ship of Malaviya on 20 August 1923. The characteristic feature of this great assembly was that it comprised all the various sects of the Hindus, viz., Sanatan Dharmist, Arya Samajist, Jains, Buddhists, Sikhs, Parsees and all others who could claim to belong to the Hindu fold in some form or other. First time people felt that there was a common platform on which different sections could meet and discuss matters relating to their welfare and safety. On the event of the *Ardha Kumbh Mela* in 1924 he began *Satyagrah* with 100 of people along with J.L. Nehru to stop changed flow of the Ganga every year in *Kumbh Mela*. Police felt helpless in front of the *Satyagrahi*.[62]

Malaviya appealed for Hindu Sangathan to support the *Shuddi* movement besides removal of untouchability.[63] Malaviya made special efforts to draw the Sikhs nearer to Hindus in the cause of Hindu solidarity. He went to Sikh Gurudwaras during his tour in Punjab. He suggested Sikhs to make Gurudwara act in 1925[64] (telegram from home department Delhi to Punjab Govt. dated 4/2/1926). On 30 December 1928, Malaviya organized *Mantradiksha* on the Lohaghat of the Ganga in Calcutta.[65] The seventeenth session of the Hindu Mahasabha held at Poona on 29 December 1935, presided over by Malaviya. In this session Malaviya stressed the need of taking back those Hindus in its fold who were converted through mistake, force by initiating them through *Mantradiksha*. On 28 June 1933, he delivered eloquent speech in Urdu, and said

61. Indra Prakash, *History of the Hindu Mahasabha, 1938*, p. 18.
62. *Aj*, September 14, 1923.
63. *Abhyudaya*, January 9, 1924.
64. Chaturvedi, S., op. cit., p. 13. Also cited in *Abhyudha*, February 9, 1924.
65. Parmanand, op. cit., p. 666.

> Unity of the Hindus and the Muslims is the first step towards freedom. It is not less shameful for all of us to look upon the foreigners to vouchsafe our safety and interest. I have a great faith in the religion that I follow but whenever I pass by a church or a mosque, my heads bows down with reverence to them automatically.[66]

On 12 March 1936, he went to Nasik for the purpose of the *Mantradiksha*. Malaviya's scheme of upliftment of the depressed class through procedure of *Mantradiksha* indirectly linked with the growth of the Hindu society. His last speech was delivered in 1946, before his death given for the safety of the Hindu *Dharma* after inhuman activity in Noakhali.

2.3.12 *Malaviya's life and Swadeshi Movement*

Throughout his life, Malaviya had passionate love for the Swadeshi movement. In 1881, a Deshi Tijarat Company was started in Allahabad to promote the use of indigenous manufactures, and Malaviya was one of the well-known supporters of this company.[67] All three decades during independence movement he consistently advocated the use of Swadeshi goods, and wherever he delivered lecture, he promoted the indigenous industries by a similar policy. Malaviya understood *Swadeshi* as a part of his religious duty to purchase country-made goods in preference to foreigner ones. For the preference of this view, he explained a cause that by sacrificing these foreign goods and buying the indigenous goods we would be able to enrich countrymen who might otherwise remain hungry. His interest in the Indigenous industrial movement shows his love for Indian Goods. He is among those who helped in bringing into existence the Indian Industrial Conference at Benares in 1905.[68] Consequently through the sincere efforts of Malaviya U.P. Industrial Association was formed at Prayag for the promotion of Indian arts, crafts and industries.[69] During the world war, a commission was appointed in May 19, 1916 to investigate into

66. Chaturvedi, S., op. cit., p. 50.
67. *Ibid.*, p. 48.
68. *Ibid.*, p. 41.
69. Mishra, A.B., in CCV, p. 118.

the Indian trade under the chairmanship of Thomas Holland. Malaviya was the member of this commission. Malaviya did not agree with the report of the Commission submitted in 1918. His notes of opposing the industrial commission presented Malaviya not only an orthodox pandit but also as a thoughtful economist. Malaviya accelerated Gandhi boycott movement; undertook an extensive tour of whole of the country in 1921, and advocated to establish the well-known All India Swadeshi Sangh. In 1934, he was invited to open the Swadeshi Exhibition at Kalpi but he could not go there due to illness. The touching message was sent by him on that occasion which proved his faith in Swadeshi as the only measure for the economic and industrial growth of India.

2.3.13 *Malaviya as a strong Political Leader and Nationalist till the end of his life*

Malaviya was gradually identified as a preferred leader on the Congress platform after participation in 1885 Congress session. This was not only due to his power of speech and debate, but due to his earnest and determined work. As for example in 1887, before the Congress session held at Madras, Mr. Hume was in stress. He was hopeful for a large strength of delegates from every province; but he was only doubtful for North-West Provinces, and uttered his hope that somebody might provoke the people to a sense of their duty. The hint was soon taken by Malaviya. He worked throughout the year to aware the Congress people; he could not allow to suffer Congress from his native province, so he toured in whole of the province and worked at city after city and made political environments by encouraging the people to participate in Congress sessions. Consequently 45 delegates came to distant Madras in that year, a number not equal to any succeeding Madras session. Mr. Hume was eager for organizing a Congress session in Allahabad. Malaviya turned his idea to invite the Congress in Allahabad, and held a successful session of it.

Again in 1892, when the Congress session was invited to hold its eighth session in Allahabad, the serious mishappening i.e. death of Pandit Ayodhya Nath discouraged the people and many suggestions were given for not to organize the Congress session here; But Malaviya did not listen to the advice of hopelessness. Therefore under the guidance of reliable old leader and wise counselor Pt. Bishambar Nath, Malaviya and other workers did all preparation and held successful session that year in Allahabad. In the year 1906, 1907, 1908 when there was the birth of Hindu Mahasabha and Muslim league came into action, there was moderate extremist split found in political platform, where Malaviya acted as a moderate leader. At the same time Malaviya attended provincial Industrial conference and prepared a plan for establishing Hindu University on the platform of Hindu Mahasabha. On 29th February 1908, he presided over the provincial political conference in Lucknow referring to his address on the issues like poverty, famines and high rate of mortality causes and remedies.[70] In 1909, Malaviya was elected as president in Lahore after a short notice which was expressed in the Manchester Guardian as

> Not so prominent a man as either Rash Behari Ghose or Phirojshah Mehata but nevertheless a politician of high standing and notable ability, a self-made man having made his way at the Bar after an apprenticeship as a school master and a journalist.[71]

Malaviya became the president of the Indian National Congress in 1918, 1930 and 1932.

In 1916, Malaviya supported Home rule also. From 1918 to 1919, Malaviya did prevention action for Rowlett Act, and by this act the effectiveness of the press was rejected. In 1919 a week after Jalianwala Bagh massacre. All-India Congress committee met in Bombay in April 20 a week after the Jalianwala Bagh under Malaviya's Presidentship and appointed a strong committee along with Jinnah. This committee demanded for the public enquiry. Malaviya was much sincere and said Punjab first, reforms afterwards.[72] Malaviya through All India Samiti collected money and did relief work for the sufferers. From 1920 to 1922 Malaviya had some clashes with Gandhi on the

70. Parmanand., *op. cit.*, p. 111.
71. *Ibid.*, p. 151.
72. *Ibid.*, p. 162.

issue of Khilafat movement but lastly he agreed and from 1920 to 1928 he was busy in visiting to different region of India for the non-cooperation movement, Swadeshi movement and for the collection of money for Hindu university. In August 1925, he addressed the convocation address in Kashi Vidyapith.[73]

In 1930, he supported Gandhi salt movement and other aspects of national movement. Consequently, he was arrested in August 1930 and was locked in Bombay jail, from where he was released after 15 days after paying 100 fine which was paid by somebody.[74] On August 27, 1930 when Congress working committee met in Delhi, by the order of Delhi administration Malaviya was arrested on the next day.[75]

He was sent to Naini jail by special train on 3rd September where approximately 2000 people gathered on Naini station. Same crowed might be seen in Allahabad but the train ran without stopping at Allahabad.[76] During 1931, Malaviya took somewhat more energetic steps to secure commutation of death sentences of Bhagat Singh, Rajguru and Sukhdev. On 14th February, he sent a telegram to the province secretary of the viceroy, and through Abhudaya he issued a special Bhagat Singh number which was confiscated under the press act in 1930.[77] In 29 August 1931, he started his journey for Landon to participate in deliberation of the Round Table Conference. At this time Malaviya carried with him his own foodstuffs, cooking utensils, stove and Gangajal. This shows his faith in virtues of Sanatan philosophy.[78]

During his three months in England, Malaviya expressed his views on 15 September 1931, the more extraordinary British rule because the people of this island have always stood for liberty. They have fought for the liberty of many people in different parts of the world: and they should establish and so long maintain a dominion over a great continent like India had,

73. *Abhyudaya*, May 31, 1919.
74. *Ibid.*, p. 770.
75. *Ibid.*
76. *Ibid.*
77. *Ibid.*, p. 782.
78. *Ibid.*, p. 795.

I submit, been an extraordinary event.[79] On 29 November 1931 at Issac Newton hall, Landon, he delivered a lecture at university of Paris, Barlin, Rome, and Venice. In 1932, he addressed the meeting of communist at Victoria Hall of south Hampton London. He also delivered convocation address in Allahabad University on the golden jubilee of the university.

After his return on January 14, 1932 at the time of declaration of communal award, Malaviya played a notable role in achieving a compromise between Harijan and high caste Hindus. On the day of Shivratri he gave mantra to about five hundred persons including Harijans at Dashashwamedha ghat, Banaras[80] (*Aj*, February 15, 1932). Malaviya appreciated the women by saying

> Almost every important center has women-president or director of local Congress committee. Young girls and old ladies, who had never before come out of their houses to join any cause, however has thrown off their veils and has walked into the active ranks of civil disobedience workers.[81] (*Aj*. June 1, 1932)

In 1932 on Poona pact, Malaviya, said,

> Removed the apprehension among the depressed classes that their case might not be substantiated strongly.[82]

In 1934, Malaviya established an independent Nationalist party due to the two subjects in which he differed from the Congress policy, namely Communal Award, and the acceptance of reforms that is separate electorate for Muslims. Malaviya expressed his grave dissatisfaction in the form of his resign.[83] In 1936, he presided over the session of the All-India Sanatan Dharma Mahasabha in Allahabad Sangam during the *Ardha Kumbha* Fair on January 23-25, in the absence of Maharaja of Darbhanga.[84]

79. *Ibid.*, p. 812.
80. *Aj*, February 15, 1932.
81. *Aj*, June 1, 1932.
82. Parmanand, op. cit., p. 882.
83. Thomas, K.P. and Roy, B.C., West Bengal Pradesh Congress Committee, (1955).
84. Parmanand, op. cit., p. 531.

In 1937, first general election held in the country in which Nationalist party got 11 seats as compared to 44 of the Congress[85] (1937: The First general election on the 5th January 1937). At the 75th birthday he said, "The condition of the country is very bad in this tidal wave of the sea of sorrow do I get time to die."[86] In the same year he addressed Allahabad University golden jubilee convocation.[87] In 1938, Malaviya went through Kaya Kalp under the treatment of Tapsi Baba (Baba Vishnu Datta).[88] Malaviya was acting as Vice Chancellor from 1919 to 1939, and after that he was rector till his death 1946. In 1939, Malaviya's failing health led him to resign the vice chancellorship and he submitted his resignation in August 20.[89] During 1942 "Quit India" movement he expressed his full co-operation and helped the freedom fighters. In 1942, when Cripps mission arrived at India along with the members of Muslim league, Malaviya with Saverkar attended the meeting in Delhi for talks on the issue of Indian Independence. As Gandhi did not like this idea and called it as post-dated cheque. Malaviya also opposed it on the cost of partition of country.[90] During his life Span he participated in much of movements like Ganga canal movement, Go Raksha movement, movement for the uplift of untouchables, movement for Hindu Mahasabha, etc.

He organized much of seva samities, scout association, mahabir dals, established many educational schools, and presided so many educational conferences and meetings. He was born in poverty and dedicated all his life for poors as he said

> I have no desire for the Kingdom, neither any desire for heaven, nor freedom for Moksha I have only desire to remove the miseries and sorrows of all living being.[91]

He left this world on 12 November 1946.

---

85. *Aj*, March 17, 1936.
86. Parmanand, *op. cit.*, p. 951.
87. *Ibid.*, p. 965.
88. *Ibid.*, p. 955. Also cited in *Leader*, February 2, 1938.
89. *Aj*, June 2, 1939.
90. Parmanand, *op. cit.*, p. 1039. Also *Quoted in Mahatama*, Vol. VI, pp. 87-88.
91. *Ibid.*, p. 1074.

2.4 Writings and Speeches of Madan Mohan Malaviya

1886: During Second Indian National Congress (Calcutta)—Malaviya said,

> No taxation without representation. That is the first commandment in the Englishman's Political Bible: how can he palter with his conscience and tax us here, his free and educated fellow-subjects, as if we were dumb sheep or cattle? But we are not dumb any longer India has found a voice at last in this great Congress, and in it, and through it, we call on England to be true to her traditions, her instincts, and herself, and grant us our rights as freeborn British citizens (Prolonged cheering).[92] (Legislative Council—Tentative suggestion the making of Malaviya)

1887: Third Indian National Congress (Madras)—Malaviya said,

> This Congress re-affirms the necessity for the expansion and reform of the council of the governor-general for making laws, and the provincial legislative councils, already set forth in Resolutions III of the Congress of 1885 and 1886, and expressed the earnest hope that the government will no longer delay action in the direction of this essential reform.[93] (Expansion of Legislative Councils: The making of Malaviya)

1888: During Fourth Indian National Congress (Allahabad)—Malaviya said,

> As the administration of the income tax, especially as regard to the income below ₹ 1000 has proved extremely unsatisfactory, it is essential, in the opinion of the Congress, that the taxable minimum be raised to ₹ 1000[94] (The Income-Tax and the Taxable minimum)

1890: Six Indian National Congress (Calcutta)—Malaviya said,

---

92. Panday, R., *The Making of Malaviya: Malaviya in the Eyes of Historians*. Varanasi: Kishore Vidya Niketan, 2010, p. 5.
93. *Ibid.*, p. 8.
94. *Ibid.*, p. 170.

> I am happy to find that today we are discussing the leading features of the scheme for the reform and expansion of the legislative councils. The only vital point of difference between us and government now, is with regard to the manner of appointing members to the Council. The government wishes to nominate all the members and we ask for the privilege of electing half of them. How evidently simple and just our prayer how utterly in-defensible the unwillingness of Government of grant it (Cheers).[95] (Reforms of Legislative Councils, 1890)

1891: Seventh Indian National Congress (Nagpur)—Malaviya said,

> Fifty millions of the population, a number yearly increasing, are dragging out a miserable existence on the verge of starvation, and that, in every decade several million actually perish by starvation. This unhappy condition is largely due to the exclusion of the people of India from a due participation in administration, and all control over the finance of their own country. The extravagant cost of the present administration, Military and civil, gradual deterioration of agriculture, short sighted system of land revenue were the factors accountable for this situation.[96]

1892: During Eighth National Congress held at the Allahabad—Malaviya said,

> On employment of Indians in Public Service Commission presented the data of the amounts of annual salaries ranging from 5,000 to 10,000 per annum there were 1207 Europeans, 96 Eurasians, 421 natives of India. He also presented the data of total salaries of above person as Europeans earned 8,77,14,431 ₹, Eurasians earns 72,96,026 ₹, and Natives 255,54,313 ₹. He also focused on the pension of the Indians and Europeans. He said gentleman we are not prompted to ask for a more

95. *Ibid.*, p. 12.
96. *Ibid.*, p. 78.

> extensive employment of our countrymen in the public service commission simply for the pleasure of seeing them there. If our country was not being drained of its money year after year by the in ordinate employment of persons whose home it is not and who would not make it their home (hear, hear), we would never have given such painful earnest attention to the matter as we are not giving (Loud cheers). But this ceaseless drain is making India every day poorer and poorer and it is duty of every well-wisher of the country to endeavor to stop or check it, as best he can (Cheers). Lastly he recommended for the fair field and for no favor.[97] (Employment of Indian Public Service Commission)

1894: Tenth Indian National Congress (Madras)—Malaviya said,

> This Congress, in concurrence with the preceding Congress, considers that the creation of a legislative council for the province of the Punjab is an absolute necessity for the good government of that province and having regard to the fact that a Legislative Council has been created for the N.W. Provinces, requests that no time should be lost in creating such a Council for the Punjab.[98]

1895: In Eleventh Indian National Congress (Poona)—Malaviya said,

> On the inquiry of the Expenditure Commission that "It will not be satisfactory to the people of this country".[99]

1896: During the Twelfth Indian National Congress (Calcutta)—Malaviya said,

> The time have arrived when a future step should be taken for the financial decentralization, by having the responsibility of financial administration of different provinces principally to local government.[100]

97. *Ibid.*, pp. 173-74.
98. *Ibid.*, p. 16.
99. *Ibid.*, p. 94.
100. *Ibid.*, p. 175.

1896: During Twelfth Indian National Congress (Calcutta)—Malaviya said,

> In mean time the Congress would remind the government for its solemn duty to save human life and mitigate human suffering aware the government on the issue of Poverty and famine code which are inadequate so he would appeal to the government to redeem its pledge by restoring the Famine Insurance Fund for the relief of famine-stricken people.[101] (Poverty and Famine)

1897: In Thirteenth Indian National Congress (Amraoti)—Malaviya focused on

> The Military expenditure and on other unproductive expenditure will be reduced and suggested such larger amount spent for the purpose of welfare of the people. He also gave emphasis on sufficient number of representative Indians in legislative councils.[102] (Royal Commission of Expenditure Commission)

1901: In Seventeenth Indian National Congress—Malaviya suggested

> that it is essential for the success of the work weekly journal published in Landon propagating the views, Journal INDIA was published and its circle was maintained in Bengal, Bombay, Madras, Kanpur, Punjab, etc.[103] (The London Committee of the Indian National Congress)

1903: In Nineteenth Indian National Congress—Malaviya said on university bill that

> Each university should have a separate act. He said that the Bill did not remove the shortcomings of the present system of higher education. Malaviya focused on the faults of senates and syndicates of the existing university and suggested for the reform.[104] (The University Bill)

---

101. *Ibid.*, p. 84.
102. *Ibid.*, p. 97.
103. *Ibid.*, p. 185.
104. *Ibid.*, p. 181.

1903: Under the president ship of the Lieutenant Governor, Sir James John Digges La Touche, KCSI—Malaviya said,

> On the Bundelkhand alienation of Land Bill on 19 January 1903 and presented the cause or situation of Land holders of Bundelkhand and positively tried to convene the government by presenting the data of little irrigation facility, dependency of crop on rain water. So, land and land owner require special treatment. Here Tenants are more in demand of the land and he requested to Govt. to reduce the land revenue reduced by 71/2 lakhs of demand and fever Rayatwari system to take revenue.[105]

April 1904: In Allahabad Madan Mohan Made a Speech on financial statement under the president ship of Lieutenant Governor, Sir James John Digges La Touche, KCSI—said,

> Why the Govt. of India have reduced the share of expenditure by ₹ 28,20,000.00 and suggested entire possibility of advancement and progress in the provinces depends upon amount of our revenues, which the Govt. of India allows to spend, as well as during his speech, he said that it is well understood that in all countries the happiness of the poor depends in great measure on their education. So in his speech he advocated the universalization of primary education in India and requested to provide sufficient funds to set a part for education system and also made complaint against the appointment and promotion of Indian in Govt. Job, gave idea to establish health centre for sanitation, and regret to Govt. to enhance expenditure for higher education, he forcibly said the need of medical college, law department, parks, hospital, college, and library etc.[106]

1904: Twentieth Indian National Congress (Bombay)—Malaviya said,

105. *Ibid.*, p. 123.
106. *Ibid.*, p. 116.

> In the opinion of the Congress, the time has arrived when the people of this country should be allowed a larger voice in the administration and control of the affairs of their country by: (a) the bestowal on each Province or Presidency of India of the franchise to return at least two members to the British House of Commons, (b) an enlargement of both the Supreme and Provincial Legislative Councils—increasing the number of non-official members therein and giving them the right to divide the council in all financial matter coming before them—the head of the government concerned possessing the power of veto. The appointment of Indian representatives (who shall be nominated by the elected members of the Legislative Councils) as members of the Indian Council in London and of the Executive Councils of the Government of India and the Government of Bombay and Madras.[107]

1905: In Twenty-first Indian National Congress (Banaras)—Malaviya said on repressive measures in Bengal, he focused on difference between Swadeshi and boycott. He said,

> I do not want to keep out Boycott movement of foreign goods, but like to continue Swadeshi movement which in my own knowledge started before 30 Years.[108] (Repressive Measures in Bengal)

8th November 1905: Under the president ship of lieutenant governor, Sir James John Digges La Touche, KCSI in Allahabad—Malaviya said on united provinces district board bill he said,

> It will be the duty of the Boards to provide elementary education for all, and it would suggest to modify the clause 42 of the bill, that ensures the purpose of the Board as construction and maintenance of railway, establishment of relief works, relief houses and the adoption of such measure relief in time of famine or scarcity as may consider necessary.[109] (Local and Rural Police Rates Bill)

107. *Ibid.*, p. 20.
108. *Ibid.*, p. 192.
109. *Ibid.*, p. 109.

1906: In Twenty-second Indian National Congress (Calcutta)—Malaviya said on Boycott movement,

> Having regard to the fact that the people of this country have little or no voice in its administration and their representation in the government do not receive any consideration, this is the opinion of the Congress that the Boycott movement inaugurated in Bengal by way of protest against the partition of that region and is lawful.[110] (Boycott Movement)

1906: In Twenty-second Indian National Congress—Malaviya said,

> On the Swadeshi movement that the it is better people of that country labour for the success of the indigenous industries and to stimulate the production of the Indigenous articles by giving them preference over imported commodities even at some sacrifice.[111] (The Swadeshi Movement)

13 March 1906: On United provinces District Boards bill under the president ship of Lieutenant Governor, Sir James John Digges La Touche, KCSI—Malaviya said,

> On power of government to appoint one third of the member of the local board and district council, and forced self-local Govt. should selected on the basis of the people representative but Sir Syed Ahmed Khan pointed out the population may consist of various creeds and various nationalities and if one section of the population commands wealth and commerce, the other may suffer so government reserving the power of the appoint 1/3 of the member of local board and District council in the only measure which can be adopted to guarantee the success of self Govt. by balancing the representation of various section of the Indian Population.[112] (The United provinces District Boards bill)

---

110. *Ibid.*, p. 194.
111. *Ibid.*, p. 196.
112. *Ibid.*, p. 114.

Malaviya's Speeches on the Banaras Hindu University Bill

When objection was raised by Hon'ble Mr. Ghuznavi and Setalvad that university has sectarian character then Malaviya replied,

> My Lord, the University will be a denominational institution but not a sectarian one. It will not promote narrow sectarianism but a broad liberation of mind and a religious spirit which will promote brotherly feeling between man and man. Unfortunately, all was aware that the absence of sectarian religious universities, the absence of any compulsory religious education in our state universities, has not prevented the growth of sectarian feeling in the country. I believe, my lord, instruction is the truth of religion, whether it would be Hindus or Muslims, whether it be imparted to the students of the Banaras Hindu University or of the Aligarh Muslim University, will tend to produce men who, if they are true to their religion, will be true to their God, their King and their country. And I look forward to the time when the students who will pass out of such universities, will meet each other in a closer embrace as sons of the same motherland than they do at present.[113]

1906: Financial Statement under the president ship of Lieutenant Governor, Sir James John Digges La Touche, KCSI—Malaviya in Allahabad legislative council said,

> On the need of higher education and financial need for the expenditure of higher education, secondary education, and need of industrial education and lastly said without sound finance no sound government possible. Without sound government, no sound finance possible. So, there will need that government of India realizes the need and contribution of the people and accordingly made financial policy.[114]

113. *Ibid.*, p. 63.
114. *Ibid.*, p. 139.

1908: Twenty-third Indian National Congress (Madras)—Malaviya said,

> This Congress desires to give expression to the deep and general satisfaction with which the reform proposals formulated in Lord Morley's dispatch have been received throughout the country: it places on record it sense of the high statesmanship which has dictated the action of the government in the matter and it tenders to Lord Morley and Lord Minto its most sincere and grateful thanks for their proposals. This Congress is of opinion that the proposed expansion of the legislative councils and the enlargement of their power and function, in the appointment of Indian member to the executive councils with the creation of such councils where they do not exist, and the further development of local self-government constitute a large and liberal instalment of the reforms needed to give the people of this country a substantial share in the management of their affairs and to bring the administration into closer touch with their feelings. This Congress expresses its confident hope that the details of the proposed scheme will be worked out in the same liberal spirit in which its main provisions as outlined in the Secretary of State's dispatch have been conceived.[115]

1908: Presidential address delivered at the second united provinces conference (Lucknow)—Malaviya said,

> I feel unhappy due to the lost of revered leader Pt. Bishambar Nath, Pt. Laxmi Narayan Vyas of Allahabad and vast number of brothers and sister who have fallen victims to plague in his presidential address he focused on poverty of the people, the evidence of famine, evidence of plague and high mortality, causes of poverty, disregard of India public opinion, present reform proposal, speak on legislative council member selection power and favour to decentralization

115. *Ibid.*, p. 24.

commission. During his address, he focuses on reform in education system also.[116]

1909: Indian Nation Congress (Lahore)—During his presidential address he said,

> On the scheme of constitutional reformation for which the country is indebted to Lord Morley and to Lord Minto. He said the educated class in India first felt the desire for the introduction of self-government, the Govt. of the people through the elected representative of the people in India. Malaviya present his view on representation, on the basis of proportion of population, and provide them political importance. He gave the example of Punjab, Eastern Bengal and Assam where Mohomedans have succeeded every seat and said it is the care of exclusion of the majority by minority.[117]

1917: At the special provincial Congress (Lucknow)—Malaviya said,

> On demand of self-government, Minto Morley reforms, the impacts of war, constitutional reforms, military training, etc.[118]

1917: On the issue of simultaneous exam in Imperial legislative council—Malaviya said,

> We want Indian youth should be subjected to the same test as English youths are subjected like Englishmen Indians allowed to test of civil services in India, very naturally I say that the test of Government of India should held in India only.[119]

1918: Malaviya at the imperial legislative council said,

> On the reduction of Railway fares in March 1918.[120] (Enhancement of Railway Fares)

1918: Malaviya addressed on presidential address of the Indian National Congress—

---

116. *Ibid.*, p. 30.
117. *Ibid.*, pp. 57-58.
118. *Ibid.*, p. 203.
119. *Ibid.*, p. 215.
120. *Ibid.*, p. 221.

> On several issue and resolution adopted in Congress under his president ship was resolution on Indian civil service, reform in Punjab, Delhi, Ajmer-Merwara, Rowlett committee, resolution on Indian Industrial Commission, Release of Ali Brothers etc.[121]

Speech on the abolition of indentured Labour: Malaviya said,

> The indenture system is thoroughly indefensible. At beginning as Mr. Gokhale observed is fraud and maintained by force. It does not benefit the labours. He can earn as much at home as abroad. It lowers the status and wages of the free population and brings the name of India into contempt, it is the source of advantage to the capitalists only who use the laborers as a tool, and the sooner system like this, which permits such a heartless exploitation of human beings, is put an end, the better will it be for all concerned. My Lord, human reason and experience alike show that indentured labour is an unmitigated curse, and the greater the inequality between the contracting parties, the longer the period of contract, the grater is the extent of evil and both humanitarian and political consideration humanitarian far more than political demand that it should be abolished as early as possible and replaced by free labour, which is after all, the most efficient form of labour.[122]

1923: Malaviya in Gaya Presidential address in Hindu Mahasabha—

> He began his address with Vedic mantras. He laid emphasis on greatness of Hindu Civilization, Four *Verns*, Four *Ashrams*, paying respect to Buddha, correlate the ten Buddhist commandments to manu rules and say no difference in Hindu and Buddhists. Also speak on Hindu-Muslim Problem, on reconversion, and on

121. *Ibid.*, p. 228.
122. *Ibid.*, p. 216.

> Suddhi movement.[123] (Presidential address: Gaya Hindu Mahasabha)

1929: On 14th December 1929 Malaviya delivered convocation address in BHU—He paid tribute to Lord Irwin. He said,

> I love to think you have a burning desire to see country free as soon as possible. He expressed the developments and achievement of the students of Banaras Hindu University.[124]

1932: Malaviya addressed to Indian National Congress session (Bengal)—When Mahatma Gandhi and many large patriotic sons of India undergone in imprisonment, Malaviya presented,

> His dislike towards the English government attitude for Congress sessions and resolution adopted in the INC was civil disobedience, Boycott, goal of independence, voice of swaraj arise in this session.[125]

1936: *Malaviya Presided over the session of the All-India Sanatan Dharma Mahasabha*—Which assembled at the Allahabad Sangam during Ardha

Kumbh Mela on January 23-25 he said,

> On the resolution about Harijans, and Mahabir Dals, Kathas, On Women, On Mantra Diksha, etc.[126]

1942: In August 1942 Malaviya as rector of the Banaras Hindu University addressed—

> The students of the Banaras Hindu University asked do you believe in Gandhi ji teaching or not? They cried yes. He said to students to follow non-violence. He said I do not want you to discredit Congress but still I may disagree to burning of Station and things like that. It is

123. *Ibid.*, p. 294.
124. Dar, S.L. and Somaskandan, S., *History of the Banaras Hindu University*. Varanasi: Banaras Hindu University Press, 1966, p. 57.
125. *Ibid.*, p. 298.
126. Parmanand. *Mahamana Madan Mohan Malaviya: An Historical Biography*. Varanasi: Malaviya Adhyayan Sansthan, BHU Press, 1967, p. 939.

> the waste of Public money and will you want to again rebuild it on the expense of Public money. I think what I say to you acceptable to you.[127]

1st November 1946: Malaviya last speech (This message deliver after mass killing 16-19 August 1946, forced conversions of Hindu in the Noakhali district) (translation from Hindi)—

> For years Hindus have been trying fully from their side to realize the true Hindu-Muslim Unity...but it saddens me to see that their tolerance is mistaken for weakness and their cooperation has been rejected mostly by the Muslims. I am making this statement, not from any feeling of intolerance but out of patience and after careful thinking. It is absolutely necessary that Hindus unite together, work closely as one, and build up a unit of selfless and patriotic workers, whose sole purpose would be service only. Forget the caste, creed, and sacrifice more and more for the protection of Hindu community. Conversion should definitely be stopped... those who have been forcibly converted and those who would like to be back as Hindus should be given special facility.... Hindus should be free from fear and become brave and strong...a central help sena should be built up for self-protection. Hindus should rise up their head against oppression.... Hindus do not like to see the death of his Dharma, the erasing of his culture, the dwindling of its number... I think it is my duty to inspire you like this because now humanity is under threat, Hindu culture and Dharma is in danger.[128] (The message sent for the publication in the *Kalyan*, Prabhu Dutt Brahmachari, p. 86)

2 November 1946: Malaviya last visit to Sodepur, on the Occasion of the Gopashtmi—

> Despite of his feeble health he went to the festival of Gopashtmi, on this occasion Malaviya in feeble voice said thanked to the Vyas for the land he had donated for the Goshala. In the Country in India, it is unnecessary,

127. *Ibid.*, p. 716.
128. *Ibid.*, p. 1069.

he said to dilate on the benefits derived from the Cow. He expressed his regret that the country children did not get milk and this shortage had been aggravated by the world war. He exhorted to the audience to organize the industry of milk so more milk was available for everybody.[129] (Speech collected from the Brahmachari book, p. 88)

2.5 Genesis of Malaviya's Personality

The life of Malaviya is a direct challenge to the Law of contradiction. He was a firm believer in ancient culture and tradition. He was also the most modern and had a deep rational and inquiring mind. It was an instance that how opposite qualities could dwell harmoniously in him that is amalgamation of idealism and realism. Many events, thoughts and persons influenced him during his life time and ultimately resulted in shaping his thoughts and thinking in a particular way which made him unique champion for the cause of national development. Thus through making of Malaviya researcher has tried to find out the factors responsible for influencing his personality.

2.5.1 *Birth Place*

Pt. Madan Mohan Malaviya was born at Prayag (Allahabad) on 25 December 1861. When Malaviya was born in Allahabad it was considered as a place where no industries and trades were found. Only pilgrims flocked for *Ganga Snan* at *Sangam* throughout the year especially in the month of *Magh*. It was recognized as *Tirtharaj*, and also as an arsenal and garrison-town. After Malaviya birth Allahabad became state capital High Court, A.G. Office and many English medium educational institutions were established. It brought revolutionization in the life of citizens. When Malaviya was in school going age there was a reputed government high school under working order. There was a college named Muir Central College established in 1872 to complete degree courses. A high court was established in 1866, which played an important role in Malaviya's Law Career to set up legal practices. It was also observed that he

129. *Ibid.*, p. 1070.

started his social work from Allahabad. Malaviya attended first religious discourse in *Kumbh Mela* in Prayag at the age of seven. He spent much of the time in organizing such *Ardha Kumbh* and *Kumbha Melas* and delivered lectures in various meetings of *Sanatan Sabhas* here. So, from *Prayag* his religious background was prepared. Therefore, Allahabad was a place where Malaviya's political, religious, social and educational views took shape due to the transitional state of the city.

2.5.2 *Family Background*

Madan Mohan Malaviya's father Pt. Brij Nath was a '*Vyas*' having a deep devotion to Lord Krishna. The Maharaja of Banaras acknowledges him as Guru. He had many ancient religious books and manuscripts, some of them centuries old and had selections of gems of literature in the form of pocket books (*Gutkas*). Madan Mohan got deep knowledge by reading again and again these books of his father and he was also interested to get this job of Mahajani as his most esteemed birthright. Malaviya's mother Moona Devi was also a simple religious lady who gave food to family members after *Pooja* of Lord Krishna. Malaviya proudly narrated about his mother Moona Devi, who was always keen to serve and help anyone in distress. Such benevolent behavior was also seen in Madan Mohan's personality. She has high skill in managing family affairs in low amount of her husband's earning. She herself fed and milked the cow which they had in the house. She had given a *Chhataak a*nd more of butter and a seer of milk to Malaviya daily since his Childhood. This habit was also seen in daily routine of Madan Mohan's lifestyle. He had been trained by his parents to follow the rules of conduct arranged in the scriptures which he conducted in his whole life as a typical orthodox Brahman. He went with his father to visit the temples to offer salutation and *Kathavachan*, which shaped religious turn of mind in Malaviya.

> He has born testimony to the qualities of his parents and recognized his thanks to them in language also, which has been recorded by Tripathi.[130]

130. Tripathi, *op. cit.*, p. 114.

2.5.3 *His Uncle Gadadhar Chaturvedi*

He was immediate senior in age than his father. He was the senior teacher of Sanskrit at Government High School, Mirzapur. In the formative years of his career he played a vital role in shaping his outlook. Through his uncle's suggestion and encouragement he continued his study of Sanskrit in which his interest would have otherwise flagged after joining an English school. Malaviya's depth of attachment with him was seen in the lines which Malaviya mourned at the death of his uncle, one of them is recorded as,

हाय गदाधार तत्वधर मालवीय कुलकेतु।
इतने थोड़ समय में प्रान वव्यो केहि हेतु।।[131] (Tripathi, pp. 10-11)

2.5.4 *Hardev ji's Pathshala*

Malaviya for his *Upnayan* went to *Hardev ji's Pathshala*, which was a remarkable institution run by a teacher of vision and aptitude. Hardev ji was a Pt. from Mathura, well versed in the *Bhagavata* and fond of music. He practiced yoga and kept cows whose milk was occasionally given to his pupils. In *Pathshala* special importance was given to build up physical strength for achieving the purpose of wrestling, and other exercises were also encouraged. Malaviya acknowledged it during general assembly in his *Pathshala,* teacher or one of senior student recited a *sloka* which was repeated by the pupils. Number of *slokas* of *Bhagavad Gita* and *Manu Smriti* and other laws of *Shastra* were committed to his memory as a result of this morning assembly. Malaviya gained knowledge of Sanskrit, *orthdox-Sanatan Hinduism* by Hardev ji. Hardev Guruji many times took Malaviya much of time with him during discourses on Sanatan Dharma. It was during his school age, at the age of seven, Malaviya was put up by one of his teacher, Pt. Devakinand, to deliver a public lecture at the *Magh Mela* of 1869. Thus, Malaviya was shaped by teachers like Hardev ji and Devakinanda. The effect of this *Sanskrit Pathshala* was seen also in institution visualized by Malaviya. Many times Malaviya acknowledged his gratitude towards his *Pathshala* and his guru

131. Tripathi, *op. cit.*, pp. 10-11.

in speech, and declared that he took training from this *Pathshala* that helped him throughout his life.

2.5.5 *Professor Aditya Ram Bhattacharya*

Next to Malaviya's own parents, if anybody had much influence in molding his character, it was none other than Professor Aditya Ram Bhattacharya who was the teacher of Muir Central College where Malaviya had studied. Malaviya wrote about his life "which was published, Sanskrit work of Shiva Sharma called "Vasudevarasanandah"[132] (Appendix Life sketch of Professor Aditya Ram Bhattacharya). Malaviya was not only influenced by his strictly following orthodox way of life but he received an active cooperation from him during the formation of Banaras Hindu University and Pro Vice-chancellorship during the formative years in 1916-18 (Sunder Lal was vice-chancellor). He lost his eyesight under its strain."[133] (Preparation for life Appendix Life sketch of Professor Aditya Ram Bhattacharya). Both Malaviya and Aditya Ram Bhattacharya have great belongingness to each other.

2.5.6 *Kundan Devi (His Wife)*

Madan Mohan Malaviya married to Kundan Devi in 1881. She was the daughter of Pt. Nand Ram of Mirzapur. She was able to read the *Bhagavad Gita* and had well knowledge of Hindi. Malaviya told Tripathi,

> She occasionally recited her Hindi verses, some of her own composing.[134]

Malaviya had neither passed his degree course nor did job when he got married to Kundan Devi. So, the condition of the family was not so good. She had to remain ill fed and ill clothed but she never complained against him and his family. Shiv Ram Pandey, who became intimate with his family, comments

> Verily, is a house hold, with such a housewife worthy of being on abode of God.[135]

---

132. Parmanand, *op. cit.*, p. 28.
133. *Ibid.*, p. 30.
134. *Ibid.*, p. 20.
135. *Commemoration*, 1931, p. 108.

So no doubt she was devoted fully for her husband and his family. Thus, Malaviya did much of social, political, educational task without any stress due to her dutifulness for family.

2.5.7 *Malaviya's colleagues of school age*

During school age in government high school, Malaviya was influenced by his cousin Pt. Jai Govind Malaviya, who was a prominent scholar of Sanskrit Grammar. Both of the brothers always discussed for the welfare of Hindu Dharma such as why Hindus did not have ample opportunities of knowing about their religion like Muslim and Christian students, which led to a state of ignorance and lack of interest regarding religion among Hindu boys. Along with him, participation in many activities like elocution, extracurricular activities, drama, etc., also influenced his outspoken personality.

2.5.8 *Muir Central College*

Malaviya joined Muir central college in 1879 for the study of his degree the medium of the school was English, therefore Malaviya's strong elocution in English was enriched due to this school.

2.5.9 *Second session of Indian National Congress*

Second Indian National Congress session held at Calcutta in 1886. It was attended by Malaviya in the company of his teacher and guide Pt. Aditya Ram Bhattacharya. On the third day of this session, Malaviya gave a maiden speech which marked a turning point in his life, and Malaviya became known throughout the India as a young leader. The beginning of his role as a National leader started from this session. After this session Raja Rampal Singh of Kalakankar was impressed by Malaviya, and offered him the job of editorship by paying 200 Rs., and forced him to leave the job of teaching. So, his career as journalist, political leader and also of advocate were somewhere related to this session.

2.5.10 *Raja Rampal Singh*

Raja Rampal Singh played a vital role in initiating his inherent capabilities. He provided him opportunity of editorship first time in reputed newspaper *Hindustan* on good payment and also when Malaviya did not agree to do job with him due to his mistake that is in drunk state he spoke some wrong words about Malaviya. But later on Malaviya accepted the editorship of English and Hindi *Hindustan*, a daily newspaper. He agreed to lose him, on one condition, that Malaviya would take the study of Law. He promised to bear all expenses so as to fulfill the degree of Law. Rampal economically helped him. This degree of law helped further in his political career. So after editing the *Hindustan* paper of Raja Rampal Singh Malaviya started a life of stalwart journalist, and edited English daily newspapers, *Indian opinion*, *Abhyudaya* and *Leader*.

2.5.11 *National Movements (1905)*

Contemporary background of Indian politics, social condition and education very much influenced Malaviya which were discussed in the first chapter, since the charter act of 1813, Curzon 1904 policy, several educational experiments had been tried on indigenous system of Indian education, and so the Indian education system started declining gradually and few new schools cropped up by Christian missionaries. The story of Indian mutiny, Jallianwala Bagh massacre movement, Rowlatt Act, non-cooperation movement, the rising-tide of Swadeshi movement etc. generated a feeling of nationalism in the masses. Due to this political awakening, the people began to realize that they could not progress without rising percentage of literacy and education. Malaviya, during his visit in the country for the participation in Congress session, observed the declining condition of Hindu religion, and education. Therefore, Malaviya wanted to revitalize India as a nation through his own view of education by reviving the ancient Hindu thought and combining with scientific and professional knowledge of the west, accordingly he dreamed and manifested it in the form of Banaras Hindu University for the sake of the motherland and Hindu religion.

2.5.12 *Annie Besant*

Mrs. Besant came in India in 1893 and since then she made India her home. Her thinking and devotion for India were seen in her answer,

> Revivify its peoples, revivify its literature revivify its religion.[136]

She was not only confined to the field of education, culture and religion, but she also stepped into politics as soon as social-political situation demanded. She joined Indian National Congress in 1914, and was elected as president in Congress session Calcutta in December 1917. In year 1898, Mrs. Besant established the Central Hindu College at the holy city of Banaras. She felt that religion is the foundation of all true education as it is the foundation of the family and state. Religious and moral instrument were, therefore, introduced by her as a part of school and college teaching. She believed in Hindu Shastra and secular education very soon, Mrs. Besant began to hope that central Hindu College would be centre of a great circle of related institution, it became Hindu University of India. She put idea in 1907 under the name of "The University of India." A scheme of university was also formulated in mind of Malaviya some years ago, and after amalgamation of both the scheme immediate formation of residential university was possible only due to Annie Besant and her sacrificing nature by which she becomes ready to commit with Malaviya and provided him, her consent and the Central Hindu School to fulfill the condition to establish Malaviya's dream university. Malaviya appealed that it was ignoring the facts for anybody to suggest that Mrs. Besant had no admirers among Hindus, or no influence upon them. Central Hindu College is noble edifice on which every Hindu has feeling of proud, and for the rearing of which every Hindu ought to feel unaffected gratitude to Mrs. Besant. On 6 Oct. 1911 due to rich support of Annie Besant and Malaviya ji, Hindu University came into existence. So Annie Besant through love of religion, education and culture, influenced Malaviya ji. The objective which was formulated for university also reflected

---

136. Dar, S.L. and Somaskandan, S., *op. cit.*, p. 34.

Annie Besant's thoughts as building up of character in youth by making religion and ethics an integral part of education.

2.5.13 *Ancient Education System (Gurukul System of Education)*

Malaviya was influenced by Ancient Vedic, Buddhistic cultural Universities such as Sandipini Ashram, Takshashila and Nalanda University, the fame of these universities extended throughout the length and breadth of India and was attracting scholars from different parts of the foreign countries like China, Tibet, Korea and Nepal. The well-known Chinese pilgrim Hiuen-Tsang who came to India in 7th century AD studied in Nalanda. Nalanda and Takshashila were institutions of high standard and advanced studies and their income was also sufficient to provide their alumni free cloth, food, beading and medicine. Malaviya listened and study about these universities thus he dreamed to establish university based on the same approach. As in *Ashram/ Gurukul* consisting about 1,00,000 students and cooperation provided them free lodging, food, etc.[137] He also dreamed to make his university a center of 10,000 students who will learn and live there.

2.5.14 *Effect of student-teacher relationship of Vedic Period*

In Vedic Period, Students lived in the ashram of the Guru as a member of his family, and Guru loved them as his own son. The teacher and the pupils shared a common life, common food, they have common purpose to increase the knowledge, and prosperity of one another. The teacher and his pupils used to awake very early in morning, went to the river or stream nearby, took their bath and performed prayer daily they again perform *Sandhya* on the same day with each other. Malaviya also wanted to create such culture in the university, so he dreamt to establish university at the bank of Ganga. He thought that through their manner teacher can develop spiritual nature and higher qualities of need and heart in his pupils, so he made residential university, where student passes complete *Brahmacharya*, and quarter was also given to teacher and pupil. He wanted university to develop students who have characteristics as explained in this *Shloka*.

137. *Ibid.*, p. 40.

सत्येन ब्रह्मचर्येण व्यायामेनाथ विद्यया।
देश भतत्त्यात्मत्यागेन सम्मानार्हः सदा भव।

Malaviya in his whole life respected his teachers. He always recited students much *Shlok* related to *Brahmacharya* and inspired them to follow strong conduct as he said rectitude of conduct is thought to be a far more valuable possession than wealth.

2.5.15 *Effect of the Bhagavad Gita*

Malaviya's life revolves around the philosophy of the *Gita*. In his personality "Gita enjoins" that is the union of *Yogesvra* and the *Dhanudhara*. In his life he acted as a man of ideals and a man of action respectively. Therefore, Malaviya blended idealism and realism both in his dream of Banaras Hindu University. In his personal life, Malaviya was dedicated to supreme and installed Lord Krishna at the centre of all his activities. Malaviya liked inaugurating weekly discourse on the *Gita* in university which reflects his faith and love for *Gita*. Effect of teachings of Lord Krishna was seen in his humanity and administration. He wanted every man to be humble to the status of Arjuna and to receive cure by the *Gita*. The attitude of Malaviya to solve any problem and reaction of *Sambhaav* in happiness and grief reflected that how much he inculcated *Gita's* lessons in his practical life.

Mostly Malaviya's speech was phrased by the *Gita Shlok* as,

न काम्येऽहं गतिमश्विरात् पराम्। अष्टद्धियुक्तामपुनभवै च।।
आर्ति प्रप्रद्येखिलदेहभाजाम्। अन्तः स्थितोयेन भवन्तुदुःख।।[138]

(*Srimad Bhagavad Gita* 9-21)

I don't pray to God to given me salvation characterized by the possession of the eight Siddhis or the highest salvation or freedom from re-birth, but what I pray for is that I may feel that sorrows of all being by dwelling within them. So that they may be free from them. He always follows,

शिवायलोकस्य भवाय भूतयेय उत्तम श्लोक परायणा जनाः।[139]

---

138. *The Bhagavad Gita English Translation* published by Gita Press, Gorakhpur Chapt. ii shlok (47), (2007).
139. *Shrimad Bhagavad Gita*, pp. 9-21.

All above described *Shloka's* related to the welfare of human were seen not only in *Vani* but also in Mansa, *Vachan, Karma* of Malaviya. Malaviya said,

न त्वहं कामये राज्यं न स्वर्ग न पुनर्भवम्।
कामये दुःख तप्तानां प्राणिना भार्तिनाश्सम्।।[140]

I have no desire for the kingdom, neither any desire for heaven, nor freedom from bondage (*Moksha*).

> I have only one desire and that is to remove the miseries and sorrows of all living being.[141]

He likes to said, "Nothing is impossible for me in this world if I recite Gajendra Moksha whole heartily." Therefore, Malaviya was a unique epitome of ideals of *Shrimad Bhagavad*. He says if Lord Krishna made all, than nobody could be an untouchable. Malaviya started a movement of *mantradiksha* for untouchable which was severely opposed by the orthodox section of Hindus. Then Malaviya convinced Hindu scholars and Conducted debates and obtained cooperation and support for his mission. He initiated *Om Namah Shivaya* and *Om Namo Narayana* mantras to several lakhs of untouchables at Kashi, Prayag, Nasik. Therefore, it could be said that his life and all his activities were inspired by the *Gita*.

2.5.16 *Effect of Hindu Sanatan Dharma*

No account of Malaviya's life and work is complete which does not determined his faith in *Sanatan Hindu Dharma*. This was the most outstanding feature of his personality. All his activities such as political, social, educational were based on it. He felt about Hindu *Dharma* as a child feels about his mother, as something essential without which life becomes impossible. Those who described him sectarian, did great injustice to him. His idea of Hindu Dharma could not be sectarian, but universal. In fact, *Dharma* and Hindu *Dharma* were identical for him. He belonged to the *Bhagavata sect*, his dressing sense,

---

140. Chaturvedi, S.R., *Builder of Modern India Madan Mohan Malaviya*. New Delhi: Ministry of Information and Broadcasting Government, 1995, p. 34.
141. Dar, S.L. and Somaskandan, S., *op. cit.*, p. 223.

way of living, all attitudes reflected him as *Sanatani*. Malaviya began his campaign for Hindu renaissance under the banner of Hindu Samaj in Prayag in 1880 at the age of 21 under the presidentship of Pandit Adityaram Bhatacharya, nearly 4 to 5 years he continued his mission of awakening Hindus against the evils, tona and totakas, and superstitions that had crept Hindu society. "During 1885, he organized *Madhaya Hindu Samaj* in 1887 January in *Bharat Dharma Mahamandal* at Haridwar."[142] He put his views for the protection of cows and environmental purity of Ganga in 1905. Mahamana laid the foundation of "*Akhila Bharatiya Sanatana Dharma Mahasaba*"[143] with a noble resolve for the moral upliftment and welfare of Hindu society from 20th to 27th January 1906. Mahamana convened the first week in *Sanatana Dharma Mahasabha* at Prayag which was attended by all religion need of all sects and ready unanimous approval of the establishment of Kashi Hindu Vishvavidyalaya. In Aug. 1923, seventh session of *Mahasabha* at Kashi Mahamana threw light on the necessity to remove untouchability, upliftment of women, dowry system, remarriage of widows, problems of social security till 1922 to 1935 his continued participation in Hindu Mahasabha. Therefore for Malaviya however *Hindu Dharma* was quite competent to supply all the principles which shaped his life.

Although many factors affected such as environmental causes, hereditary factors, etc. his personality. But in reality, he was self-motivated and self-esteemed personality having high will power and moved by inner self. His father Pt. Brijnath had six sons and two daughters but only Malaviya attained name and fame. Thus all the power and qualities of Malaviya, were initiated by his religious father and mother but some of them were already provided to him by God in the form of his ideal self, which made his whole personality great. Some of his characteristics as curiosity for higher knowledge since childhood, great attention for spiritual meditation, his sharp memory, regular habits, proper dressing style, code of discipline, high moral values, social life, high determination, patriotism,

142. Chaturvedi., S.R., *op. cit.*, p. 35.
143. *Ibid.*

high ambition, and elocution power made him different from others, which were somewhere got affected by outward factors and situations, but finally it was his inner self which controlled him, so it could be said that he was a self-made personality.

3

Philosophical Thoughts of Madan Mohan Malaviya

3.1 Introduction

This chapter presents the thoughts of Madan Mohan Malaviya regarding society, economics, politics, religion, morality, and spirituality in the frame of his social, economic, political, religious philosophy. It was thought necessary to study critically the core concept of philosophical thoughts of Malaviya before studying his educational philosophy.

3.2 Core Concept of Malaviya's Social Philosophy

The thoughts of Malaviya about society were based on the principle of well-conversant society which follows the indigenous culture and traditions of *Sanatan Dharma*. What Malaviya meant by *Sanatan Dharma* was a *Dharma* which is eternal and followed since ancient time and which will be followed till eternity. It is followed by the truthful, altruistic, unprejudiced, and scholarly persons. The social order of the *Sanatan Dharma* is based upon *Vern Ashram Dharma* that means everybody should follow his duties peculiar to their *Varna* and *Ashram*. His thoughts mostly revolved around contribution of *Sanatan Dharma* in framing an ideal society. Malaviya was not rigid philosopher but he believed in dynamism of society and religion simultaneously. In the 20th century religious reformers and saints like Vivekanand, Swami Dayanand, Gandhi, Tagore, Aurbindo, Ramathirth, and others laid emphasis upon humanism, monotheism, world unity of all religions, etc.[1] Similar to these visionaries, Malaviya also interpreted his view on Hinduism as a religion of humanity.

His social thoughts meant for whole mankind. He believed that the same spirit dwells in all living beings. Therefore, he was not only identified himself with the men, but also with other living beings. As a democrat, his understanding about society and social laws followed basic principle of democracy as freedom, justice, equality, fraternity. He understood society as a complete picture in which each aspect like education, religion, politics, economics are equally important. As a functionalist, he provided scientific principle for the formation of society which was based on the religious approaches.

As an idealist philosopher, Malaviya tried to find out the link between the human society and ultimate reality of life. He critically evaluated and analyzed the *Veda*, *Upanishad*, *Gita shlok* and developed widespread thoughts about universe and life. He thought that the nucleus of the society is man, or society is the dynamic organization of the individual. So he wished

> Every men and women should practice fearlessness, truthfulness, abstinence from stealing, continence, patience and mercy. He always spoke that one should never forget that the result of good deed is good and of evil deed is bad and that one has to take subsequent birth according to ones actions in this life.[2]

For the development of the harmony in the society he paid honor to all religions and their followers. Malaviya was of the view one should be determined in one's faith, should never to talk unwell of others, be open-minded to one's opponent (whether in matters of religion or social relations). Malaviya said that

> Do to others as you would done by. Never do to others what you do not want to be done to yourself. It is the duty of strong man to ward off the sufferings and miseries of others. So for an ideal society in Bharat it

1. Singh, Y.K., *Sociological Foundation of Education*. New Delhi: APH Publication, 2007, p. 155.
2. Chaturvedi, S., *Madan Mohan Malaviya*. New Delhi: Ministry of Information and Broadcasting, Government of India, 1988, p. 37.

> is important that one should work shoulder to shoulder with the patriotic Parsees, Muslims, Christians and others for the upliftment of the nation.[3]

Malaviya assumed that society must be based on religion. He was not against the development of society based on the community. He thought if people followed their religion truly whether Hindu, Muslim, there is no need to make effort from outside to acquire peace. He paid respect to legislation but gave more emphasis on religious values for social harmony. Both the *Shastra* and the *karma-kand* or rituals were dear to him what however distinguished him; from his orthodox lifestyle, i.e. he always interpreted *Shastra* in logical and scientific way. Malaviya said that

> He does not like to build up moral value education as a part of education and society but claimed never leave from the path shown by the Shastra, and honestly liked people should follow to the purest norms of the Shastra. Because in his view the old system which was followed in ancient time was not half as bad as it is today.[4]

Therefore, for the construction of ideal society, Malaviya's outlook was matched with the *Vedic* system in which the main string to weave the framework of the society was religion. He wanted every human should follow four *Ashrams* system in life, as in his lecture of religious discourse and on natural appeal for students, he furnished the importance of *Brahmacharya* (first stage of life), as the age, in which youths got physical stamina and he advised for the installation of *Akharas* in villages for the wrestling. He cited the example of Lakshman to create discipline and love for the *Brahmacharya* in the youths of Banaras Hindu University. However, Malaviya was not superstitious for the social customs, norms of Hindu society which were harmful for the Hindu community. He took a number of pains periodically to remove the social evils of the Hindu society. For example, even he was opposed by many orthodox *Brahmin* for the entrance of *Sudra* in temples and equal right as upper caste Hindus but

3. *Ibid.*, p. 38.
4. Bakshi, S.R., *Madan Mohan Malaviya: The Man and His Ideology.* New Delhi: Anmol Publication, 1991, p. 272.

he never changed his opinion and did the best according to his voice of understanding. Even he had faith in *Verna* system of *Manu*, but his understanding of the *Varna* system was followed by the view in which social development was based on the ability and performance instead of birth. Thus, Malaviya's attitude did not reflect cultural inertia that is the blind beliefs, customs, and tradition which came down from forefathers and which could be defined as rigid, conservative, and narrow outlook which made an individual static and averse to any change.[5] It was reflected by his social works and programs which he initiated for the uplift of untouchables.

During his social conferences, he delivered speeches against dowry, animal sacrifices, and lack of women's education, *purda* system, sati, widow marriage, problems of untouchables and various social evils, etc. Malaviya's views were divergent on child marriage as he logically presented his ideas against it and said

> It greatly affected the physique of the youths and practice of early marriage mismatched with Brahmacharya concept. He forcefully said that the youth got married at the age of 25, and then they will be able to reproduce strong young ones while the offspring of persons married at the age of 12 or 13 was bound to be weak, sick and short lived, so it is harmful in relation to the society to marry the youth in early age. For girls he said not to marry before the age of fifteen.[6]

He wanted to enhance social and economic prosperity by raising educational standards of the society. His views on education were innovative and according to the need of the society. Malaviya's social philosophy was based on understanding of human situation, or it was as imperative as human demand. In his social philosophy, logic was the main dogma as his support to widow-marriage, girl's education, opposition of child

5. Singh, Y.K., *Sociological Foundation of Education*. New Delhi APH Publication, 2007, p. 148.
6. Parmanand, *Mahamana Madan Mohan Malaviya (An Historical Biography)*. Varanasi: Malaviya Adhyayan Sansthan, BHU, 1985, p. 624.

marriage or the explanation of any ritual or *Sanatan* value. On the issue of social and personal security of the women, his views are relevant for today. He said

> I desire that all women of our country should possess pistols and guns liked English women and should learn to fire so that they can protect their personal sanctity (Satitva) against any attack.[7]

Again for widows, he said

> If a widow desires, she should be married.[8]

His social and political ideas were guided by the ideals of social harmony and cooperation. Malaviya not only resided in the heart of Hindus but also he found equal respect by another community such as Muslims, Sikhs, etc. Many times as a fine orator, he influenced the British bureaucracy by his powerful and comprehensive arguments. He fought over and over for the fundamental right of Indians which included education, adequate representation in government services along with the Britishers and the demand of *Swaraj*. Malaviya's social philosophy never differed from his actions and political movements. For him the meaning of nationalism and concept of religion was the same, not different to each another. So in elocutions on religious discourse and in social works done by Malaviya the feeling of service of motherland is reflected.

Malaviya opposed social reform through legislation and believed that any social reform should come from within. So when he represented himself in any social conference, he presented himself as an active *karyakarta* not as a party leader and tried to unify and strengthen the society. When the social work of Malaviya is critically analyzed, it was found that his views were based on a well-defined community-based society where objectives of the community was clear and based on religiosity. He also thought that if such a society developed, then the values like belongingness, respect to other people and their

7. Tiwari, U.D., *A Short Biography Mahamana Malaviya*. Varanasi: Mahamana Malaviya Foundation, 2007, p. 46.
8. *Ibid.*

religion can be easily inculcated. He propagated social reform on many issues some are discussed as under.

3.2.1 *Work for the Upliftment of the Untouchables*

Malaviya initiated movement for the upliftment of the untouchables along with Gandhi. He visualized that the socio-economic status of the untouchables can be raised only by providing them equal or honorable position in society. When he initiated positive actions through his movements he faced much opposition by orthodox *Sanatan Brahmin*, but he logically cited different examples of *Shastra* and tried to prove that *Shastra* does not believe in monopoly of one class, that even *Sudra* should not be denied to study. To explain this context while speaking on the *Varna Ashram Dharma*, he told,

> In the time of Raja Bhoj even Palki-bearers and fishermen knew Sanskrit. So, it is our duty to educate everybody.[9]

In order to re-establish the dignity of the marginalized section of untouchables in the Hindu Society and to associate those in the mainstream of the educational and social development Malaviya founded the *Antyajodhara Sabha* in 1921. He began an innovative experiment, i.e. *Mantrodiksha* for untouchables, which was when violently opposed by the orthodox section of the Hindus, Malaviya organized the meetings to convene Hindus scholars of different parts of the country and participated in debates and gained assistance and held his mission. In 1927 he propagated the "Om Namah Shivaya" and "Om Namo Narayana" mantra to more than a lakh of untouchables at Kashi, Prayag, Nasik, Calcutta, and Haridwar and saved them from becoming non-Hindus.[10]

During session of the Hindu-Mahasabha in the premises of the Central Hindu College, Banaras Malaviya articulated to depressed class that the Mahasabha was the sabha of the Hindus, Brahman, as much as of Chandals.

> I look upon the Brahman and the chandal alike as my brother and salute him. May God pardon me if I do not

9. Parmananad, *op. cit.*, p. 623.
10. Tiwari, U.D., p. 39.

have a tender feeling when a chandal's child approaches to me?[11]

He was able to lock the agreement of both the *Pandits* and *Sadhus* before announcing any concession to them. For example during addressing a gathering of *Pandits* and *Sadhus*, Malaviya pleaded that sweepers should be allowed to draw water from the wells, by citing a story of Raja Ranti Deva who, after having given away his food to a chandal, was preparing to satisfy his hunger with the washing of the plate off which the chandal had eaten, then the lord appeared to bless him so by this way he tried to agree Pandits of Mahasabha.[12] During the same conference Malaviya showed his mind set in front of Hindu leaders or leaders of Arya samaj, representatives of Buddhist, Sikhs, Jains, etc. against the proselytizing activities of the Muslims and Christians. Thus, Malaviya thought that to save Hindu religion, it is important to continue movement in regarding rights of the untouchables and also *Shuddi* programmes. The vision of both the programmes was to stop the conversion of the Hindus into Islam and other religions.

In 1924, during Maghmela Malaviya mainly stressed on the measures of Untouchability. He appealed to Hindusangathan for support of the *Shuddi* movements besides removal of untouchability.[13] In April 1928, Malaviya again planned and executed *mantradiksha* programme at *Dashasvamedh Ghat* at Kashi. Again at Calcutta he initiated thousands of untouchables and Dalits to mantra *diksha*.[14] *Mantradiksha* programme run by Malaviya appreciated and supported by Gandhi. *Shuddi* programme which was organized by Malaviya not opposed by the Gandhi, as in 1922 during All India Shuddi Sabha joint session of Hindu and Rajput Mahasabha on Feb. 13, 1923[15] four and half lakh Muslim Rajputs known as Malkans in the district of Agra, Mathura return into Hindu religion. In

11. Parmananad, *op. cit.*, p. 625.
12. *Ibid.*
13. Abhyudaya, February 9, 1924.
14. Tiwari, U.D., *op. cit.*, p. 39.
15. Prakash Indra: *History of the Hindu Mahasabha*, pp. 36-37.

response Gandhi stated nothing objectionable in the *Shuddi* of the Malkans and wrote in his article of editorial of the *Harijan*:

> If Malkans wanted to return in Hinduism they had every right to do so; but there should be no reviling of the other creed.[16]

In December 1927 publically Malaviya declared that there was no section in the *Shastra* for Untouchability and advocated relaxation of the rigid restriction on untouchables using the public road and wells and entering temples in a special session of Hindu Mahasabha.[17]

Therefore, it can be concluded that Malaviya as a visionary knew liberation of the untouchable classes would be recognized as a burning political issue in coming days for Indian society, which further appeared during Poona pact where *Dalit* leaders demanded for representative electorate in government on political stage in the form of communal award. Thus, Malaviya understood the fact that the political importance of any community would correspond to its numbers in the population and the Hindus could retain their dominant majority only if the depressed classes remained attached to them. So by knowing this fact he decided to aware Hindu community, through political stand or Mahasabha conferences resolutions, some measures to improve the condition of these classes.

Therefore to strengthen Hindus at political, social, educational front Malaviya convoked these conferences and programs. Consequently, the deprived, marginalized, segregated section of the Hindu community, i.e. untouchables and Dalits regained their respectful status in the majority of the Hindu society and got liberty to get water from public wells, ponds, entrance to temples for *devdarsan*, right to walk on streets with raised heads, to get education in the same institution of learning of high class Hindus, to watch and rejoice religious festivals.

Malaviya, requested to all Dalits to preserve cleanness, in their manner of living. He initiated a plan of some positive steps in this direction,

16. *Gurukul University Dimond Jubilee Brochure*, 1960, p. 8.
17. Abhudaya, May 5, 1927 and *Leader*, May 18, 1927.

In 1918, during the Kumbha gathering at Prayag; he tried for collective agreement of two thousand scavengers for engaging in cleanliness work and inaugurated the Seva Samiti as social service activity. After the end of this fair, he told all the scavengers to take bath in the Ganga and presented *dhotis*, towels, and blankets to each of them; recited scripture at Sangam and finally arranged a community feast and took food sitting along with them in line. Contrary to anticipation that Malaviya would change his cloth and take a bath before taking his meal he did nothing like this and took his food as their guest, i.e. Dalit of Seva Samiti.[18]

On December 25, 1932 when he presided over the "*Antyajoddhar Sabha*" at Bombay where untouchable put *chandan* and *tilak* on his forehead and garland him.[19] Many decisions were acknowledged in that meeting for Untouchables. Gandhi organized a conference of *Harijanodhar* in 1934 at Kashi, during this event Malaviya in his speech made violent attacks against the false imitation of the orthodox section of the Hindu society who did not welcome the reforms heartedly and were rigid in their attitude.[20]

In 1936, on the occasion of *Shivratri*, he organized a march for the deprived untouchables riding on elephants and horses, in this march thousands of untouchables participated, it was about one kilometer long.[21] So such activity manifested Malaviya not only wanted to raise the status of untouchables in Hindus but his goal was to change the attitude of higher caste Hindus for untouchables and also to change the mind set of untouchables for their status. For the sake of this noble goal Malaviya accepted the challenge of the Shankaracharya and he participated into religious debate with Shankaracharya in presence of 60 thousand people. In 1935, he preached his sermons on the topic "*Dharmo rakshati rakshitah*" at *Hari ki*

18. Parmananad, *op. cit.*, p. 354.
19. Tiwari, U.D., *op. cit.*, p. 40.
20. Tiwari, U.D., *loc. cit.*, p. 39.
21. *Ibid.*, p. 41.

pauri for untouchable and high caste people.[22] In the Banaras Hindu University, he had made ample provision as free education for untouchables they were given monthly stipend and were also given blankets and clothes every year. It is the contribution of Malaviya that a number of *Dalit* students got higher status in society, like Babu Jagjivan Ram, after getting their education at the Banaras Hindu University.

3.2.2 *Malaviya's Reaction for Communal Award and Depressed Class*

The communal award was declared on August 16, 1932, when Malaviya and Gandhi came back from round table conference. Hindus of Bengal started agitation against it under the support of Malaviya.[23] Gandhi started fast against this provision of government by which Britishers wanted to weaken Hindu community and tried to create cleavage between Hindus for the purpose of long stay in India. Although Britishers tried to express the goal of equality in their administrative policy by giving recognition to the Hindu depressed class as a separate community with their own electorate. But Malaviya and Gandhi understood their aim and analyzed fact that such separate electorates were applied by the government for the detachment of the depressed class from the Hindu society. No doubt the principle of separate communal electorates primarily divided Indian population into 17 unequal parts by extending their concession of separate electorates to several communities—Europeans, Anglo Indians, Indian Christians and depressed-class Hindus including labour and women. European wanted to develop a microscopic minority of the population in the presidencies of Bengal, Madras and Bombay.[24] So both expressed their firm determination to oppose it.

Gandhi started his opposition through fast and writing article in *Harijan* while Malaviya depended on the Mahasabha works with depressed classes and they tried to play a key role to save this grim situation for best of the nation. Finally, in order to improve the feeling and the condition of the depressed classes,

22. *Ibid.*
23. Parmananad, *op. cit.*, p. 875.
24. Mehta and Patwardhan, *The Communal Triangle*, p. 72.

and to satisfied their needs Malaviya and Gandhi started to talk with leaders of the depressed classes.[25] Malaviya in relation to this award actively worked and he announced to all Hindu leaders on September 17, 1932 he said:

> I honestly believe that the feeling of patriotism, and devotion to religion among us would help us to achieve an agreement which will satisfy the desires of depressed class and he took immediate step to open the temples of his native town Allahabad including two belonging to his own family for the entry of the Harijans.[26]

Consequently, an instant response resulted in all over the country at Bombay, Calcutta famous temples were open for the Harijans.[27] Gandhi expressed his willingness not only to concede the reservation of seats but also something more than Ambedkar asked.[28] Malaviya was the first signatory on this pact. Ambedkar not only thanks to Gandhi but also said warm praise to Malaviya as

> I must also thank to Malaviya for the courtesy and forbearance that he showed in the hot exchange of words and acrimonious debates that went on during all these negotiation. I hope, he said it would be possible to device ways and means whereby it would be possible for the depressed classes not only to be part and parcel of the Hindu community but also to occupy an honorable position, a position of status in the community.[29]

Therefore by the actions of Malaviya it is concluded that he wanted to remove the blot of Untouchability from the Hindu religion and his zeal was not only to remove this social evil by providing measure of reservation but he wanted to eliminate the untouchable feelings from both upper caste and lower caste the society.

---

25. *Ibid.*, p. 876.
26. *Ibid.*, p. 877.
27. Pyarelal, *The Epic Fast*, p. 277.
28. Prashad, R., *Autobiography*. New Delhi: Sasta Sahitya Mandal, 2013, p. 350.
29. Parmanand, *op. cit.*, p. 882.

3.2.3 *Malaviya's Social Journey in Allahabad*

The native place of Malaviya was Allahabad, so his social life was started from this city. From the very beginning age as in 1889, the Bharati Bhavan Library was founded by him in the locality where he resided.[30] Malaviya served as a social worker in his native town as member of Municipal Board from 1900-16 and did a lot of social work for the welfare of the society.[31] Malaviya's first concrete achievement in the field of education was the establishment of the Hindu Boarding House at Allahabad. Behind doing this task, the aim of Malaviya was to help the students who generally came from the distant places and from rural areas to pursue higher education in the colleges of the Allahabad and faced the problem of lodging.

So he contemplated for the establishment of a hostel where they could live in comfort and security.

Before foundation of Hindu boarding house (1899) a Musalmaan boarding house was promised by Sir Antony MacDonnell in Allahabad and its construction was completed in 1892 on the ground of the Muir Central College for the residence of Muslim students by Auckland Colvins.[32] The construction of the hostel for the welfare of Muslim community influenced the brain of Malaviya consequently he started to effort for the establishment of the Hindu hostel in the same city. Here a question arose in the mind of researcher why Malaviya's social work followed by the social welfare of the Muslims work? This was the first incidence, but when his other great social activities are observed as for example his eagerness for the foundation of Banaras Hindu University after provision of Aligarh Muslim University or establishment of Hindu Mahasabha after foundation of Muslim League all were reflected that Malaviya's zeal was always ready for healthy competition in relation to social, educational, political development of both Hindu and Muslim community.

30. *Ibid.*, p. 77.
31. *Ibid.*, p. 112.
32. *Ibid.*, p. 114.

The foundation of Hindu boarding house was laid with due ceremony on July 27, 1901 in the presence of MacDonnell, who said,

> Intellectual culture is handicapped when the students' lives amidst sordid surroundings, and cut off for a large part of each day from intercourse with instructors and fellow-students. The association of young man with each other in a properly managed residential college creates a standard of honor which affects the character of each student throughout the life.[33]

No doubt the impression of MacDonnell speech made impression on the brain of Malaviya and his experience of construction of this hostel further resulted in the form of Banaras Hindu University which was residential in nature.

The Mintopark, now renamed "Madan Mohan Malaviya Park" is another monument built by Malaviya in 1910.[34] Other social activities were mainly done by him in the capacity as the chairman of the Allahabad municipality board, he took a deep interest in the alleviation of the plague-affected people's suffering by establishing plague camps. He also worked a lot for the housing and sanitation schemes.

3.2.4 *Malaviya's Attention for Communal Harmony*

Before discussion on communal harmony, it is essential to understand secular and communal approach in Indian context. During pre-independence, Indian Constitution was not formed so there was no actual meaning defined for secularism, but somewhere it exists in living style of Indians in the form of *Serve Dharma Samabhava* that means equal regard for all faiths and creeds. If Malaviya social religious speeches analyzed from above point of view, it is detected that his social philosophy was based on humanitarianism which leads secularism. Britishers planned to divide both the Hindu and Muslim community over religion and enjoyed control over fractured society. Thus, a number the

---

33. Selections from Speeches of Sir A.P. MacDonnell, G.C.S.I. Lieutenant-Governor N.W.P.P., 205.
34. Padamkant Malaviya in *Jhalkian* pp. 61-62.

community leaders such as Jinnah, Malaviya, etc. made effort for community development as well as for communal harmony.

As when the British Government tried to provoke communal stress and antagonism between the Hindu and Muslim communities by providing extra privilege to one of the communities as Muslims and harm Hindu interest of welfare, Malaviya raised his quick reaction for justice. In Malaviya view national unity was basic need for attainment of success in the fight of freedom, and was also the spirit of harmony and peace in a multi-religion country, where numerous religion, namely Hindu, Muslim, Christian, Sikh, Jain, with their different sects, sub-sects, cast, creed and sub-creeds co-existed.

Malaviya said, Act in such a way that all may unite. Let develop mutual trust. The only way of survival and growth after independence is to continue with long-term inter-communal unity, so essential for peace and harmony. He said we will have to make such a law and such a constitution that no body may be afraid of anyone else in the country in whatever circumstances are placed. When we succeed in doing so there will be no question of majority or minority. I again repeat go on discussing and explaining. Never say,

> Now we break. Never say, die. One day fight brings permanent loss to the country. It brings disgrace upon us.[35]

This statement reflected Malaviya's opinion on the communal harmony and his understanding of significance of national unity in the form of religious, cultural, political unity in diversity of India. He dreamt about Indian past in the form of ideal of *Chakravarti*, language unity in the form of Sanskrit, Prakrit language, political unity in the form of among emperors such as Chandra Gupta, Ashok, etc. so he never liked the cleavage of the country in two nations, but favors communal could be replaced by community unity.

Undoubtedly, he was eager for the progress and welfare of the Hindu community but was never anti-Muslim in his

35. Maine, S.K., et al., *Visionary of Modern India Madan Mohan Malaviya*. New Delhi: Commonwealth Publisher (2011), p. 40.

approach. Mohammad Ali Jinnah, the architect of Pakistan held very high esteem for Malaviya. It is believed by a lot of Indians if the Hindu-Muslim problem would have been left in the hand of both above visionaries, country would not face the problem of division. It was analyzed by data that when communal riots broke out in country at any place, Malaviya was the first person to reach there and provided all help to both Hindus and Muslims with the same mind set. As

> In 1910 when Indian National Congress met third time at Allahabad, Malaviya played a prominent role to heal the differences arisen between Hindu-Muslim, moderates and extremist. At the same year Wedderburn addressed Hindu-Muslim conference in which Hindu and Muslim representatives discuss on the question of communal representation and separate electorate, and on language Malaviya faced much opposition but he took stand against the separate electorate of Muslims in politics. Malaviya criticized by many Muslim leaders for his stand. But Malaviya continually organized Hindu Mahasabha at Lahore and Hardwar.[36]

He presided over the All India Hindu-Muslim Unity conference at Nagpur. In March 1916, he participated in the session of Muslim League at Lucknow. In 1921, he visited Malabar, Mopala and other places during serious communal riots and extended his all effort and helps to both Hindus and Muslims and appealed for unity and harmony. In September 1922, a very serious riot took place at Multan and he wept resentfully after seeing barbarous and brutal scenes. He presided over a Hindu Muslim Unity Conference at Lahore on 16th September and appealed for unity. Again in September 1927 he got convened the Unity conference at Shimla; on 5 April 1931, he made speeches on Hindu-Muslims unity at Kanpur.[37] Thus, through his political span he visited to all over India and tried to strengthen Hindus and unity between Hindu and Muslims. The National Muslim Meet (October 1932) was organized by Malaviya suggestion, in the same year the Ektta Conference

36. Prakash, Indra, *History of the Hindu Mahasabha*, p. 18.
37. Tiwari, U.D. *op. cit.*, p. 31.

on 3 January 1932, organized at Allahabad. Malaviya role was always moderate and of negotiator between Europeans, Muslims and Bengali's and Hindus. Malaviya's attempt for the unity was appreciated by Dr. Mahamadullah, Kunjuru, etc. after 1932.[38]

Malaviya was regarded by Tagore, Gandhi, Munsi Iswar Saran, etc. for his action towards communal harmony. Malaviya's relation was good with all community leaders like Sikh leader of Punjab always showed their faith in Malaviya. During the Nowakhali (Bengal) riots in 1946, he appealed to the Hindus to get united and delivered his last message to Hindus before his death.[39] In Hindu University, Malaviya declared general holidays in the entire university on Muslim festivals and on the birth of the Prophet Mohammad even only seven Muslim students studied at that time. So even Malaviya was recognized as a well-wisher of Hindu community but whole of his life he also devoted for the unity between different communities for the sake of nation building.

3.2.5 *Malaviya's Agro-Economic View for Goraksha Movement*

Malaviya's cow-protection (*Goraksha*) movement was not initiated only due to the faith in Hindu religious virtues, but he visualized cow's importance from economic, agricultural, health point of view. He defined his '*Goraksha*' movement as 'peoples protection (*Manava Raksha*) movement'. He said,

> The children of the nation cannot make sufficient intellectual and emotional development without cow milk. The malnutrition of children will weaken nation's both present and future growth.[40]

In 1887 at Hardwar under the shadow of Hindu Mahasabha a resolution passed to protect the cow and establish *Goshala* throughout the country. Malaviya visited to all over country for collection of fund to achieve the objective, i.e. cow protection movement. He founded a cow-shelter (*Go-shala*) in Kitaganj locality in Prayag in 1889. On the *Gopashtami* day, October 25,

38. Parmanand, *op. cit.*, p. 894.
39. *Ibid.*, p. 1070.
40. Tiwari, U.D., *op. cit.*, p. 41.

1925, he presided over the 39th '*Goraksha*' conference at Kashi. In 1928, he played an important role in acquirement of about one thousand acres of land between Mathura and Vrindaban and establishment of a trust named '*Hasanand Gochar Bhumi Trust*' named after a famous *Go-rakshaka*.

Shri Hasanand.[41] On 15 September 1928, Malaviya presided over the '*Go Sammelan*' organized at Alfred Park in Calcutta.

In 1932, he made an arrangement for supplying the fodder on a large scale during severe famines in Haryana and Gorakhpur *janapad* and founded the 'Go-raksha Mandala' at Delhi.[42] In 1933, he said, "People can survive without meat but there is no substitute for milk." On 15 March 1936, Malaviya inaugurated the '*Panchvati Pinjarapo*' (cow shelter) at Nasik. On that occasion he said,

> For the welfare of India the cow protection (*Go-raksha*) is a compulsory requirement. Without it this country cannot attain the *Purusharthas*.[43]

In an appeal published in 1934, he said, "For the protection of the cow calf-slaughter must be banned." He had established a cow shelter (*Goshala*) at the Banaras Hindu University in 1916-17. He advised all people to take cow milk.[44] His famous slogan was always repeated by the students of Banaras Hindu University not in those days but also today that is "*Dudh piyo kasrat karo nitya japo hari naam, Maan lagai Vidya padho pure honge har kaam.*"

In 1941, he constituted 'The Bharatiya Go-Raksha Mandala' and got it registered and after purchasing 65 bighas of land at Shivpur established a *Go-shala* there named as Chyavan Ashram.[45] After founding the aforementioned '*Mandala*' the programmes of cow-protection (*Go-raksha*) were going on a huge scale in U.P., Bihar, Bengal and M.P., hundreds of dedicated

41. Chaturvedi, S., *Builder of Modern India, Madan Mohan Malaviya.* New Delhi: Ministry of Information and Broadcasting, Government of India, 1988, p. 41.
42. Tiwari, U.D., *op. cit.*, p. 41.
43. *Ibid.*
44. Chaturvedi, S., *loc. cit.*, p. 41.
45. Tiwari, U.D., *op. cit.*, p. 42.

workers were engaged in this programme; cow-shelters (*Go-shalas*) were established at several place and cow-week (*Go-saptah*) programmes were started every year. Several articles, statements, and speeches of Malaviya regarding cow protection were published in newspapers and periodicals. Malaviya in his speech forcefully said to stop cow-slaughter because India is an agricultural country where 90% of the population live in the village and depends on the agriculture, he believed for agriculture the cow dung of cow and other animal use as fertilizer, milk, ghee used for health and good calf and oxen used to the cultivators.

Along with Malaviya Gandhi also took keen interest in cow protection and founded a central *Goraksha* committee under the sponsorship of the All India Goraksha Samiti at Sabarmati. In 19th century, cow protection was not only dear to Hindus but Muslim also participated in this movement as Syed Nazir Ahmad, a leading Muslim citizen of Sitapur U.P. founded Islamic *Goraksha* Sabha.[46] The credit goes to Malaviya who toured round the country for this purpose. Malaviya himself got a number of cows in his house and paid attention for the care and comfort of cow.

When Sardar Sir Yogendra Singh, Food member of the British Government came to Banaras Hindu University for the visit at that time Malaviya focused his attention to the fact that a number of pregnant cows were slaughtered for obtaining skin of the still unborn calves and sold in high rate in European market, after this he took action that the animals of less than 10 year and pregnant cows should not be slaughtered.[47] Government also began interest in promotion of *Goshala*. Malaviya had deep wish that his life should come to end while serving the *Go-mata*. It was coincidence Malaviya delivered his first public speech in sixteen year on the cow-protection (*Goraksha*) at a religious conference at Mirzapur and just ten days before his death he deliver his last speech on cow protection Nov. 02, 1946, at Shivpur (Varanasi), which he founded in 1941, at the occasion of *Gopashtmai* from where he returned in the night

46. Chaturvedi, S. *op. cit.*, p. 41.
47. *Ibid.*, p. 42.

and suffered from cold became fatal and he passed away.[48] So Malaviya stressed from economic, agriculture view it's important to save cows.

3.2.6 *Ganga Canal Movement*

Malaviya consider Ganga water as Holy mother Ganga, when he went to England having Ganga water along with him. Shortly after the drafting of Banaras Hindu University Act, Malaviya in his busy schedule took the command of the agitation for the free flow of Ganga at Haridwar in which Maharaja of Jaipur, Darbhanga, and members of Hindu Mahasabha were involved. Malaviya visited along with Lala Sukhbir Sinha to the Maharaja of Jaipur and presented his feeling how the sentiments of Hindu despised by government.[49] Maharaja wrote the letter in such reference, Malaviya collected the public protest by sending the copies related to resolution to other Maharajas as Jaipur, Udaipur, Mysore, Jammu, etc. so from 1914 to 1916, Malaviya effectively began along with other Hindu Sabha members the movement against government plan of stopping Ganga water to *Har ki Pauri* and diverted it to the canal dug at Bhimonda. For this purpose he stayed at Dehradun for one month in 1916 and organized a memorandum which was offered to the state governor.[50] For the proper maintenance of the *Har ki Pauri* and necessary assistance and services to pilgrims he established a society known as 'Shri Ganga Hindu Sabha' which prospered well and is active in its mission till today.

In 1922 and 1927, Malaviya had to take an initiative to remove the temporary bridge on the Ganga near *Har ki Pauri* because English Government servants used to look at the ladies taking bath from that bridge. In 1927, he sent a telegraph covering 1300 words to the provincial governor to get that bridge dismantled.[51] Due to his winning leadership during Ganga Canal Movement for dismantling the bridge and his services to save Ganga and sentiments of Hindu religion and culture, his statue has been installed at *Har ki Pauri*. Therefore,

48. *Ibid.*, p. 43.
49. Parmanand, p. 249.
50. *Ibid.*
51. Parmanand, p. 263.

from this movement it reflected that pain of mother Ganga pained Malaviya as like son so he took immediate action to protect her purity and availability.

3.2.7 *All India Sewa Samiti a Manifestation of Love for Sufferers*

Malaviya saying was

> I have no desire for the kingdom, neither any desire for heaven, nor freedom from bondage (*moksha*). I have only one desire and that is to remove the miseries and sorrows of all living beings.[52]

Seva (service) was reflected in Malaviya thoughts, actions, and belief. Malaviya who is an individual of the society, tried to shape society by establishing much of Seva Samiti. In continuation of his social work without any selfish motive, in 1914, Malaviya established well-known 'Akhil Bharatiya Seva Samiti' at Prayag,[53] which aimed to make a survey of social and economic conditions of the country citizens and prepares its data, to provide necessary help and services to deprive and weak marginalized people of the society. Seva Samiti also aimed to organize service societies after training of social workers, to spread out the educational programme, harmony, cooperation, cleanliness, and physical development of the people, make efforts for improvement of the depressed and downward sections of the society. The Samiti also provided medical facilities in rural areas and runs social institutions especially aimed at welfare of the mothers and children, run Ashrams for widows, homes for downtrodden, deprived women, centers for people affected with leprosy, blinds, and shelter for elderly people. The workers of this Samiti also organized extension services at the time of fairs, famines, floods, and epidemics. To achieve these more than a few branches of the Seva Samiti were started in different regions of the country.

Malaviya with hundreds of workers of the Seva Samiti served to the sufferers and extended all kind of necessary help to the people at the tragic incident of Jallianwala Bagh of 1919, Chauri

52. Tiwari, U.D., p. 52.
53. *Ibid*., p. 43.

Chaura incident of 1921, Kohat riots of 1925, firing incident at Peshawar of 1930 and Bihar earthquake of 1934, flood-havocs in U.P., Bengal and other places.[54] Seva Samiti workers, Malaviya as president, Hridaynath Kunzru, and Shiva Prasad Gupta joint secretaries provided regular services to the people at Kumbh fairs at Prayag, Nasik, and Haridwar.[55] The Samiti provided services and help to Burmese refugees about 2500 in 1942. Under the behalf of the Samiti, Malaviya organized Boys Scout Association in 1918 of which he was nominated as the Chief Scout.[56] This organization had a team of more than 25 thousand dedicated young workers. On behalf of the Samiti, an arrangement for an ambulance and emergency treatment was also made. In 1920, the Samiti started a publication of monthly magazine named *Seva*. Several books relating to social services were also published periodically. The Seva Samiti founded a library, a student's hostel, a lodge and a gymnasium at Allahabad. The Harijan Seva Sangh, Servants of India Society, Marvari Relief Society, Calcutta, and Tata Institute of Social Sciences, Bombay, were associated with the Samiti. Along with Malaviya many esteemed associates in the Seva Samiti as Dr. Amarnath Jha, Hridayanath Kunzru, Venkatesha Narayan Tiwari and other eminent people,[57] this society was established for the services of all beings irrespective of any caste, *Varna* and sectarian group.

3.3 Economical Thoughts of Malaviya

Generally, Malaviya has been regarded as a man of religion or an orthodox Hindu but when his action and reactions were keenly observed and analyzed from economic point of view then misconception about Malaviya that he was only follower of *Sanatan Dharma*, and orthodox traditional Hindu, all cleared and he appears as a visionary in relation to the development of the nation from economic views. His interest about the economic expansion of India was not less profound than his concern about other things, although he was not a financial expert like Naoroji, Gokhale, John Stuart Mill, etc. but he could

54. *Ibid.*, p. 44.
55. *Ibid.*
56. *Ibid.*, p. 45.
57. *Ibid.*

determine very well and logically the massive loss of India due to British economic policy. He understood that

> finance is not mere arithmetic; finance is a great policy. Without sound finance, no sound government is possible without sound government, no sound finance is possible.[58]

It was Malaviya, who constantly changed himself with changing time and according to the needs of society. His progressive attitude was reflected when Gandhi would not like assimilation of machine and technology, Malaviya did not blindly support him, but he stated for the development of nation and to overcome from poverty it is necessary to welcome scientific culture of the West with indigenous mind set.

> Malaviya's economic philosophy was influenced by the nationalist views like John Stuart mill, Digby, Naoroji, Ranade, as purposely he quoted them in his speeches.[59]

So Malaviya's economic thoughts were full of Indianization. Malaviya's basic aim was to ensure that the state should promote Indian industries and that there should utilize Indian raw material, and be seen with Indian capital by Indian personnel and under Indian control. It was reflected while Malaviya presided second time Congress session he said,

> While generally welcoming the recommendation of the industrial commission and the policy of the government which promoting the industrial development in the country the Congress hopes the practical application of this principle in the country and with the sole objective kept in the view that this policy will encourage Indian capital and protect this country against foreign exploitation, with the sole aim of making India industrially and economically self-contained and self-dependent.[60]

---

58. *Annual Proceeding of U.P. Legislative Council*, Apr. 11, 1906, p. 62.
59. Singh, Shivalini, "Resurgence of India Economy: Mahamana Vision", *Pragya*, 2011, Vol. 56, Part 02, p. 304.
60. Bakshi, S.R., *Madan Mohan Malaviya: The Man and his Ideology*, New Delhi: Anmol Publication, 1991, p. 245.

His economic thought was critical, when he argued and presented data in front of the British Government and suggested how India could regain prosperity. He analyzed the position of the country in the following words in his speech presented in Indian National Congress Lahore session in 1909 as,

> The national income is low and therefore the national prosperity is low. People are dying in the vast numbers from plague and malaria. Famines are calming a large toll and people are poor and unhappy. That is the condition of the country. On the other hand, you find that it is a country most richly endowed with natural resources. It is a country whose people are not lacking in intelligence and industry, and living most simple life, they are not addicted to crimes as some of the most advanced countries are. Can there be anything more sad and disappointing than to find that people are still in such an unfortunate condition that this country should lie so low in the scale of the nation? And if this is so what is our duty to the motherland.[61]

Malaviya participated in a number of meetings and bravely expressed the economic vision for India. Malaviya in his basic approaches loved to Indian past, tradition and culture, so most of the time he presented India as rich nation which was not merely based on agriculture but also on its natural resources and Indigenous talent. Malaviya expressed richness of past days of, as India had trade relation with Babylon in 300 BC and Indian Mulmal had exclusive market in Egypt and Greece two thousand years ago whereas cotton textile industry started in Britain in 17th century. India was also superior in technique and quality of Iron and steel the world famous Damishk Swords were made by the Indian steel.[62] He also cited another example to prove Britishers that don't compare yourself with Indians as competitor and said,

61. Zaidi, A.M. *The Encyclopedia of Indian National Congress*. New Delhi: Indian Institute of Applied Political Research, 1906-1910, Vol. V, p. 475.
62. Parmanand, *op. cit.*, pp. 457-62.

> When Robert Clive entered in Murshidabad, the old capital of Bengal in 1857, he wrote the city is an extreme, populous and rich as the city of London, with this difference that there were individual in the first processing infinitely greater property then the last city.[63]

Therefore, Malaviya understood for poor condition of the Indians, Britishers were accountable and for industrial supremacy of the England, Indian resources, Indian people were responsible who acted as stepping stone to attain prosperity by Britishers. Therefore to overcome from this poor situation of the people, Malaviya advocated the promotion of the indigenous industries as a remedy. So the central theme of his economic philosophy was the regeneration and development of Indian economy which faced exploitation in British colonial rule and their policies reducing the stamina of the Indians to overcome from the miserable poverty.

3.3.1 *Malaviya's Economic Opinion during Industrial Commission*

In 1914, the whole country got itself buckled up to protect the honour of the British and her allies with money and men during First World War. During the war a commission was appointed on 19 May 1916 to investigate the affairs of Indian Trade and Commerce under the chairmanship of Thomas Holland. The objective was to consider and suggest the measure to be adopted for the growth and development of industries in India. This commission having nine members with Sir T.H. Holland as president and R.D. Bell as secretary. It had three Indian members appointed by the government beside British industries and civil servant. Malaviya was also member of the commission as the sole representative of the Indian people.[64] The commission collected evidence for almost two years and submitted its report in 1918. But Malaviya did not agree with many of the recommendations made by the commission. Hence,

63. Malaviya, M.M. Note by the Hon'ble Pt. Madan Mohan Malaviya in Indian Industrial Commission Report, 1918. Reprinted as Panday, D.B. and Singh, S. (Ed.), *Industrial Growth and Development in India*. Varanasi: Mahamana Malaviya Mission, BHU, Unit, 2006.
64. *Ibid.*, p. 27.

he added his note of disagreement to the report which was considered to be an important and complete document on the economic development of India. The recommendation suggested by him is so important that even it serves as practical guide for the development of Indian industries and stabilization of economic growth today.

In the initial chapters of Industrial Commission, Malaviya focused on the material, technological, and intellectual superiority of ancient India, by citing example of cotton textiles, iron and ship building sugar, glass, and handicrafts; it was this trade and prosperity which led traders of Europe to India, including the East India Company. But after the battle of Plessey there was a sudden rise in the industrial supremacy of England due to the vast hoardings of Bengal and Karnataka being made available for her use. So, Malaviya felt that the British Government of India followed a deliberate policy of encouraging the exports of raw production which resulted in India becoming more and more agriculture. The Railway too more constructed only to promote English trade and commerce with India. The decline of Indian industries, the growing imports of British manufactures and increasing export of raw production from India which led increase the poverty of Indians. This forced the people to depend on land and exposed India to the damage of extensive famines.

Malaviya's indigenous economic philosophy was evident in the conference, when he rejected the idea that Indian were accountable for the decline of their indigenous industries and the European were by nature more fit than Asiatic for success in manufacturing pursuits. He quoted extensively from various sources, to prove that

> Up to the middle of the 18th century England herself was an agricultural country, that for the thousands of the years and up to the beginning of the last century India excelled in manufactures as well as in agriculture, this was due to the special treatment to which she had been subjected and not due to any want of industrial capacity and enterprise among her people.[65]

65. Bakshi, S.R., *op. cit.*, p. 22.

In the Indian Industrial Conference, Malaviya approved the word of Sir Fredrick Nicholson

> I beg to record my strong opinion that in the matter of Indian industries, we are bound to consider Indian interest firstly, secondly and thirdly—I mean be firstly the local raw products should be utilized by Indians secondly, the industries should be introduced and by thirdly that the profit of such industry should remain in the country.[66]

So by expressing his views, he wanted the British Government to realize that Indian backwardness was not due to scarcity of national resources but due to selfish planning of Britishers and poor condition of education. Thus, Malaviya advocated the enhancement technical education, development of indigenous industries, industrial education, and commercial education throughout the country. In Malaviya's opinion, India had three important economic advantages as plenty of agriculture and mineral raw materials, huge natural facilities, resources, and vast home market which could absorb all the production of indigenous industries.

3.3.2 *Malaviya Opinion for Agrarian Economy*

Malaviya wanted government collect the land revenue not more than 6%. Malaviya was always against to tax on agriculture yield, as he said,

> If the land revenue paid by the farmer is the form of revenue tax then again payment of tax on yield is a type of double taxation.[67]

In relation to irrigation facility, he was not satisfied by the policy of Britishers and he said adequate attention was not given by the government on irrigation facility in India, in spite of repeated Famine Commission of 1880, 1901 and 1903. He suggested that government should advance taqavi to tenants for making wells and supported his argument with the saying of ancient sages who had stressed on the importance of storage

66. *Ibid.*, p. 30.
67. *Annual Proceedings of United Province Legislative Council*, April 07, 1908, p. 61.

of water.[68] He forcibly tried to realize the British Government that his expense on railway seven times more than on irrigation though irrigation which yielded five times more than the railways. He strained for the acceptance of scientific agriculture as it would rise per hectare yield, but he also opposed to blind imitation of Western methods of agriculture. He authorized Mackenna's view that,

> As in the case of plant, the improvement of the local material which the cultivator can himself make and repair and which his cattle can draw seems the more hopeful line of improvement.[69]

In 1926, Malaviya invited agricultural commission, where he suggested some practical ways and means to improve the lot of Indian cultivations and to hasten the growth of Indian agriculture.

3.3.3 *Malaviya Faith in Swadeshi for Economic Improvement*

Malaviya from the earliest years of his public life single-mindedly worked for the revival of indigenous industries to relieve the grinding poverty of the masses, he delivered an outstanding speech on *Swadeshi* in 1893 and moved a resolution at the 1898 session. He thought sadly that this is the destiny of India today intrinsically rich country India should become dependent on the other countries for articles of daily use like a knife was a matter of shame and sorrow for them. So in 1881, a Deshi Tijarat Company (Indigenous Trading Company) was floated at Prayag through Malaviya's effort to encourage Indian industry and to patronize craftsmen who had supported in this enterprise. This company nicely worked for six years and was accredited the manufacturing of Indian cloth, buttons, soap, knives and other articles of daily use.[70]

Malaviya in 1906 on twenty-second Indian National Congress session held at Calcutta delivered an emotional speech said that

---

68. *Ibid.*, March 30, 1907, p. 53 also cited in *Proceedings of Imperial Legislative Council*, Vol. ii, Feb. 27, 1914, pp. 603-04.
69. *Ibid.*, March 30, 1907, p. 60.
70. Tiwari, U.D., *op. cit.*, p. 18.

> The Swadeshi movement is a movement to promote the use of goods of manufactures of our own country. Why does it arise? He said it was born in poverty. Let try to understand how is the poverty brought about you? He gave answer in such a way. You know that 20 crores have to be paid every year in the form of salaries and pensions, etc. This is one of the large drains of the country wealth.[71]

So he always advocated for the high recruitment of Indians in administrative post and also for the other opportunities to strengthen Indians economically. Malaviya opposed to create an Imperial Industrial Service and a cadre of scientists styled "Imperial Chemical Service" for carrying on scientific research in aid of industries. Such step he apprehended would place the future of Indian industries in the hands of bureaucrats recruited in England like the existing imperial. He referred, indignantly, to the service working such department as agriculture, veterinary, meteorological, and geological survey, which were intended to be manned by Indians but having workers having been recruited from abroad due to lack of Indians with requisite qualification, which not been available at that time. He argued to the British Government that they recruited seats by European even educated Indians available; he cited example of eminent scientists as Sir Prafulla Chandra Roy had not been admitted.[71] He presented the data of export about 120 crores than the imports of 85 crores, he firmly said

> You saw the market of India was full of foreign article and this article made by the raw material of India which is exported and for our own thing we Indian paid, this is another large drain. So the question arose that what we did, the answer is to use swadeshi goods to overcome the poverty.[72]

Thus, he always encouraged the people to use Swadeshi goods in all his speeches that he had made in the Congress session[73] (Support for Fund XIII, p. 11). Malaviya undertook

71. Bakshi, S.R., *op. cit.*, p. 343.
72. Parmanand, *op. cit.*, p. 293.
73. *Ibid.*, p. 11.

extensive tour during 1920 to 1921 when Gandhi was in jail and advocated for the use of Swadeshi goods and established a well-known All India Swadeshi Sangh. All his efforts espoused his wide knowledge of Indian affairs, and contributed to him as great economist. In 1934, he was invited to open the Swadeshi exhibition at Kalpi but he could not go there owing to his illness. The nursing message that he sent on the occasion was a conclusive proof of his ardent faith in the use of Swadeshi as the only measure for the economic and industrial growth of India.

3.3.4 *Malaviya's Efforts for Improvement in Education System for the Economic Prosperity*

Malaviya along with Swadeshi approach on various stages also focused for the improvement in education system and favoured technical, scientific vocational industrial education. He demanded universal, free, and compulsory primary education and laid emphasis on development and extension of scientific medical and other related education yields. Again in 1909, he demanded in the provincial council to establish industrial training college for laundry dye work, smith craft, carpeting gold smithing and similar to other cottage industries, crafts and standard engineering colleges for industrial chemist, mechanical engineering, cloth manufacturing, preparation of sugar and several other technical branches of learning.[74] In 1911 in the Legislative Council during his speech, Malaviya making emphatic demands for women's education, said,

> It is very painful, in India half of the society deprive of the light of knowledge. Like boys he wanted to provide adequate arrangement should also be made for the compulsory education for girls.[75]

Therefore, no doubt in Malaviya's visualized for an economically prosperous country for which it would be necessary to have material wealth as well as spiritual riches along with modern education. Thus to uplift the society economically he

74. *Presidential Address*. Lahore 1909 cited in Panday, R., *Making of Malaviya: Malaviya in the Eyes of Historians*. Varanasi: Mahavir Press, 2010, p. 59.
75. Bakshi, S.R., *op. cit.*, p. 331.

established Banaras Hindu University. It was also admired by, Dr. Radhakrishnan, on the occasion of the birth centenary celebration on December 25, 1961 said,

> Yesterday, I was at Jamshedpur and I was told that the town had 200-300 graduates of Banaras Hindu University working there in mining, metallurgy, mechanical and electrical engineering. As an outstanding study patriot, he realized that our country suffered on account of technical backwardness, lack of public spirit, and inattention to our own great culture. These were the defect which he attempted to remove by the establishment of this university.[76]

So Malaviya's economic thoughts were not based on blind race of materialistic development but as Gandhi says in *Harijan* in 1937 "Square of Swaraj determine by four angles, viz., political independence, economic independence on one side, and morality and religion." Malaviya also had the same view to regain the prosperity of India. So he said,

> Being able to earn wealth by honorable means, they will be above temptations to unworthy conduct, and being inspired by high principles imbibed from Sanskrit learning, they will be men of unswerving rectitude and incorruptible integrity.[77]

He wanted to make such youths by education who gave back more to the society than what they have acquired from the society.

3.3.5 *Malaviya Critics on Some Major Issue which Affect Economic Affluence of the Nation*

Malaviya touched those points analytically in his speeches, by which economy of the country affected positively and negatively. As he spoke issues like on custom policy, tariff policy, currency, high prices of food stuff, irrigation, banking system,

---

76. Singh, D.P. and Nath, P.R., "Mahamana Pt. Madan Mohan Malaviyaji, Economic Vision Industrial Development through technical Education", *Pragya*, 2011, Vol. 56, Part 2, p. 260.
77. Singh, D.P. and Nath, P.R., "*Prateechi Prachi ka Male Sundar*". *Souvenir (Indian Pharmaceutical Congress)*, 2007, pp. 1-4.

credit facility, on reform of peasantry and labor, railway, salt tax, agriculture tax, on communism, co-operative societies, consolidation of land, education, expenditure on higher education, etc. Malaviya in above points when suggested, to government or arguing the policies of the British Government, one point is common that was welfare of common man.

His economic principle was based on the fact that government should not allow one section of the society unnecessarily large profits at the expense of other sections of the society, particularly in the case of food stuffs, and the food supplies should be more easily available even through imports.[78] His economic thoughts were not only based on the ancient ideology but he always focused on reform as for example he said although Indians were not having habit to handle bank system but to bring tremendous change in India like other countries bank played a greater role, so it is important that India adopted vast "Banking system which entirely accountable to legislature",[79] lastly he said as the bank would affect future destiny of the people so bank should be constituted in such a manner that the interest of the common people entirely understood and safeguarded.

When Britishers developed sound transport system in the form of railway, his reaction came out with the following statement that

> It opened in India for the proper utilization of raw material in Britain and rapid economic exploitation of the Indians. He never regarded railway as a purely commercial concern for Indians while he blamed to Britishers that they introduced it in India for the promotion of English trade and Commerce.[80]

Again he logically proved it by citing an example that

> Government developed a vast system of railways in India, but they did not develop the Iron and Steel

78. P.I.I.C., Vol. VIII, Sept. 15, 1919, p. 207.
79. P.I.I.C., Vol. LVIIII, Sept. 23, 1919, pp. 436-37.
80. L.A.D., Vol. IV, Part IV, Sept. 17, 1924, p. 3682.

> Industry. Because they do not want to develop Indian Industries.[81]

Not only on railway but he argued for the betterment of the third class passengers who are common men. He awaked the Britishers to stop mismanagement and wastes of Indian money by depositing outside the country. He opposed on the point separate railway finance from the general finance because he thought it will be an evil for the country if railways were entirely free from the control of the finance department of Government of India, because by this way the people become deprived from the common opportunity. So lastly his approach for the railway is

> Railway meant for public utility not for the profit.[82]

In relation to currency, Malaviya strongly opposed eighteen pence to a rupee ratio in place of sixteen pence to a rupee. He convinced on the point that rupees was appreciated prejudicially in relation to the manufacturer of the country.[83] On labour problem Malaviya's approach was neither as anti-capitalist and nor as communist but he is liberal economist. He endorsed the view that

> The state should have the duty to safeguard the interest of the industrial workers and secured them a living wage, healthy condition of work and protection against old age, sickness and unemployment. Malaviya wanted to create peace in the industrial field not by the strike but peaceful conciliation. He contended that strikes mean a great deal of injury not only to public but also a man who goes for it.[84]

Malaviya also attacked as nationalist on salt tax because he understood salt as a prime necessity. He did not agree with the tariff policy of the government because it sacrificed Indian interest. Malaviya heartily attached with the welfare of the

81. Hunter, W.W., *The Marquis of Dalhousie and the Final Development of Company Rule*, Oxford, MDCCCXCV, p. 198.
82. P.I.I.C., Vol. LVI, March 12, 1918, p. 886.
83. Report of Indian National Congress for 1893, 1898, 1902.
84. L.A.D., Vol. Sept 6, 1927, pp. 4105-06.

peasantry, although he did not belong to the peasantry house. He published a separate weekly Hindi journal *Kissan*. Opposing to Jinnah view, he said the farmers paid the land revenue, why they paid agriculture tax. He always motivated to educated person to pay a day for the upliftment of the peasantry. In relation to high prices of food stuffs, Malaviya promote co-operative grain stores and co-operative grain banks, protection of the cultivator from local Sahukar, scientific agriculture. He emphasized on education of agriculture and he suggested to adopt effective measures to stop the export of wheat from outside of the country except, when it can be spared without pinching the people. Beside this he favored for the establishment of indigenous companies in food grain in which these companies purchased the food directly from the cultivator and provided appropriate market value to the cultivator.[85] As regards to the rate of interest Malaviya forcibly presented view that it should not exceed more than the six percent.

Malaviya's economic thoughts were not favored communistic principle in Indian concept. As a nationalist he did not support to the pure capitalist approach but he belongs to liberal school of thoughts which was devoted for the welfare of the common people. So national interest and the good of common man were the common things on which his economic thoughts were based.

3.4 Political Philosophy of Malaviya

Before knowing Malaviya as political leader and his political philosophy it is necessary to overview his political voyage. Malaviya started his political voyage by the Calcutta conference in 1886. His performance at this session made him known throughout India and marked the beginning of his role as a national leader. After this session, the friends and advisers, including Raja Rampal Singh urged him to devote a little more time to political affairs. They were convinced that in Malaviya they had discovered a political leader of great promise. Raja Rampal Singh greatly impressed by Malaviya offered him a job of journalist and forced him to do LLB, practice in bar, which are discussed in earlier chapter. His fearless editorship and practice in

85. P.I.I.C., Vol. LVIII, Sept. 16, 1919, p. 207: Malaviya Speech, p. 220.

high court expressed his hidden leader who devoted each second for the nation's welfare. Malaviya suggested various means to obtain freedom. He wanted to do things constitutionally. Later on, he exhorted every one of his countrymen to declare that he will owe no allegiance to the government. He maintained that it was permissible to write to the government that unless they gave us responsible government they would declare open war. Throughout his life Malaviya worked hard for unity within Congress and was identified as a moderate political leader. He accepted the modification of national interest and wanted to develop Congress partially as ear of country which always alarmed, awakened the individuals against repressive policies of Britishers and boom sacrificing tendency in the individual for nation welfare. He was prepared to take risk and would not hesitate to advising his countrymen to join any movement for the sake of motherland.

3.4.1 *Presidentship of Different Congress Session and Participation in Different Movements*

He was individual who honored by the Congress being elected as its president three times, the first at the Lahore session (1909), the second time at Delhi (1918) and the third at the Calcutta (1933). He could not, however, preside over the 1933 sessions as the meeting was banned and he was arrested even before he reached Calcutta. Throughout his long political career he responded with determination, willpower and strength of unique character which impressed several leaders who were senior than him like A.O. Hume, Naoroji, Gopal Krishna Gokhale and his younger as Gandhi. This was not only due to his political image but it was also due to his attitude which was much negotiating, understanding, and moderate. Several times in Indian politics, he acted as bridge between the extremist and the liberal group. He did not belong to activist group like Lala Lajpat Rai, Bipin Chandra Pal, and Bal Gangadhar Tilak and also was not like the older leaders who were still trying to achieve dominion status through constitutional and peaceful means. He belonged to the moderate school and in spite of acting as extreme nationalist approach to deal any problems. Although later Malaviya had differences with the Congress programme and made a separate

Nationalist Party but further he was worked in Congress and do work for nation welfare. After Gandhi was in prison during 1922 many of the leaders show their agreement on the name of Malaviya for the leadership of non-cooperation movement. In 1930, when Gandhi launched the Salt Satyagraha and the Civil Disobedience Movement, he actively participated in it and arrested. In the Quit India Movement, he could not participate due to his sufferings, but he always gave suggestions to Congress during critical situations.

In the long-drawn political struggle in India, the role of Malaviya was of more than seven decades. As a politician he always helped in the unstable days of Congress, as for example, during 1908 he was presided Lucknow conference and in the same year, the Indian National Conference was held in Madras. The next session held in Lahore in 1909. Pheroj Shah Mehta name was declared for president ship of this Lahore Session, but he refused the offer just six days before its beginning, Malaviya addressed as president in such critical situation. The *Manchester Guardian* wrote about this new Congress president as,

> The president of the Indian National Congress, which meets at Lahore, is not so prominent a man as either Dr. Rash Behari Ghose, the president of the last year or Phiroj Shah Mehta, who has just withdrawn. Nevertheless, Mr. Madan Mohan Malaviya is a politician of high standing and of notable ability. He is a self-made man, having made his way at the Bar after an apprenticeship as school teacher and journalist. In politics, there is no Congress orator more generally admired then Malaviya's age are 47.[86]

Malaviya's speech at Lahore session was full synthesis of enthusiasm and self-control. He criticized the oppressive policies of the British Government and called upon the Indians to pay their sincere devotion for the goal of independence.

His role in Congress Session 1905, Surat Split, First World War, Congress-League Pact, Home Rule League Movement, Rowlett Bills, Jallianwala Bagh Episode, Hunter

86. Parmanand, p. 162.

Report, beginning of Swaraj Party, Simon Commission, Nehru Report, Allahabad Unity Conference, Second Round Table Conference in, Gandhi Irwin Pact, Harijanoddhar movement, Chauri Chaura Case, Non Cooperation movement, Swadeshi movement, Indian Industrial Commission, etc. exhibited him as prominent political leader whose political philosophy was built around the development of nation. Therefore, it is important to discuss what Malaviya understood by nation, and what type of important rule, regulation and ideas he preferred for ideal nation. Even Malaviya did not write any book on democracy, constitution, fundamental principles, or on political issues such as governance, secularism, decentralization of funds or funds allocation, etc. but when his speeches delivered in Indian National Congress, religious stages were analyzed, it is concluded that basically he was a firm political thinker and his thoughts are categorized as follows.

3.4.2 *Malaviya's Analytical Views about India as a Nation*

Although Malaviya was considered as moderate political leader but in relation to his basic instinct of political philosophy, he was a staunch nationalist. He was not agreed with Tagore in disapproving nationalism as a great threat. But he positively agreed with the thought that "Country is not greater than the Humanity."[87]

So his views were not reflecting him as a blind nationalist like Hitler and Benito Mussolini.

During initial political career Malaviya suggested to Britishers but when he realized the biased policy of Britishers, his hidden nationalist views burst out in the form of love of nation. He understood the rulers of India whether Muslims, or Britishers were not ready to accept India as a nation, because India was

87. Khattry, D.P., *Report of all Asia Educational Conference, Benares*, Dec. 24-30, Allahabad (undated), pp. 114-17.

divided politically, culturally and religiously.[88] Malaviya claimed India to be a nation, and proved it by citing Geographical unity by saying its fixed boundaries, "India is one integral country, surrounded by the sea and lofty mountains."[89]

Malaviya said,

> We people of India are nearly all of one race and have lived under the influence of a common government for over 150 years.[90]

So it was Malaviya's appeal from the political stage nation is that where people however divided by religions and creeds, but lives in one country, who is the subjects of one ruler, who are ruled by one system of rule, by one set of laws which affect them equally. So Malaviya claimed that

> We are such a nation. We have long been a nation and shall continue to be nation despite all difference that divides us.[91]

Thus, Malaviya considered India as a nation.

3.4.3 *Democracy Perceived by Malaviya*

By democracy, he meant it is the right of every person to govern him/her self. Since second Indian National Congress he had been demanding for representative government. Malaviya due to his faith in Ancient culture in his writings and speeches disclosed his positive reference to monarchy,[92] but his thoughts

88. "To talk of India as an entity is as absurd as to talk of Europe as an entity.... There never has been such a nation. Whether there ever will be such a nation, future alone can show." Lord Birkenhead. See, Parliamentary Debates, V. series, Vol. LXI, House of Lords, Second Volume of session 1924-25, July 7, 1925, p. 1078; see also, Releigh, T., Lord Curzon in India—Being a selection from his speeches as Viceroy and Governor-General of India, 1898-1905, London, 1906, p. 231. Lord Curzon's Convocation Address delivered at the Calcutta University on 13 Feb. 1904. "I do not think, it can yet be said that there is any Indian nation."
89. Lekh, pp. 125-28 also cited in Gajrani, S. and Ram, S. Ed. *Pandit Madan Mohan Malaviya*, Varanasi BHU Press, p. 33.
90. L.A.D., Vol. V, Part II, 19, 1925, p. 1268.
91. L.A.D., Vol. VI, Part II, Sept. 07, 1925, pp. 996-97.
92. Lekh, pp. 22-24; 162-64 also cited in P.I.L.C., Vol. XV, March 23, 1917, p. 806.

were based on limitations of monarchy also.[93] Malaviya told when king, neither wielded absolute power nor exercised their authority randomly, there was a council of ministers to advice the kings. The displeasure of the people might cost a King his throne.[94] But finally he said that such one ruler ruled kingdom with lake of freedom, full of demerits. So he licensed the concept of people's dominion as proposed in the Nehru Report which said,

> All powers of government and authority, legislative, executive and judicial, are derived from the people and the same shall be exercised in the Commonwealth of India through the organization established by or under, and in accordance with this Constitution.[95]

Therefore, Malaviya convinced with view no government can be so good as the government of the people by their own people, i.e. government of the people, for the people and by the people.

3.4.4 *Malaviya's Idea to Attain Democracy*

Malaviya maintained vote as a powerful factor in raising the political status of the voters.[96] Though Malaviya was highly educated, but he was not firm on education being made a condition for voting.[97] He would like to extend license to the illiterate villagers, by saying his words as,

> Commonsense is not the monopoly of those who live in towns; those who live in villages are not wanting in commonsense.[98]

---

93. Lekh, pp. 162-68. It is reported that Maharaja of Jodhpur inquired of Malaviya as to what rights are to be given to the public, in the new context of reforms. Malaviya gave him a character of rights which left hardly worth the name in the hands of the ruler. Maharaja was quick to remark: "Ruler should better retire."
94. Abhyudaya, Margsirsha Krishna 2, 1964.
95. Nehru Report, p. 101, Clause 4(1).
96. I.R.T.C., Second Session, Vol. I, p. 196.
97. *Ibid.*
98. P.I.L.C., Vol. LII, March 19, 1914, p. 917.

He opposed the idea to provide extra grant to any community.[99] Thus, he opposed the regulations made under the Indian Council Act of 1909 which gave preferential treatment to Muslims and Zamindars.[100] He wanted men belonging to different communities have their place in the council. The best way of providing representation was to elect those in whom they have confidence.[101]

In relation to nomination of members for election Malaviya did not prefer strict restrictions on contesting members for election. According to him, the valid ground for preventing a man from seeking the suffrage of this fellowmen could be moral turpitude and not conviction or detention.[102] He gratified the simple fact "That a man is serving a sentence of imprisonment should not count with regard to the dignity of the House," and that "mere fact of detention should not count against him."[103] It was a matter between the candidate and his constituents. Therefore, in view of Malaviya, it was the democratic right of an individual to stand for election and of the electorate to choose a man out of several in whose ability, character, integrity, and public service they had confidence. Therefore, to attain the right meaning of democracy, Malaviya opposed the idea of *Brahminical rule* or the political domination of upper classes or any particular community in administration. He definitely opposed to the conception of Hindu Raj or Muslim Raj. He stood for Indian Raj to be established on the basis of common citizenship, equal right, and joint electorate. He took stand for representative, responsible government where the rulers had limited powers. Malaviya gave the right sense of democracy for nation in which all were in state of power by representing their representative. So to achieve this aim he preferred that the constitution should be framed in such a manner which, will

---

99. A.P.U.P.L.C., April 13, 1919, pp. 65-66 also cited in *Report of Indian National Congress*, 1908, p. 56.
100. R.I.N.C., 1909, pp. 32-33. See also A.P.U.P.L.C., April 3, 1909, pp. 65-66.
101. P.I.L.C., Vol. XLIX, Jan. 24, 1911, p. 134.
102. R.I.N.C., 1909, pp. 29-30. See also, P.I.I.C., Vol. XLIX, Jan. 24, 1911, pp. 137-38.
103. I.R.T.C., Second Session, Vol. ii, p. 889.

contain representatives of all sections of Indian public opinion with due regard to the interests of minorities.[104] Thus, Malaviya meant democracy as the representativeness of all section of Indian society.

3.4.5 *Malaviya Opinion for Federal Constitution*

Malaviya presented himself as a man who wanted declaration of federal constitution in India in the second round table conference. He demanded a federal polity for India whose constituents were the British Indian provinces and the princely states than the unitary system developed by the Britishers. By citing example of the ancient administration he stated that it was a picture of "*A United India*",[105] united, though divided States having full autonomy to manage their own affairs, except in so far as they agree to delegate their problem to the federal government. Here the people of the states would combine loyalty to the rules of their own states with loyalty to our common Motherland.[106] Malaviya understood this dissimilarity of the units of the federation did not present any irregularity. Therefore, he suggested for such system in politics. Besides he emphasized the need of considerable degree of elasticity in the financial framework.[107] Therefore, it conclude that in any how Malaviya wanted the power to come in the hand of local people and they govern own self according to their needs and desire. Thus, his approach of democracy was local to global.

3.4.6 *Malaviya's Estimation on Secularism*

Indian concept of secularism was based on the *Sarve Dharma Sambhava* that means having equal regard for all faith and creed. As Gandhi says, "My veneration for other faiths is the same as for my own faith,"[108] if a question is raised, why Malaviya regarded India as a Nation in spite of religious differences? The answer to this is that he believed in religious unity by

104. *The Hindustan Times*, Dec. 28, 1936, *Malaviya Speech at the Faizpur Congress.*
105. I.R.T.C., Second Session, Vol. ii, p. 193.
106. *Ibid.*
107 *Ibid.*, p. 561.
108. Singh, Y.K., *Sociological Foundation of Education*, New Delhi: APH Publication House, 2007, p. 2.

giving respect to all religion. His repeated statement "India is the common motherland of all Hindus, Muslims, etc."[109] that means "He did not wanted India to be a Hindu State nor a land of Hindus exclusively."[110]

As late as 1941, he said to the students of Allahabad University to aim at an Indian State. "The days of Hindu or Muslim State had long passed," he said them to not.[111] He opposed the demand for Pakistan on the ground that Hindus, Muslims, Sikh, and Christians all lived like good neighbours' side by side.[112] Malaviya was also a signatory to the Nehru Report which enjoined that,

> There shall be no state religion for the commonwealth of India or for any province in the commonwealth, nor shall the state either directly or indirectly endow any religion or give any preference or impose any disability on account of religious belief or religious status.[113]

Along with this Malaviya's secular attitude reflected by certain incidents such as collection the funds from Muslim Nawab's, or declaration of holidays on Muslim festival through university had only few Muslim students, getting regard by all the leaders of other community, Jinnah's faith in Malaviya.

3.4.7 *Malaviya's Insight on Liberty*

As an idealist philosopher Malaviya's faith in Indian scriptures was very firm so his views on liberty was somewhat motivated by the view of 'Sankhya' and 'Vedanta' school of thought. The former defines liberty as a 'state of mind,' a 'discriminative knowledge,' a reason called *Vivek* which helps a person to discriminate and distinguish himself from the environment.[114] Malaviya meant by, freedom as the capability of the individual by which he can alter his circumstances, and individual not

109. Lekh, p. 24. See also, R.I.NC., 1890, p. 24.
110. Abhyudaya, 13, 1963.
111. AAJ, Oct. 10, 1941 (Malaviya Speech before the Allahabad University Students Union).
112. AAJ, Aug. 16, 1944.
113. Nehru Report, p, 123; also in *Hindustan Times*, Nov. 11, 1932.
114. Lekh, pp. 207-09.

dependent upon others for fulfillment of their needs, but is his own master. He said what is true for an individual is also true for an independent nation. After realizing this meaning of freedom, he appealed to the Britishers that Indian in general believed in 'natural rights' don't try to provide them meaning of liberty depend on any particular charter or constitution.[115] Malaviya supported the Hegel's thoughts, i.e. '*Dharma*' and 'Freedom' are synonymous terms which also reflected in Vivekanand's *darshan*. In his words, "Religion" is nothing but evolution of humanity from animalistic approach to divinity.[116] In other words, *Dharma* or freedom is that which converts man from evils and animal instinct to good and divinity. The same view was held by Malaviya, as he described meaning of bondage first, to describe freedom. Bondage to Malaviya is not only the negation of freedom but the most harmful thing in the world,[117] because it drives away humanity from both the winner and the defeated. To him, "Loss of freedom means loss of opportunities; loss of opportunities means degeneration and degeneration means death."[118]

Thus, in his view to preserve human dignity it is necessary to pull up both the seed of bandage and the will to dominate other people. Malaviya realized under a foreign rule, the mental, physical, economic, internal willpower of an Indians were destroyed and the individual living there in is deprived of opportunities. Malaviya explained the meaning of liberty in British time as, they deal public like property, who were survive on their mercy. He said these rules were not meant for the safe of people but meant for the humiliation. Further he suggested to British Government to make rules which did not attack over elementary liberties otherwise the people have right to disobey the rule and then right is known as right of disobedience or

115. *Hindustan Times*, Feb. 5, 1932. *Malaviya to Lord Willingdon*, dated Jan. 29, 1932.
116. Lekh, pp. 204-06.
117. L.A.D., Vol. iii, March 28, 1930, p. 616.
118. Lekh, pp. 204-06.

resistance.[119] Thus, its Malaviya's willpower and faith in liberty which did not allow him to sleep against any exploitation.

3.4.8 *Liberty as Practiced by Malaviya*

In the life of Malaviya, it had been observed that on many occasion he fought for his own views. As a journalist, he was showing his awareness for his idiosyncratic opinions, without taking any tension to the risk of official displeasure as well as penalty to close the newspaper, and worked as an excellent journalist of the Press. He considered the utility of the newspaper, for awaking the people, so in his view press need lawful liberty and if the newspapers would be forced to write under a greater sense of control for the popularizing the goods of the administration, it was not fair therefore, he had to fight for the freedom of the Press.[120] As a lawyer, he had always protected political injustice suffered cases, and as a legislator, he had to be even watchful of individual liberty. As a political leader working for the freedom of India, he was always firm on his individual stand whether it was differences from Gandhi on non-cooperation movement or boycott movement. Malaviya's viewed on liberty of opinion as lawful discussion which was highly beneficial to both the people and the administration.[121] Therefore throughout his life he fought for the cause of individual liberty and liberty of opinion.

3.4.9 *Malaviya's View on Religious Liberty*

Though he was serious and dedicated for liberty of religion, but his sense of religious liberty was full with the sentiments of the people of all religion. He opposed the demand of Muslim religion as right to cow-slaughter and to offer prayer chanting Azan from a house or a mosque by speaker. He stated it is the duty of the magistracy to stop music before mosque or keep peace.[122] Malaviya also focused on discussion regarding religion as,

---

119. Gajrani, S. and Ram, S. Ed. *Pt. Madan Mohan Malaviya*. Varanasi: BHU Press, p. 45.
120. P.I.I.C., Vol. XLVIII, Feb. 8 (1910), p. 133.
121. P.I.I.C., Vol. XLVIII, Feb. 8 (1910), p. 33.
122. AAJ, Oct. 4 and 10, 1926, *Malaviya Public Lecture at Allahabad, and Ramlila Controversy*.

> Tenets and doctrines of the religion a prophet preached or uprooted might be open to free discussion and consideration, and one should not discuss founders of religions or Avatars or religious leaders in a light-hearted manner.[123]

Malaviya admitted propagation one's religion or conversion is understood as religious freedom but with some argument he stated "Every individual or group is at liberty to convert or reconvert another by argument or persuasion," but then "one individual or group should attempt to do so or prevent its being done by force, fraud or other unfair means such as offering material."[124] So by these statements it realizes that he respected the sensitivity of all religious creed and respect them heartily.

3.4.10 *Malaviya's Reflection on Equality*

Malaviya during addressing Congress session many times argued to Britishers for the impartiality or providing equal of opportunity in public services, he requested to British Government to implied equal treatment in regard to recruitment, office of power, honour, exercise of any trade, salary, etc. without differentiating them as Britishers or Indians, Hindus or Muslims.[125] Malaviya said that

> In every sound system of administration, every member living under it is equally important, entitled to chain protection and equality of treatment in the eyes of law.[126]

He opposed to subjective or excessive powers being given to the executive, and along with others he invariably protested against exercise of exceptional powers by the executive, just as he opposed the executive being installed in place of the judiciary.[127] So Malaviya insisted and urging the government to follow 'ordinary law' and 'ordinary procedure' in the interest of good government and justice. He advised the government to

---

123. Banaras Hindu University minutes, Vol. iii. B. Jan. 1911, July 1919, p. 91.
124. R.I.N.C., 1927, p. 62.
125. L.A.D., Vol. I, Feb. 7, 1929, pp. 592-93.
126. P.I.I.C., Vol. XLIX, Jan. 24, 1911, p. 135.
127. L.A.D., *op. cit.*, p. 588.

do that justice between man and man and between community and community irrespective of race, creed and colour.

3.4.11 *Malaviya's Consideration on Theory of Trusteeship*

In 1909, in article of Abhyudaya Malaviya proposed the concept of trusteeship. His concept was different with Gandhian philosophy of *Swaraj* or *Ramrajya*. He suggested to rich people to regard all their property as an award from God, and not their own. So they should spend the property, for the welfare of his creature. He said by this saying,

> I did not mean it as that the rich should give out their wealth among the poor of feed them free. But it meant they should spend their money for the spread of educational purpose of the people so that in the future people are become capable of earning their bread.[128]

In one more article, he said that it was the '*Dharma*' of the judicious and wise people who are strong and the rich, to use their God-given gifts in the service of the poor and the weak. If they do not do this, they will be charged of violation of trust of Godly donations which in itself is '*Adharma*' or sin. Therefore, the vital meaning of trusteeship is that those who are gifted with knowledge, power and wealth should use that power for strengthen to the weak, as part of their duty, relatively using them for personal self-seeking interest. Malaviya in whole trend of his life inspired for service to humanity which reflects his believe in the theory of trusteeship.

3.4.12 *Issues on which Malaviya Stated his Political Ideas*

On some of the issues like I.C.S. Service, defense or promotion of military, decentralization of power and utility of Local Self-Government, Malaviya was not satisfied by the policies of British Government. So he expressed himself on such issues frequently on political stage.

(a) *Malaviya's Nationalistic Approach for the I.C.S. Services*

In administrative system of British India, I.C.S. job had unique status with salary of 2250 ₹/month. But the condition of Indians in such job was not satisfactory. The entrance exam

128. P.I.I.C., Vol. LIII, March 18, 1915, pp. 473, 491.

rule, syllabus of entrance exam, age limits, partiality due to family status, ratio of Indians verses Britishers all things were not favours' to Indians. Malaviya was much tortured on the above issue because at that time the chief beneficiaries of this high salary and generous service were mainly Europeans.[129] To keep the Indians out of the I.C.S., the age of entrance examination was reduced from twenty-two to twenty and competitive examinations were held in England. Therefore, Malaviya condemned the government policy as unrighteous, suicidal, and criminal, and sinful.

Malaviya was also critical on the preferential treatment given to Europeans in subordinate services under the cover of 'Natives of India'. In his opinion, the syllabus for the I.C.S. examination was for from satisfactory from the Indian point of view.[130] Hence, Malaviya urged the necessity of introduction useful subjects in the syllabus. He would suggest to cut out Latin and Greek, allow more marks to Sanskrit and Arabic and introduce Indian Law including Hindu and Mohammedan Law, and Indian History. Malaviya demanded 25% reduction in pay of the officers drawing salary above ₹ 2250/- per month.[131] Therefore, Malaviya stood for an Indian character of the administration. He wanted the Indian administration to be, "Especially, particularly and definitely Indian." So all his demand of administrative job favoured the welfare of Indians.

(b) *Malaviya's Views on National Defense*

After the revolt of 1857, the Indians was significantly reduced in the army, and for future 'loyal classes' and 'safe areas' and all materials stores, had essentially to be purchased from England and higher posted of command were kept by

---

129. Strachey, Sir John, *India—Its Administration and Progress*, London (1911), 4th revised ed., p. 547.
130. Gupta, J.N., *Life and Works of Romesh Chandra Dutta*, London, 1911, p. 21. Indian students were at a disadvantage as compared to the English students. The letter offered in Latin and Greek getting full marks 750 marks compared to the Sanskrit which carried 500 marks.
131. Islington Report, Vol. IX, p. 82, Q. No. 4319.

Europeans. Further, the people were disarmed,[132] such a policy not disheartened the people. It also made them helpless and pusillanimous. Malaviya's observed there was reservation of some post of army for Indian and all the high salary post kept by Europeans consequently Indian economy lost. He said, "The key to Swaraj was the control of Military." He rightly observed that

> Unless Indians made them fit to manage their own Military affairs, they could not expect Swaraj.[133]

By Swaraj he meant 'self-dependence,' that is 'self-defense.' So as long as a nation's army is under the control of some other country, the nation cannot be said to be free. Malaviya was much impressed by the Japanese Army and wanted a military or a citizen's army for India on similar lines. Therefore, Malaviya visualized that,

> If responsible Government is to be established in India, the first, and the most essential reform to be carried out is building up of Indian army.[134]

(c) *Malaviya's Approach for Decentralization of Power*

Tilak and Malaviya were described the relation between the Supreme Government and the Local Governments, as between husband and his wife. Here the husband first having indulged in all his extravagant habits, asked his wife to surrender all her savings. Therefore, they consider the provincial governments were like housewives while the imperial government was the master of the house, but added that the Government of India was more like a "rack-renting landlord" who leaves just enough to keep alive and to toil to raise revenue for his master than like a guardian of the people solicitous to advance their happiness and prosperity. Malaviya understood that the development and pleasure of the people depended more upon provincial governments than upon imperial government. He demanded that the provincial governments should cease

132. *Organization of Indian Army*, Report (1859), cd. 2515, pp. ix-xv, cited in Lekh, pp. 199-203.
133. *New India*, April 10, 1922.
134. I.R.T.C., Second Session, Vol. ii, p. 98.

to be merely delegates of the supreme government. Instead, they should be made semi-independent. He pleaded that the unitary system of administration of finance be replaced by the federal system.[135] Malaviya wanted the imperial government to be mainly concerned, defense and foreign relations, currency tariff, post telegraph and railways. The provincial governments were to make contributions to the imperial government in case of shortfall in the latte's revenue. He maintained ultimate aim "Was to give to the Provincial Governments independent sources of revenue and separate power of taxation subject to general control of the Government of India."[136]

So Malaviya by decentralization wanted to establish democracy for common man and equity to overcome super dominance of the Centre Government over provincial government.

(d) *Malaviya's Views for Local Self-Government*

Malaviya was himself as member of local self-Government as a chairman of Allahabad Municipal Board served various capacities in nineteen's. His interest in local self-Government bodies was both loving and dearer. He was influenced that the local bodies being nearest to the people could do a lot for the welfare of the locality.

He was distressed with the state of both municipal service and municipal finance which were inadequate. He opposed to communal representation being extended to local bodies. For the happy and smooth running of municipal administration, amity, and fellow-feeling among different communities the municipal board was essential. He accepted success of this grand scheme of local self-Government depended to a larger extent upon its chairman. Malaviya wanted freedom in this regard from official control.

Thus, it is concluded that Malaviya in his political philosophy showed attributes of progressive political leader who greatly contributed to shaping India as modern progressive country from a dependent colonial economy to face the challenges of

---

135. L.A.D., Vol. V, Sept. 17, 1929, pp. 1001-05.
136. L.R.C.D., Vol. VII, pp. 72-73.

a newly dependent nation. His ideas of liberty, democracy, equality, self-defense, were in consonance with the modern human right. His political dream was concerned with selfless politics which was devoted for the welfare of common man. The poverty of the masses, illiteracy, economic, mental, physical exploitation of Indians, suffering and sorrows of common men greatly perturbed him and throughout his life till the death he worked for the betterment of country and countryman. So Malaviya considered as a builder of the nation who belonged to moderate school of political thought with nationalist touch. His political philosophy reflected Ethico-religious thought because he discussed political, social issues by citing examples or norms described in Veda and religious scriptures.

3.5 Religious Philosophy

India has produced innumerable saints and sages, ascetics and mystics, seers and philosophers for whom the quest of the self has been long-lasting search of life. Malaviya was a true Brahman who considered patriotism as a part of his religious dogma because, to him, India was not merely a geographical unit or a political gospel but a spiritual force, a divine spirit to be adored by all who take birth in this land. Hinduism to him was not merely a way of life followed by a certain fraction of people but a philosophy covering the whole range human reactions of all over the world.[137] Malaviya was essentially a man of religion. There is no doubt, Malaviya guided by a discriminating faith of the Hindu scriptures and philosophy which enjoined by each individual to sacrifice his dear and near ones for the sake of righteousness and protection of human rights and privilege. According to Malaviya, aim of religion or *Dharma* is to hold "What is real". Because he believed that by integration of religion in education people can realized their individual soul from inside. He was the follower of *Sanatan Dharma* and *Bhagvad Gita*. In his view, *Sanatan Dharma* means the eternal religion, the ancient law and Hindu view of life. This is based on the *Vedas* and oldest among all living religions.

137. Chaturvedi, S., *Builders of Modern India Series Madan Mohan Malaviya*. New Delhi: Publications division Ministry of Information and Broadcasting, Government of India Patiala House, 1988, p. 39.

3.5.1 *Malaviya's Views on Sanatan Dharma*

Malaviya was the embodiment of the ancient virtue. In his view, *Sanatan Dharma* is the moral law combined with spiritual discipline that guides one's life. *Sanatan* ethical teaching is lofty, unique, and sublime. According to Malaviya, the more you know of it, the more you will honor and love it. The more you study it; more it will enlighten you and satisfy your heart.[137] Malaviya delivered many lectures on *Sanatan Dharma*, and expressed his views as *Sanatan Dharma* has a culture, civilization, and religion millennium older, than those of any century. He exclaimed God did speak, *Sanatan Dharma* through India's rishis, yogis, mahatmas, acharyas, sanyasis, and saints.[138] According to *Sanatan Dharma*, the social code and regulation of India are founded and if yoga, religious conviction minus from *Sanatan* regulation, India will not be what it has status from millennium years ago? In his article in weekly magazine *Sanatan Dharma*, Malaviya said

> *Sanatan Dharma* is the oldest and scared religion on the earth. It has been originated from the *Vedas*, *Smriti*, and *Purana*. It is unique among all the religions of the world. He had faith in God and said God can dress Himself into Visnu, the sustainer; Brahma, the creator; Mahesvara, the god of destruction.[139]

So through interpretation of three Gods and their three functions and three *Gunas*, i.e. *Sattva*, *Rajas*, and *Tamas*, Malaviya tried to explain the Supreme reality. He described them by separate name, viz. Brahma, Hari, and Hara. So through Bhagavat explanation he cleared the doctrine of transformation (*Parinamavad*) and evolutionary process of subtle creation. Malaviya believed process of evolution entails *Prakarti* as an efficient material cause, and *Kaal* (time), *Svabhava* (nature) and *Karma* (total action performed by *Jivas*). *Sanatan Dharma* is defined by a Western philosopher named Wilhelm Halbfass (2009) as "*Sanatan Dharma* is the eternal religion, the religion

---

138. Y.A. Sundaram, *Homage of Malaviya ji*. Varanasi: BHU Press, 1949, p. 84.
139. *Ibid.*

in or behind all religions.[140] In his view, it is a kind of Meta religion. It has structural potentiality ready to comprise and reconcile within itself all the religion of the world. Malaviya considered this religion as the group of major virtues, such as donation, mercy on all living beings, truth, kindness, patience, forgiveness, etc. Malaviya also has faith in the division of the *Varna* and *Ashram* which are discussed in *Sanatan Dharma* philosophy, which is also chanted by Lord *Krishna* through his sacred mouth in *Gita* as,

> *I have created the four Varnas as Brahmin, Kshatriya, Vaishya and Sudra on the basis of virtue and action.*[141]
>
> चातुर्वर्ण्यं मया सृष्टं गुण कर्म विभागशः।
>
> (गीता, अध्याय-4, श्लोक-13)

Malaviya in his religious speeches also explained the concept of liberation from rebirth, religious praxis, and ontology. He believed in inclusiveness and strived for ontological inclusiveness. Consequently, he tried openly to reconvert Christian Hindu, into Hindu and converted Muslim to Hindu after *Shuddi* and also stressed to upgrade untouchables with equal right as upper cast to entering temple, drink water, to take education, etc. This reflected that Malaviya was a religious philosopher, who did not believe in conservative force of religion. He said by performing holistic deeds, man achieves sublimity in *Varnas* and by doing mean deeds; he falls down in the category. As it has been said in *Shastra* also as even *Sudra* with pious and virtuous character, can became a *Brahmin* and when a *Brahmin* leaves his religion, he becomes worst than *Sudra*. Thus, from these view it is crystal clear that Malaviya was not the blind imitator of the rituals and dogmas of religion. He has right understanding about *Sanatan Dharma*, and because of this, in his life activity, harmony was found between instinct, mind, and spirit. It is also reflected from his activities such as although he faced much opposition from *Sanatan*ies but he was deeply involved in removing the Untouchability, i.e. is an evil for Indian society. Therefore, Malaviya having a true knowledge of *Sanatan Dharma* which

140. Wilhelm Halbfass, *Tradition and Reflection*, pp. 52-53.
141. The *Bhagavad Gita English Translation.* Gorakhpur: Gita Press, *shloka* (47).

he achieved by detached objective and impersonal approach. During his life time, his personality was reflected as union of *Yogeshwar* and *Dhanurdhara*, i.e. man of ideal and man of action.

So Malaviya wanted to develop a right wisdom in Hindus by religious discourses. He had faith in the view, i.e. God becomes man so that man become God. Thus, he tried to remove the duality between man and God through his lectures on *Bhagavat*. He understood that unchecked activities and blind rituals of religion became destructive and produced cynicism in men. Consequently, dual-minded society developed, and no harmony was found in mind, instinct, and spirit of individuals. So according to him through inculcation of religion values, it was possible to promote pure spirit in men, which resulted in peace, love, and impersonal nature and saw oneness with others. So through expansion of *Sanatan Dharma* he desired to clear human uniqueness and its relationship to God and path of salvation.

3.5.2 *Malaviya's Universal Approach for Religion*

Malaviya's lectures during different ceremonies reflected him as a person who believed in universal religion eclipses from sectarian diversion. In relation to *Sanatan Dharma*, Malaviya was meek as a lamb, gentle almost to a fault but a proud Hindu conscious of the treasures of his inheritance. During the foundation laying ceremony before Lord Harding in 1916, he said,

> We cannot divest our consciousness that we have inherited a culture and civilization of our own, which reaches further back in time than that of any other people, and which possesses, as we believe in a special degree, the elements of social stability as well as the fundamental principles of physical, intellectual, and spiritual progress and welfare. Amidst all the vicissitudes through which Hindu society has passed, it has, in all essentials, clings to that civilization and has even been governed by it. There was naturally a widespread desire in our community that we should

> have a central educational institution of our own to preserve and promote our distinctive civilization and culture, and to instruct our youth in the sacred precepts of our religion.[142]

This speech of Malaviya reflected his faith in Indian tradition, culture, civilization, and religion. He felt for Hindu *Dharma* like child feels for his mother, as something indispensable without which life becomes impossible.[143] Lifelong his love for *Sanatan Dharma* did not reduce and was reflected in his multifaceted works.

Was Malaviya having sectarian touch in relation to Hinduism? When different religious, social, political activities of Malaviya analyzed it revealed no account of Malaviya's vision and work is complete without mentioning his faith in Hindu *Dharma*. This was the most outstanding feature of his personality. In fact, it was the very breath of his life. It pervaded his whole life as nothing else did. All his activities, political, social educational were centered in it. Yet there was nothing sectarian in him.

He was not confined to any creed or dogma. Malaviya as a *karma yogi* believing in the saying of Lord Krishna,

> Your right is to work only and never to the fruit there of do not be the cause of the fruit of the action nor let your attachment be in action.[144]

So all actions were done by him in an impersonal way, having detached, and unbiased attitude. Those who describe sectarianism to him do great injustice to him. His conception of Hindu *Dharma* could not be sectarian, it was universal. In fact, *Dharma* and Hindu *Dharma* were identical for him, and if the conception of *Dharma* was that of something universal, that of Hindu *Dharma* must necessarily be so. To confine it to any sect would be to limit its universality, which Malaviya

142. Dar, S.L. and Somaskandan, S., *History of the Banaras Hindu University*. Varanasi: Banaras Hindu University Press, 1966, p. 447.
143. Mitra, S.K., "*Madan Mohan Malaviya*", Mahamana Malaviyaji Birth Centenary Commemoration, Vol. ii, p. 95.
144. The *Bhagavad Gita English Translation*. Gorakhpur: Gita Press, Chapter ii, *shloka* (47).

could never do. There was a *Bhagavat* touch in him. But that does not mean that he belonged to the *Bhagavat* sect. So for a moment Malaviya was admired as secular, communal leader as during formulation of objectives of Banaras Hindu University as to conserve, promote, and enriched the Hindu religion he was checked by British Government. But later it proved that he had no compulsion related to attend the religious instruction in Hindu University. There was no obligation of written and oral test prescribed in university exam related to ethical disciplines of *Shastra*.

During first court meeting, Malaviya addressed and said,

> Yet there is much controversy whether a denominational or sectarian university would or would not be beneficial.

Malaviya said

> "I myself not have such apprehension that it is sectarian, it depends upon the spirit that animates the workers, and now the question is whether spirit is one of competition or of cooperation. In the later nineteen century teaching of religion unhappily not corrected having unhealthy spirit of cooperation in reversibly and a desire of domination, the result of which we see today in the hideous and devastating war that is convulsing entire continents". Gentlemen, "I am sure that it is not the spirit of religious education to develop blind competition instead of cooperation. True religion is based on the belief of the supreme being, the almighty God and essence of all morality founded upon such a faith of charity and good will towards all.[145] The same was written in Vedas which reflect how much cooperation exists if a person is religious sees the God in yourself and in all, see all in God that is yourself and therefore do not unto others as you would be done by, and do not unto them what you would that they should not unto you."[146]

145. Dar, S.L. and Somaskandan, S., *op. cit.*, p. 244.
146. K. Chandramauli, "Malaviya ji's and his relevance" *Pragya*, Vol. 56, Part 2, 2010, p. 301.

Malaviya played role as a peace maker for the communal harmony. He organized all party conferences to bring communal amity in Allahabad in 1910 and Bombay (14 Jan. 1922). Malaviya convened a conference of all communities at the request of M.C. Chagla and, Abdul Kalam Azad in 1932. M.C. Chagla commented about him as "It was largely due to his able guidance and the conference got marked success." Rabindranath Tagore said,

> Your efforts have had a perceptibly wholesome effect on other communities and we feel grateful for your assistance to country in its present crisis.[147]

Dr. Mahamadullah commented for Malaviya's contribution as highest service to the country in 1932, i.e. he brought an understanding between the various communities in India. So in his religious conception he was not polluted by sectarian touch while he had lofty, holistic, humanistic, and futuristic vision, for society and *Dharma*.

3.5.3 *Malaviya's Humanistic Approach for Religion*

The axiology of his religious philosophy exhibits values like passionate love, humanity. He read *shloka* as

> "न कामयेऽहं गतिमीश्वरात् पराम।
> अष्टद्धियुक्तामपुनर्मव वा।।
> अति प्रपद्येऽखिलदेह भाजाम्।
> अन्तः स्थिति येन भवन्त्वदु:खा।।"
>
> (*Srimad Bhagavat* 9-21-12)[148]
>
> I do not pray to God to give me salvation characterized by the possession of eight *ridhis* or the highest salvation or freedom from re-births, but what I pray for is that I may feel the sorrows of all beings by dwelling within them, so that they may be free from them.

This faith of Malaviya reflected his humanizing behavior. Malaviya as a humanist stands for peace, prosperity, and happiness of mankind, as well as purity of means and end. He

147. *Ibid.*, 300.

148. *The Bhagavad Gita English Translation.* Gorakhpur: Gita Press (2007). *Shlok* (22-23).

propagated scientific and humanistic ethics along with religious faith.

Malaviya regarded religion as an essential factor for socialization and emotional integrity of men. In his view, religion was codified by the founders and glorifies the tradition and custom of any civilization. So when a society followed a practical code and conduct given by religion, then there is no conflict between individuals of society. Malaviya gave preference to the past traditions and culture but he was not against the innovation of science which make human life easy. He appreciated those who enjoyed balance between past and present ideals. By praising the liberalism of *Sanatan Dharma*, Malaviya said "सर्वे भवन्तु सुखिनः सर्वे सन्तु निरामया। सर्वे भद्राणि पश्यन्तु मा कश्चिद्दुःखभाव भवेत्॥" which meant all the creature may remain happy, each and every remain healthy, each and every one see happiness to others, none may remain unhappy. So expressing his views on *Gita* and *Bhagavat*, Malaviya wanted the world citizen to believe that God is one. He is partially present not only in men, but present in all the creation. So the best worship to him is to see the God in each and every creature, have companionship with all.

3.5.4 *Malaviya View on God, Goodness and Morality*

What Malaviya answered about God and Goodness? When Malaviya's views were analyzed to extract answer of above excavation, it is detected Malaviya worshiped Lord Krishna as God and had faith in *Gita*. He believed that God itself defined all his characteristics in *Gita*. So he recommended pupil to study *Gita*. He forced Hindus, if you want to know God and way to deal life peacefully study *Gita* because all answers occur in *Gita*. He exclaimed God presented His identity through Krishna in *Gita* as (Chapt. xii Lord Krishna)

> I am equally present in all being; there is nothing hateful or dear to me. They however who devoting worship I abide in me and I too stand revealed to them.[149]

149. *The Bhagavad Gita English Translation.* Gorakhpur: Gita Press (2007), Chapter x, ii *shloka.*

So God exist in every creature. Malaviya in his speech explained the existence of God through an example as

> Among modern writers those who were agnostic have come to believe in the existence of a God. One such person, will particularly name Hegel, the greatest scientist of Germany and zoologist. He has in his 'Little creation' fought against the idea of God, but when he has said all he had to admit that there is one supreme, all-pervading energy to be found in the whole of the universe. That matter and energy are constant, that you find that is indestructible and that its energy pervades all the whole creation from time immemorial. Hegel does not acknowledge that there is a God in the sense in which others do. But he has the idea of a God in Nature and he has shown that he cannot find a solution for this question without accepting the idea of such a God. Hindu religion teaches us that God is imminent in all created beings. Its meaning is that in Hindu religion God is not defined as engineer who is erecting a building on a plan which he has conceived. God is defined as being immanent in the whole creation and it is a wonder that the men of science as they go on studying their problems of science are becoming more and more theists and convinced of the existence of God. Now I want to ask you how the matter stands. The idea of matter is not different from God, in Hindu religion the idea of God is not that of a man working like an engineer upon material different from himself. He constitutes the material. He creates it. He brings it into existence by indescribable, almost unimaginable which represent him.[150]

He thought as human being regulates his body and control his environment similarly there is a Universal Mind which rules and regulates the whole universe. Whatsoever moves in the moving world is pervaded by God (ईशावास्यमिदं सर्वं यत्

150. Y.A. Sundaram, *Homage of Malaviya ji*. Varanasi: BHU Press, 1949, p. 43.

किञ्चित् जगत्यां जगत्।) He cited example of Veda as (यतो ईमानि भुतानि जायन्ते तदैव ब्रह्म।) that means this universe is a manifestation of that Universal Mind or spirit. All these created creatures are Brahman. The same was declared by Lord Krishna in Gita as

> *I am the seed of all the elements and beings.*
> (बीजमाम् सर्वं भूतानां।)[151] (p. 104) (Bhagirathi Sahu).

So it concluded that Malaviya view about God is much scientific not based on religious stories. He believed in spiritual reality not material and material world is manifestation of spirit.

The next inquiry arose in the mind of researcher as what Malaviya views on "Is Goodness without God good enough?" When the opinion of Malaviya analyzed to answer this query, it is concluded that Malaviya defined good through golden teaching of *Sanatan Dharma* as

> Not to do that unto others what you wish others not to do for you. God having holy and loving nature provides an absolute standard of moral value, everything before and around proclaims the existence of God. He is one without second and he is alone real. To know him is the great joy of life[152] (V.A. Sundaram—Homage).

Malaviya again defined goodness as,

> Where is the merit in men, who returns good for good? The wise call him only good who does well for evil doer. They alone are good who do good for those who do harm to them and these good souls adorn the earth, for it is better for their birth[153] (Golden words of Mahayana in Homage Malaviya by Y.A. Sundaram).

For moral accountability and Goodness, Malaviya believed in God and said if it is the objective of education in to make a good citizen, it is important to integrate religion in education. Malaviya said,

> Being able to earn wealth through honorable means, by avoiding temptation of unworthy conduct, and

151. *Ibid.*
152. *Ibid.*, p. 45.
153. *Ibid.*, p. 42.

> being inspired by high principals only imbibed through Indian ancient language Sanskrit and religious learning, then they will be men of unswerving rectitude and incorruptible integrity, i.e. Goodness.[154]

So Malaviya's concept of God and Goodness was inspired by the ancient Indian *Veda*, *Puran*, *Gita* and *Sanatan Dharma* philosophy.

As an inquisitor, next inquiry was to know the Malaviya's view on the issue moral goodness without belief in God rationally stable or not. When Malaviya's moral philosophy or his theistic view analyzed then it found he trust that moral values are rooted in God. He is the locus and source of moral value. God's own loving nature supplies the absolute standard against which all actions are measured. He is by nature loving, generous, just, faithful, kind, and so forth. Thus, if God exists, objective moral value exist (Speech of Malaviya on Immense of God, p. 81).[155] He negates the claim of moral education and suggested moral will exercises a control over impulses and desire to maintain harmony. So he exclaimed there was no need of moral education if any person has faith in religion.

On countless occasions, he exhorted his students to be faithful towards God and their religion, for him a life devoid of religious impulse was an empty vessel, a mere husk without the seed of reality. This indifference of the modern youth towards *Dharma* gave him genuine pain, and nothing pleased him more than the sight of religious spirit amongst the students. According to Malaviya no call is higher than that of *Dharma*, i.e. right living. He never found indifference in morality and religious values. In his opinion, the purpose of morality and religion is common, i.e. to deal life harmoniously and peacefully. Malaviya how correlate between these two it cleared by his living style. When Malaviya's action was observed, it was revealed that his moral obligations towards himself and towards his fellow beings were not two folded but he achieved a synthesis between personal excellence and civic virtues. So Malaviya was not an

---

154. *Ibid.*
155. Y.A. Sundaram, *Homage of Malaviya ji*. Varanasi: BHU Press, 1949, p. 84.

extremist, who formulate inconsistent values against man's nature while his moral and religious code and conduct judged by their consequences.

So in his view when a human being has faith in his religion and right understanding of its code then religion endorses moral behavior in the form of selflessness, courage, self-purification, non-attachment, and impersonal outlook, which ultimately produce positive attitude towards life and the world. So if educational institutions are able to inculcate these virtues then it can surely bring salvation in learners. He opposed the views that God motivated immoral behavior. Malaviya believed in the three claims. First, God's holy and loving nature provides an absolute standard of moral value; second God's commands are constitutive of moral duty, third God's providential control of world history guarantees for moral accountability. So without believe in God moral stability is not possible.

Malaviya composed and remind always.

> Ram that dwells in every heart
> Be he your constant remembrance,
> Bear no ill will towards any,
> And speak no falsehood,
> Pilfer not what does not belong to you,

And take no intoxicant.

> Take no eye not gamble.
> Do not cost eye on women.
> This alone will be your true austerity
> Let Ram that abides in all life be
> Your constant remembrance.[156]

Each line of this poem composed by Malaviya expressed moral education.

Malaviya worshiped *GO, GANGA* and *GAYATRI*. Malaviya's had strong faith in Gayatri because he thought his innersole became pure by chanting Gayatri mantra. He loved to Ganga not as simple water, but he considered her as Maa, and

---

156. Shastri, G.D., "*Mahamana Madan Mohan Malaviya*" *Mahamana Malaviya Birth Centenary Commemoration Souvenir*, Vol. ii, 1966, p. 207.

worshiped her holiness. He worked with the people for Ganga *raksha* and cow protection movement. All these works of his life reflected his thought, how he correlated moral values and God in his life. He did daily *Sandhya* and Morning Prayer and inspired university students to devote their one and half hour for each Sunday to listen *Gita* lecture not only for his own religion but for moral and spiritual development. Malaviya was interested to build a temple, within the grounds of the university reflected that he thought it may radiate wholesome influence inside the university area. Thus, in Malaviya's opinion for moral progress, it is important to have faith in God, because God provides you right way of living. In one of his famous extempore speeches he once confessed,

> "It is one of the settled convictions of my life that religion is at the foundations of all greatness and Goodness, and that without an abiding religious faith no affair of man can succeed. But he tells you that he is impatient with the corruption of religion, codified superstition and he abuses of it, to enforce social discriminations."[157]

Thus, in Malaviya's opinion God and religious thought is only reason to realize a man omnipotent but instead today man feels quite helpless to the external circumstances. There is natural ignorance of man about himself. Materialistic desire is the weeds in the mind and till they are uprooted and cast off, proper spiritual culture cannot be thought of. So it is important to sow the right seed. The seed should choose discriminately because chaff may give shoots only not grain. In brief for the restoration of our inner divinity of human race it is important today to faith not only one-sided materialistic development which increase greed, cartelism, lust, ego, etc. which are obstacles in attaining perfect humane but faith in God and religion.

3.5.6 *Views on Science and Religion*

By integration of religion in education, Malaviya wanted to generate the opinion in the individuals that there is a relation between science and religion. In his opinion both are not

---

157. Dar, S.L. and Somaskandan, S., *History of the Banaras* Hindu *University*. Varanasi: Banaras Hindu University Press, 1966, p. 381.

antagonistic, they are at least compatible. Malaviya realized the truth of ancient religious teaching, and it is simply due to the reason that he used to test the validity and reality of his ideas in the light of ethical disciplines of *Shastra*. He understood religion is not the result of the crudest, barbaric, and fancies imagination; on the contrary, it is eternal, supreme, and sublime. So he felt that in order to develop true Indians who had national and spiritual approach, religion must be the part of training of every child, must be the basis of ethics of everyone. He wanted to promote social consciousness by amalgamation of religion and science in education by which every individual binds himself, with the higher ideals of social service for the cause of social uplift. So Malaviya seems to agree with the point that for the establishment of non-corrupt value-based society, along with science it is important to expand high moral and religious values of Eastern.

He was not only a firm believer of ancient Indian culture and tradition and but modern than ultra-modern in his future vision of higher education. This is revealed from the objectives of Banaras Hindu University, which is initially formulated by Malaviya, as to promote the study of Hindu *Shastra* and of Sanskrit literature generally as a means of preserving and popularizing for the benefit of Hindus in particular and of the world at large in general and to enrich knowledge of science and technological education. Thus, accordingly, Malaviya framed curriculum of Banaras Hindu University. He established departments for Mechanical and Electrical Engineering, Glass Technology, Pharmaceutical Chemistry, Mining and Metallurgy, Chemical Engineering as well as Sanskrit and Ayurveda, apart from many other courses which existed in other institutions in India.

3.5.7 *On Religion and Education*

Malaviya as a metaphysical traditional thinker who emphasized on virtue, which are the essential characteristics of perennial truth or goodness. The core of his educational philosophy is eternity, divinity, which is behind within and beyond passing flux of all existence. His religion is hardly separable from any aspect of life. Malaviya had an abiding faith in the value of religious instruction. Malaviya said,

> An education which does not provide instruction in the religion of one's forefathers can never be complete and convinced that a Hindu will be better Hindu, a Christian a better Christian and a Mohammedan a better Mohhammedan.[158]

It reflected Malaviya had implicit faith in God and religious education.

Malaviya felt that religion was being neglected everywhere and patriotism was impossible without religion. He considered that religious education is essential for the unity of society and morality and true patriotism. Malaviya by integration of religion in education wanted to build such human who one ready to struggle against evil and sordidness. He did not believe in Macaulay theory of education. As, Lord Macaulay addressed to the British Parliament on 2 Feb. 1835,

> I have travelled across the length and breadth of India and I have not seen a person who is beggar, who is thief, such wealth I have seen in this country; such high moral values. People of such caliber, that I do not think we would conquered this country, unless we break the very backbone of this nation which is spiritual and cultural heritage and therefore I propose that we replace her old and ancient education system, her culture, for the Indians think that all that is foreign and English is good and greater than their own, they loss their self-esteem, their native culture and they will become what we want them, a truly dominated nation.[159]

Yet Malaviya was born after the Macaulay period but he better understood the aim of Macaulay, so he repeatedly said to redesign the Indian education system which is contaminated due to English education system. He realized to bring back our ancient education practices moral as well as spiritual values

---

158. Mishra, K. "*The Purpose of Hindu University*", Mahamana Malaviyaji's Birth Centenary Commemoration, Vol. ii, 1961, p. 120.
159. Dar, S.L. and Somaskandan, S., *op. cit.*, p. 301.

integration of religious education is necessary. In October 1917, Malaviya while delivering the second convocation address of the Banaras Hindu University, said,

> It was an object of the university to promote the building up of character in youth by making religion and ethics an integral part of education, because, we believe religion is to be the surest foundation of character and the trust source of human happiness. Has it not been said that a man without religion cannot be said to belong to himself?[160]

Therefore, it can be said that in order to revitalize India as a nation, Malaviya thought that it was necessary to feed her youth with the old spiritual and moral food, and that religion must be a part of the education founded upon Indian Ideals. It is reflected in Banaras Hindu University. Malaviya on Sunday's *Gita* lecture delivered a correlation between science, scientific thought and religion. So by the religious discourses he did not want to create any propaganda but desired to develop sense of enquiry sense in learners to know what is true. In religious discourses not only the teachers of *Dharma* delivered lecture of religious belief but the great scientist also exchanges their views. So Malaviya tried to develop such atmosphere in the university which helps in scientific, moral and spiritual development. As he believed through religious understanding, humanistic values, sense of duty and reverence could be inculcated in men which are the finest qualities of a civilized person.

The same culture was developed by next Vice Chancellor Dr. S. Radhakrishnan who said,

> When moral education process pushed from outside, there a radical dualism found between men and Nature. As long as this dualism remains, real harmony cannot be achieved. Religion is only one which removes this dualism and restores the last unity between man and eternal. For us Indians a study of the Upanishads is essential, if we are to preserve our national being and character. To discover the main lines of our traditional life, we must return to our classics, the Vedas and

160. *Ibid.*, p. 244.

> the Upanishads, the Bhagavad Gita and the Dharmapada.[161]

It saves us from the greed, lust and hatred. It releases the moral power in human.

3.6 An Estimate of Malaviya's Philosophy of Religious Education

A common critic of religion, in general appeals to their bad consequences. Generally, in informal discussions claims are made that religion is most harmful social institution, religion has caused most misery than anything else in human history, and religion belief is bad because it has caused the death of millions of people. This kind of argument probably has been given by common people. In reference to this, many philosophers like Dawkins (2008) have attacked religion as "the root of evil."[162]

Similarly, Grayling (2009) contents religion as it is harmful for society, and therefore we would be better without of it.[163] But such common consequential critique is claimed due to some political ideology. Keeping this view most of the philosophers attempted to avoid expressing views which hurt religious sentiments, so that they do not involve in any trouble. Malaviya, however, acted to the contrary and consequently he became sometime the controversial figures for the sake of Hindu religion in India. He faced hostility from the society and became famous as sectarian, but religious tolerance is more than the concordance between the adherents of different creeds. Thus, as a metaphysical traditional thinker he passed his life on the norms of *Sanatan Dharma*.

Malaviya perspective reflected that by incorporation of religion in education, he could prepare citizen who richly known their culture, heritage and scriptures. Along with this he wanted to develop such culture in university, where student follow discipline and having high moral character. Due to his religious inspiration, the Hindu University exist as a seminary,

161. Radhakrishnan, S., *Bhartiya Darsan*, New Delhi: Rajpal and Sons, 2009, p. 675.
162. Dawkins, *The God Delusion*, 2008, p. 23.
163. Grayling, *op. cit.*, p. 52.

where intellectual osmosis and cross pollination of ideas could take place, resulting in the endowment of new moral and intellectual qualities to the people of this land. Malaviya by integration of religion in education not only developed Indian culture but also nourished *Vasudhaiva Kutumbakam* feelings in the students. According to him, the moral code of religion is completely sufficient to solve the problems faced by the people of today. It can be resolved only by progress through right means and this will be brought only in the tenets of *Dharma* or righteousness which would shape the values and strengthen the core of one's personality.

Through his quote

> India is the common motherland of all Hindus, Muslims and pareses[164] (AAJ Apr. 12 1924).

Malaviya wanted to promote universal thinking. He advised to people of India to "Follow your *Dharma* and respect others and work closely with Parsees, Muslims, and Christians for the progress of the country."[165]

All statements reflected Malaviya's love for universal religion. No doubt in present scenario when the critical approach trying to point out the harms of religion and argue that they compensate all of its benefits easily by science and money. But the loss of authority of religion is producing deviant behavior in man. Modern knowledge is accelerating doubt and jealousy. The abundance in amenities of life is increasing mental diseases and emotional tension. This increases multitudnal activities has segregated life into so many compartments so the unity and integrity of life can hardly be comprehended: nothing seems to be solid and stable in the world. Life has become complex and complicated. There is tremendous growth of industries, bureaucratic organizations, nepotism, favouritism, multiplication of wants increases with inadequate means, create much unhappiness and frustration in human beings. Under these circumstances, man looks for the spiritual rehabilitation. Malaviya supposed that if man wanted

164. *AAJ*, April 12, 1924.
165. Chandramauli, K., "*Malaviya ji and his Relevance*", *Pragya*, Vol. 56, Part 2, 2010, p. 299.

to overcome such problems, it is important to have faith in religion and its code. Criticism of religion by illogical way does not promote constructiveness in man. Malaviya assumed in ancient time all such greed's controlled by the institution of religion. So to check all these unwanted, unlimited desires of men it is essential to integrate religious education. So he focused to minimize more narrow sectarian thinking in relation to religion and start to think broadly on religion and God. In his view, a true religious person is, who loves all and respects to all religions and performs his duty as worship of God.

It is also concluded that Malaviya regarded morality and religion not as segregated, separated pole. But he considered the separation of one from another makes them ineffective and the men who practices such morality without faith of religion split his personality. He believed that religious faith raised sense of self-dedication, self-sacrifice in human being. This faith adds piety and divinity in men's action. The social pressure, social code alone cannot produce it. In Malaviya view, to regulate the men's behavior along with social pressure, religious sentiments are essential. Without divine source of authority, moral education becomes superficial. So Malaviya denied from the fact that only moral education are sufficient for value inculcation.

Therefore, in Malaviya's opinion, religion is the custodian of the virtues which played a significant role in the development of civilization and culture. It has laid down all the rules of conduct which practiced by men. So it is essential to attain stable, peaceful society incoming generation follow these rule or code of conduct. It is religious education which teaches people their duties and obligations, and act as bridge between different generations. It is not only the practice of virtues but it teaches what is right and wrong. In modern time, when the society realized moral crises lost past spiritual heritage, when holiness regarded as an evidence of weakness, truthfulness regarded as foolishness and goodness regarded as simplicity. The only hope in such sinking civilization is returning to the port of religion and in India because *Sanatan Dharma* followed by ancient time so it is important to boost *Sanatan Dharma* for preserving its spiritual wealth.

4

Educational Philosophy of Madan Mohan Malaviya

4.1 Introduction

Among the educational thinkers of India, Madan Mohan Malaviya was one of the visionaries who significantly contributed to education, educational theory and practice. The contribution of Vivekananda, Tagore, Gandhi and Aurobindo Ghose have been critically examined and they have been recognized as well-known educational philosophers. No doubt, Madan Mohan Malaviya is an outstanding figure, who profoundly influenced the history of modern India by playing different roles as a great politician, lawyer, journalist, and as an orthodox Sanatan Hindu. But Malaviya was basically an educationist, who after seeing the social, political, economical and cultural situations could not restrain himself and participated in different roles for restructuring the Indian society. But his main goal was to reform education which ultimately aimed at directing the other processes of social change and development in Indian society. But his contribution was not properly evaluated in different branches of knowledge in general and in education in particular. Therefore, in this chapter, an attempt has been made to study the educational thoughts of Madan Mohan Malaviya. As observed by A.S. Altekar,

> "Any educational institution is usually the mirror of the ideals of a nation, and enables us to understand the spirit of civilization."[1]

1. Altekar, A.S., *Education in Ancient India*, Varanasi: Manohar Prakashan, 1996, p. 1.

This is especially found to be true in ancient educational institutions as well as in case of Malaviya, who put his educational philosophy in the practical form by establishing his unforgettable contribution, i.e. Banaras Hindu University. Malaviya understood the role of education for the change in a static society into a dynamic one. He believed, if people wanted a major change in the society without violent revolution, there is only one sole instrument, i.e. education. He realized that the path of success lied in educational organizations and in the dedication of people to the wider loyalties of national development, and not through selfish and narrow loyalties to personal or group interests. Malaviya devoted his whole life for the establishment of social, educational organizations and selflessly worked for the welfare of common people. He started his educational activities by setting up the Bharati Bhavan Library at Prayag in November 1889. He enriched the cause of education in the country by opening hostels, libraries, social centers, educational institute and *pathshalas*. He took great pains and made more sacrifices to clarify the function and objectives of higher education in Indian mode.

The work of Malaviya was not confined only in the areas like politics and the welfare of Hindus only, but he may be considered as "reconstructivist" who always tried wisely to manage the significant constraints such as caste, ethnicity, class, language, religion and regionalism on each political and religious platform. Many hectic efforts have been made by him to solve language problem to achieve social and national integration. Malaviya's educational view categorized him as a thinker, who was keenly interested in building up an egalitarian society by providing equal opportunity to all. In his educational views Malaviya is considered as realistic, pragmatic, idealist and eclectic philosopher. Thus, Malaviya is a visionary who acted as torchbearer for the people who live in society and formulated ideals of education. He gave his logical opinion about values, human nature, curriculum, economic system, etc. Malaviya's philosophy of education was interwoven with his conception of social welfare, which furnishes an apt response to the moral question raised by the social order. Education to him was not mere incident of social existence but essential function of cosmic order.

4.2 The Genesis of Malaviya's Educational Philosophy

Malaviya's ideas regarding education did not strike suddenly in his mind but it had been the outcome of many years of sustained thought processes and experiences. As the philosophers said that the educationists did not have students as *tabula rasa* upon which they might inscribe what they wanted to. They had to deal with deep-seated dogmas of students, underdeveloped tendencies inherited from the past which are still to mature, to strengthen and sometimes to correct. Malaviya's educational views were very much influenced by Aryavartha's concept of education, culture and tradition. Like other philosophers Malaviya was very sensitive towards social issues, so he could not resist himself by the social, political, educational changes and events of his times. Consequently, his thoughts evolved due to his vast experiences of the political, social and economic life.

He was the philosopher of an age, when India was under British rule. He was born just after mutiny of 1857. In the next two to three decades, following the first war of freedom, the entire country was passing through a national renaissance in every corner of life, viz. social, economic, political, religious and educational. The spirit of revolt was aroused against the British rule in the hearts and minds of Indian people. Malaviya was one of them who faced and felt all hostility and humiliation of British Government. So, he joined the Indian National Congress immediately and actively participated as helping hand of A.O. Hume. Gradually, he became known as a champion of Indian Nationalism. During different political movements, Malaviya toured the whole country and understood the real needs of society and deeply analyzed the causes of many problems like poverty, famine, drought, diseases, and poor agriculture, economic and religious conditions of the country. When he visited frequently to different places, he found that religion was being neglected everywhere and Western culture was dominating the Indian culture and religion. Subsequently he delivered lectures on the essence of Hinduism. Adverse situations of the nation and deteriorating religious conditions encouraged him to struggle to find the solution of various problems. Thus, many of these situations were responsible for the genesis of Malaviyan thoughts.

Malaviya's philosophy of education was deep-rooted in the belief of *Sanatan Dharma*. Basically, Malaviya's family background was also responsible to make him admirer of Sanatan philosophy, as described in chapter second. He had faith in the thoughts that realm of metaphysical being is traditional in nature and possesses the characteristic of truth, beauty and goodness. He himself believed in *Rith* (spirit), *Dharma* and Action (Yoga). He was mainly influenced by the *Gita* which he listened from his father in childhood in religious discourses. Thus, factors such as family background, his birth place, friends, and social-economic-political conditions of the country, all were responsible for the genesis of Malaviya's educational philosophy.

When other Indian philosophers' thoughts were studied and analyzed, it was found that either these visionaries were influenced by the highest spiritual persons or gurus or they experimented their own thoughts in their own educational settings, for example Vivekananda's educational thoughts were particularly influenced by his guru Ramakrishna and Vedantic philosophy. So by creating Ramakrishna Mission he provided his service to the motherland, likewise Aurobindo and Tagore, both were poets in the beginning and they came in contact with Western culture during their education when they stayed overseas. They belonged to rich family. So as Gandhi was also educated from abroad, and influenced by Tolstoy experiment of education. In case of Malaviya things were different. He was not influenced by any religious guru or school of thoughts and had never gone abroad to take education, his home culture was not egalitarian. He was a man of crisis, who suffered from many economical crisis since his childhood. Thus after analyzing his sayings and views on different issues it can be concluded that Malaviya's poor condition of the family, sufferings and learnt high moral values of childhood were the factors which played a positive role in making Malaviya's mind into an ambitious one. Hence, he was motivated to do hard work since his childhood to achieve respect in the society and when he was recognized by many respected people of that time, he became conscious about his innate qualities and made efforts to manifest and utilize them for welfare of nation. His high moral values and willpower were also got motivated by great faith of *karma* philosophy of the *Gita* which he used to recite in his daily routine.

Indeed, Malaviya belonged to common middle-class family, but his ambition always motivated him to dream like those powerful and rich people who could do their best for the welfare of the nation without worrying about the problem of finance. Although he always faced economic crises but his enthusiasm never yielded to any barrier related to lack of money to accomplish any great task for nation. Malaviya had firm faith in himself and was much positivist towards the blessings of God. As, He firmly said,

> if I recite *Gajendra Moksha* once by my heart, any obstacles which act as barrier would be removed from my way of desires."[2]

This reflected his optimistic personality and strong faith in God. Malaviya's very good control over English, Hindi, Sanskrit and Urdu languages made him a good orator due to which he was able to counter Britishers' policies logically. So, all such factors forced him to think that if all Indians could get a better education like him, they would be able to fight against Britishers rationally and also their living standard would be upgraded by education. As a result Malaviya discussed the issue of education at any possible platform and always focused to strengthen education system.

Malaviya's educational opinions were committed for Indianization of education system. As he got education from an English medium school, he realized the difficulties faced by Indians in understanding the English language and the goal of English missionaries. He observed that Britishers tried to strengthen their clutch over the educated classes of the country

2. Halna, Bhagwan Das. Jhalkian, p. 25. Halna was connected with the Abhuyudaya and got the account from Malaviya himself. This is the story of the rescue of the elephant King from the clutches of the Alligator of Lord Vishnu.

by developing a pattern of education in which the tradition of Sanskrit and Arabic scholarships and values of great Indian religion found no place. His upbringing always attracted him towards the culture of the ancient time which he inherited from his parents. During the memberships of various commissions he analyzed Britishers' aspirations in industrial areas, during the expansion of Railways, export of raw materials from India, taxation of land agriculture, tragedies of Bengal and Punjab, lack of opportunities of Indians in status job, Hindu-Muslim split and riots, etc. where Malaviya played a crucial role. All such incidents forced him to accept the fact that the Britishers and their policies were the only reason for the deteriorating economic, educational as well as religious condition of the country.

A spirit of cynicism and flippancy was encouraged by Britishers towards Hindu religion to spread Christianity. Malaviya observed that the Hindu society was utterly disorganized and disintegrated due to foreign policies and blind imitators; consequently he became anxious for developing a strong religious faith, among Hindus, in their own religion and virtues of *Sanatan Dharma*. Malaviya also realized that along with education, protection of Hindu Dharma and expansion of *Sanatan* rituals were essential to save Indian culture. Many social reformers and visionaries like Raja Ram Mohan Roy, Swami Dayanand and Keshab Chandra Sen urged the countrymen to look within order to discover and uproot the evils that had exhausted the power of Indian society. Therefore such awakening inspirations also motivated him for doing the same but with a different approach. He did not develop any new kind of *samaj* as *Brahma Samaj, Arya Samaj*, etc. but he fought for the regeneration of *Sanatan Dharma* by establishing Sanatan Dharma Hindu Mahasabha. Malaviya tried to unite all the communities to get freedom. He united untouchables, Sikhs, Buddhists, etc. and attempted to remove all discrepancies of Hindu religion to strengthen Hindus. Thus his educational thoughts were primarily originated from his faith of *Sanatan* religion, which he considered as the basic need of a Hindu's life.

Consequently, it can be said that Malaviya's educational philosophy was based on his patriotic sentiments, love of *Sanatan Dharma*, Indian culture, values and ethos. Still Malaviya became very controversial figure in relation to Hindu Dharma. He faced much antagonism by the Muslim leaders due to his some activities like Shuddhi movement and conversion of Muslims into Hindu, etc. Britishers' activities, such as dividing policies, more preference to Christianity, etc. convinced him to believe that Britishers' aspirations and their education system were pushing India in a wrong direction, that's why Indians, his own people were incapable to enjoy their own religious wealth and happiness. He therefore decided to bring about a change by implementing his own educational model in which he integrated religion in education for rejuvenating the society along with amalgamation of scientific vision of the West. Finally, his all experiences were manifested in the form of his educational thoughts which proved him as an Eclectic educational philosopher.

4.3 Malaviya's Educational Activities

Malaviya organized a large number of educational activities. Those were not confined to the narrow academic world but reflected much variations in all aspects of life as he delivered lectures, attended seminars, conferences on various multidimensional subjects, construction of hostels, *goshalas*, libraries, schools, *pathshalas*, colleges, *rishikuls* also he published journals, books, pamphlets, papers, magazines, lectures on religious discourses, etc. Details of his educational activities are given as—

- Malaviya was fond of doing social activities along with the teaching profession. With the help of donated books on literature and philosophy he made an important and good collection, which after some time came to be known as the Bharati Bhawan Library. "It was established by him in Prayag in Nov. 1889. Malaviya's name is so closely associated with Bharati

Bhawan that it generally considered to be his personal achievement."[3]

- In 1887 when Allahabad University came into existence with the Muir Central College as its nucleus, it attracted a large number of students. This led to a shortage of hostel accommodation. So, Malaviya decided to build a hostel for the Hindu students, coming to Allahabad University for studying various courses. In March 1901, he collected two and half lakhs rupees and laid the foundation of hostel 'Hindu Boarding House' at Prayag with 200 rooms which was completed in 1903.[4] In 1922, 50 more rooms were added to it.
- In 1904, he established the Gauri Pathashala at Prayag which later on became Inter College.[5] After collecting the contribution from people, he laid the foundation of Minto Memorial proclamation pillar and park at Prayag on 9 November 1910 which was completed in 1918.[6]
- In 1908, on the initiation of Sanatan Dharma Mahasabha, Malaviya decided to establish the Rishikula Brahmacharyashram College at Haridwar to impart education for the young children on the basis of ancient residential schools.[7]

  This ashram is spread over some 65 acres of land. In 1909, again in Haridwar he played a key role for the establishment of Jai Bharat Sadhu Mahavidyalya. This name is inscribed on the foundation as co-founder of this college.[8]

---

3. Tiwari, U.D., *A Short Biography Mahamana Malaviya,* Varanasi: Mahamana Malaviya Foundation Varanasi: (2007), p. 49.
4. Parmanand, *Mahamana Madan Mohan Malaviya an Historical Biography,* Varanasi: Malaviya Adhyayan Sansathan BHU (1967), p. 113.
5. Tiwari, U.D. *op. cit.* (2007), p. 50.
6. *Ibid.*
7. *Ibid.*
8. *Ibid.*

- "On 9th February 1935, he inaugurated the Seva Samiti Vidya Mandir at Prayag which was established by him. This Vidya Mandir has now been developed as college."[9]
- Malaviya wrote a small booklet called

  "*Hindu Dharmopadesh* in which he had prescribed the ideal life which ought to be led by each member of Hindu Society and at the same time to be tolerant to other religions and patriotic groups."[10]

  In this book Malaviya described the principles of social reformation in relation to villages. He said,

  I first make obeisance to God. I wish that meetings should be organized in each village for the welfare of the people, for punishing the wicked and for conducting rules of righteousness. *Kathas* (religious discourses) should be arranged in each village. Schools and gymnasiums should be established in each village and all the people should jointly celebrate religious festivals. All the inhabitants of the village should join hands in protecting orphans, widows, religious places and the cow. Compassion should be shown to the needy and oppressed. No, animal which does not harm anyone should be killed, women folk should be held in reverence. Those persons should be brought to book (who perpetrate crimes, assault women, or try to harm the property of any one). If one's life and property is not considered safe without doing any with such wicked persons, it is essential to annihilate these class.[11]

  Thus through this book he suggested suitable educational, social measure for the removal of the evils from society.

---

9. *Ibid.*
10. Chaturvedi, S., *Builder of Modern India, Madan Mohan Malaviya*. New Delhi: Ministry of information and broadcasting Government of India (1988), p. 37.
11. *Ibid.*

- Throughout his life Malaviya delivered lectures in so many important conferences and meetings. He remained chairman and member of so many institutions and societies, the list is appealing. During his student life he delivered a lecture in the meeting of students in Madras in 1884.[12]
- In 1903, Malaviya was nominated as fellow of the university of Allahabad and member of the managing committee of the Prayag public library.[13]
- In January 1916, he delivered a lecture in the U.P. educational conference held at Lucknow.[14]
- He was the Vice-Chancellor of Banaras Hindu University from 1919 to 1938, and thereafter he was its rector till his death in 1946.

Some of his other important works are as follow—

He delivered convocation addresses in the Banaras Hindu University in 1920 and 1929.

- In 1920 a lecture on land revenue at all Indian economic conference held at Banaras Hindu University.
- In August 1925, he addressed the convocation in Kashi Vidyapith.[15] In the same year he presided over All India Vaidya Conference at Jaipur, pervaded over All India Student Conference at Lahore in 1929,[16] chairman reception committee of All Asia Educational Conference at Banaras Hindu University, addressed the meeting of the student council on 29th November.[17]
- "He delivered lectures at the university of Paris, Berlin, Venice and Rome on January 1931."[18]

---

12. *Ibid.*, p. 50.
13. *Ibid.*
14. *Ibid.*
15. *Ibid.*
16. *Ibid.*, p. 51.
17. *Ibid.*
18. Parmanand, *op. cit.*, p. 858.

On the advice of his friend, Andrew, Malaviya paid a visit to Manchester where he made a good impression by his speech.[19]

- In 1932, he addressed the meeting of the communist University at Victoria Hall of Seventh Hampton Raw, London on 5 November 1935,[20] presided over the all-India Joytish conference held at Banaras Hindu University, "He established the Jyotish mandal and decided for the publicity of the world calendar (*Vishvapanchang*),"[21] based on solar principle (Suraya Sidhant) (which is being published by Banaras Hindu University till the date).
- In November 1935, he was nominated as Chairman Reception Committee of All India Vaidya Conference at Indore.
- In 1936, he presided over the public celebration of the Dayanand Anglo-Vedic College,[22] Lahore.
- On 15 December 1937, he stepped away from the tradition, delivered his convocation address in Hindi for the first time on the occasion of the golden Jubilee of the University of Allahabad.[23]
- In 1938, he presided over the all-India political sense conference at Banaras Hindu University.

Thus, Malaviya's approach towards education was not merely theoretical but he always tried to give a concrete shape to his ideas. He was always worried for all Indians to get educated and he thought that education must be brought within reach of every one. His activities reflected that he was a humanist in his approach and the main center of his educational philosophy was man, the empirical man, who always believes in experiments, rationales and in social relationships. Establishment of Seva Samiti by Malaviya proved that he identified the sufferings

19. Birla: Diary, September 30, (1931).
20. Tiwari, U.D. *loc. cit.*, p. 51.
21. *Ibid.*
22. *Ibid.*
23. *Ibid.*

faced by humanity in imperial world and he tried to liberate the people from the rules of exploitation, religious fragmentation and superstitions. Malaviya's educational activities acquired a practical form because of cooperation of the people. So, he stressed on the need of a broad outlook in life and discouraged all extremes of selfishness, individualism, communism, self-indulgent, materialism and visual spiritualism. Thus Malaviya, by his works and educational activities, wanted to form an integrated human personality.

4.4 The Foundation of Malaviya's Educational Philosophy

Malaviya was a nationalist, democrat and orthodox Brahmin. His philosophy of education is hardly separable from beliefs of *Sanatan Dharma*. As it had been discussed in chapter second that Malaviya was brought up and socialized in a traditional orthodox Brahmin family. His social thoughts had strong faith in Indian classics, culture and spiritualism, which he had seen in the atmosphere his home. It is one of the settled convictions of his life that religion is the foundation of all goodness and greatness, and without an abiding religious faith no one can succeed. Thus before knowing his basic thoughts on education, it is important to know what Malaviya meant by *Sanatan Dharma*. Why he took pain at any critical situation, even in sufferings, for the sake of *Sanatan Dharma*? Why all his activities of life whether political, religious, social, economic and educational were based on the concept of Nationalism and *Sanatan Dharma*? Was *Sanatan Dharma*, only Hinduism or anything beyond this reflecting there in his eyes? If the answers of all above questions could be detected, it was possible to describe the foundation of his educational philosophy.

In third chapter during discussion on Malaviya's religious philosophy, his faith, understanding about God and *Sanatan Dharma* have been discussed. After analyzing all that it can be said that in Malaviya's view, *Sanatan Dharma* is the eternal *Dharma* which had been followed since ancient times and will be followed till eternity. It was followed by the truthful, altruistic, unprejudiced and scholarly persons. Such a religion was propounded by the *Vedas,* describing perfect realization of God and defined nature of bondage, and various ways for removal of bondage or achieving liberation. According to Malaviya, it is the universal religion of the *Upanishads*, the *Gita* and the *Bhagwatam* which represent *Bharatvarsh* in whole world.[24] In his opinion such actions, thoughts and practices that promote physical and mental happiness in the world (*Abhyudaya*) and ensure realization of God (*Nishreyas*) in the end is called *Dharma*. So, when Malaviya's views are collectively analyzed it is clear that *Upanishad* + *Geeta* + *Bhagwatam* + *Bharatvarsh* + *Whole World* perspectives are the important aspects of his understanding. So, throughout his life Malaviya made efforts to protect the above conceptual parameters of *Sanatan Dharma*.

He understood that the rulers of India whether Muslims or Christians do not love Bharat like motherland, because their origin was not from India. They recognized Bharat as India and they regarded this country only as a source of earning and residing place and they never respected Bharatvarsh like any other Sanatani or Bharatvasi who considered it as Dev Bhumi or Motherland. Therefore, Malaviya worried about the preservation of Indian culture and civilization, which was characterized dominantly by the followers of the Hindu Dharma or Arya Dharma or Hindutava. He agreed with the fact that any civilization is characterized by the continuity of culture, norms, educational institutions, models of thinking, customs, and practices by which successive generation took shape, so these were the primary needs of any nation to save its own culture and civilization.

Through progress of Sanskrit, Devanagari lipi, Hindu Shastras, etc. Malaviya wanted to preserve and regain spiritual, religious precious treasures of India. But his whole thinking was not full of the sense of Hinduism only. Because his concepts of Hinduism and Hindutva were very clear as the former was having mere religious sense, while the latter had a more encompassing sense that was based on geography, culture, history and spiritual sense. He considered Hindutva not only a religion but as a nation and way of life. His views did not reflect narrow

24. From www.thevedicfoundation.org/authentic-hinduism/sanatan-dharma-part-ii.htm retrieved July 14/2012.

sense towards Hinduism. He acknowledged Hindu Dharma in such a way which completely accepted and assimilated *karma*, *Dharma*, *yoga*, *dhayan* into its philosophical framework and had much liberal and cumulative character. He considered Sikhism, Buddhism, Jainism as the sister and daughter branches of Hindu Dharma. Therefore his approaches for such *Sampradaya* were similar to Hinduism and he described such religions from the common point of view, i.e. having common objectives such as *Nirvana, Kavalaya* and *Moksha*. Finally, in relation to diversity of religion, his thinking reflected Hinduism as one eternal Meta religion which manifested itself as *Anekantvad* or manifolded *Vedanta,* today it is defined as Hindu pan-inclusivism.[25]

If Malaviya's action during political movement is observed, it will be found that he always worked for the welfare of the Sikh's in Punjab and attempted to unite untouchables, etc. All such efforts were done not only for excellence of the society but indirectly it strengthened the followers of the Hindu Dharma. During the ceremony of Banaras Hindu University foundation, Guru Granth Sahib had been chanted which showed his love for the Sikh religion. So, he considered India always as a country which had its own culture, with a historic Sanatani past, where various religious minorities existed and were claiming for separateness but they all descended from the Hindu or Muslim religion. He said that such followers of Islam descended from the outside of Indian geographical boundaries when ruled here about 700 hundred years and tried to propagate Islam in India but the culture of *Sanatan Dharma* never diminished. He agreed with the fact that while some people changed their religion by heart or due to religious pressures they became different but culturally they remained the same.

So in Malaviya's mind it stroked that due to Christian's rule prosperous India became a poor country where people were dependent for earning on agriculture resources and were also not academically strong to manage their own customs, culture, administration in future. When he fully understood the desires of the Britishers, using India as resource of income and increasing the follower of Christianity, his love of *Sanatan*

25. *Sanatan Dharma as a Whiteheadian Religious Pluralism*, 2006.

Dharma, Indian culture, civilization, and sufferings of Indians forced him to think about a serious and right solution for the problem. So Malaviya, according to his basic instinct, tried to do all his best efforts to rediscover India by Hindus on their own terms for their own people, not as sense of Christianity, or Islam.

His foundation of educational philosophy was moreover pragmatic, he ignored all of Western culture but heartedly, accepted science and technological and industrial education for the development of India to emancipate the poverty-stuck people of India from their low socio-economic status. Thus, his educational philosophy was founded on the values of *Sanatan Dharma*. Malaviya's attitude, as Sanatanies, never favored the division of the country in two parts on the cost of freedom, but he showed his religious tolerance and agreed to accept all Muslims as a part of India or as Indians. Malaviya, during various Unity Conferences and on political stages, always respected diversity of India in terms of religion but it had become a great fear of minorities for their future and British policies; due to which India was partitioned into India and Pakistan, and further into Bangladesh.

Therefore, the principle of his educational philosophy was to spread *Sanatan Dharma* along with teaching with wide acceptance of science and technology of the West for materialistic development. Thus by education he wanted to develop both the concepts of *Sanatan Dharma*, i.e. *Varnaashram Dharma* or *Apravidya,* and *Paravidya* or *Bhagwat Dharma*. *Apar* word means secondary or general or preliminary because it is not the absolute or prime *Dharma*. In short, it can be understood as all kinds of good deeds and humanitarian works that are beneficial to the society.[26] Malaviya wanted both of the *Dharma*, i.e. *Para* and *Apra* to attain by the Indians in their lives. Consequently in his educational ideas or discourses he always focused on enjoins of the Gita. This principle of action is envisaged in *Gita* as "*Yogash Karmash Koshlam*" was appeared in Malaviya's educational philosophy. His educational thoughts were the combination of his religious faith and zeal that would make a

26. From *www.thevedicfoundation.org/authentic Hinduism/* sanatan-dharm-part_I.htm 2/2. retrieved July, 14/2012.

man really healthy, wealthy, and wise. Malaviya's educational thoughts were deeply attracted by the philosophers and ancient saints of India. He never favored the thoughts of Lord Macaulay who was appointed as the president of the general committee of public instruction and made the future course of education based on English approach in colonial India. Like Mahatma Gandhi, he too had a vision of a *Sarvodaya Samaj*. But the difference was lied in their meaning, Gandhi tried to establish a *Sarvodaya Samaj* through trusteeship, Malaviya on the other hand attempted through educational imperatives to establish a society in which all could enjoy happiness and everyone could become a source of happiness to others, all could see auspicious days and no one suffered any injury. Thus his philosophy of education is co-oriented with his conception of social welfare. Thus his educational philosophy was based on the parameters such as humanism, tolerance, progressiveness, liberty, *Sanatan Dharm's* teachings, science, technology and industrial development.

4.5 Manifestation of Educational Philosophy of Malaviya in the Form of Banaras Hindu University

His educational philosophy took shape, when his idea was manifested in the form of his noble creation of Banaras Hindu University. When Lord Curzon appointed an Indian University Commission in 1904 to check out conditions of higher education, his report recommended that all the universities should be brought directly under the government control, and his negligent attitude towards Indian representation in Indian University Commission aroused suspicion in the minds of the Indian people. The Indians felt that this commission was only a perpetuation of the narrow, bigoted and inexpensive rule of the experts. Therefore many of the private enterprises came forward simultaneously to establish schools, colleges and universities with their own economic bases because they understood that the educational institutes set up by the government could not cope up with the increasing demand of higher education.

Malaviya also dreamt to establish a university at Banaras under the flag of Hindu Mahasabha. Malaviya from his student life had a high belief in Indian ideals and the Hindu way of life and dreamt of series of *Ashrams*, along the river from Prayag to Kashi.[27] Malaviya first propounded the idea of founding the Hindu University in the year 1904 when a meeting was held at the Mint House under the presidentship of the Maharaja of Banaras.[28] The idea took some years to mature and was led in 1911 to the formation of the Hindu university society which was registered under that name.

Malaviya, in his vision of higher education, came to a point that it had become essential to establish a national university where oriental and accidental arts, humanities and sciences could be taught without losing contact with Indian culture and thoughts. Throughout the India, during 1905 to 1920, nationalism was the priority of people. At the same time,

> Sir Syed Ahmad Khan the founder of Aligarh Muslim College had steady planning to establish Muslim college and along with this Bareilly College, Khalasa College of Amritsar, Tata Ratan Institute with famished equipment were also founded.[29]

Malaviya immediately gave up his law practice in November 1905, in order to devote his full attention to the new project.

> For one full month he practiced at Hanuman Temple at Triveni by chanting the Gayatri Mantra for achieving success in establishing the cherished university.[30]

Then he approached his venerable father for his blessings. In addition to his sincere blessings, his father gave him a token donation of fifty-one rupees for the university.

In the same year, the Indian National Congress had decided to hold its session at Banaras under the presidentship of Shree Gopal Krishna Gokhale.

> During this session of the Indian National Congress at Banaras, a public meeting was convened on 31 December

27. Parmanand, *loc. cit.*, p. 192.
28. *Ibid.*
29. Rawat, P.L., *History of Indian Education*, Agra: Ram Prasad and Sons (1991), p. 210.
30. Chaturvedi, S., *op. cit.*, p. 56.

> 1905, at Town Hall under the presidentship of Shri B.N. Mahajani of Berar, the scheme of the Hindu University was placed before the representatives of all religious and renowned educationists. It received unanimous approval and the resolution for the establishment of the Hindu University was publicly announced on 1st January 1906, in the Pandal of the Congress.[31]

The resolution was reiterated at an assembly of Hindu religious leaders and scholars held at Prayag, on the occasion of the Kumbh fair *sammelan*, under the presidentship of Jagadguru Swami Shankaracharya who approved the idea of Malaviya, and suggested to prepare religious teachers for the propagation of *Sanatan Dharma* to encourage the study of Sanskrit language and literature and to assist scientific and technological studies by Indian languages and Sanskrit was also proposed in Hindu University.

In approved resolution the following institutions had been assigned as Vedic Vidyalaya, where instructions would be imparted in subjects like *Vedas, Vedangas*, *Smrities, Itihas* (History) and *Puranas* (old Indian annals). In the conference the decision was taken for the establishment of following departments, as an observatory for studying the movements of the stars, planets and satellites in the department of astronomy, an Ayurvedic Vidyalaya with a laboratory and an arboretum or botanical garden of medicinal herbs for the study of medicinal botany, school of architectural engineering and economics with three departments: (i) Physics department, (ii) a laboratory for experiments and researches, and (iii) a workshop for imparting training in mechanical and electrical engineering. A plan was made for engineering department, where articles of daily use would be manufactured.

It was also decided in the resolution that, those departments shall also impart education in accordance with the latest experiments and researches. A college of languages, where English, German and other foreign languages should be taught so that the treasure of the literature of Indian languages,

31. *Ibid.*

enriched by new treasures, was discovered through them and further developed by the new researches in the field of sciences and arts. It was also decided that the working of the religious institutions of the university and the Vedic Vidyalaya should lie in the hands of those Hindus alone, who are ardent followers of the *Sanatan Dharma*, as enjoined upon by *Shrutis* (the Vedic Literature), *Smritis* (codes of personal and social conduct), and the *Puranas* (old Indian annals). Only such students should be admitted to this college who were admissible according to the injunctions of the *Varnashrama Dharma*.

At the same year in 1907, Mrs. Annie Besant had gained worldwide status for the establishment of a great centre of learning in the form of Central Hindu College. She also submitted a plan of university of India with power to affiliate college of all dominations throughout the country.

> When the promoters of the Muslim University had collected the separate amount for the establishment of the Muslim University, Annie Besant announced her willingness to join hands with Malaviya for the establishment of the Hindu University.[32]

Mrs. Annie Besant had great faith in Hindu *Sanatan* religion and culture.

Maharaja of Darbhanga had concurrently launched a scheme for founding a *Sanatan Dharma* university. In the year 1911, the Maharaja of Darbhanga incorporated his scheme with that of the Hindu University proposed by Malaviya and both of these great men met Lord Hardinge, the Governor-General of India during that period willingly gave his approval and agreement, and promised a whole hearted support on behalf of the government. Parallel to these schemes there was developed a communication between Malaviya and Mrs. Besant in April 1911 at Prayag, the three schemes were fused into one. As Kashi was an ancient seat of learning, so the Hindu University could not be established at any place other than Kashi, it was declared by Malaviya. There was deviation in the opinion among the trustees of the Hindu College. But as soon as it was reported

32. Parmanand, *op. cit.*, p. 196.

to all active founders that the establishment of a Muslim University in Aligarh had reached its final stage, they thought that it became more necessary to speed up the foundation of the Banaras Hindu University, for which much part of work had already been done and public opinion had already been created. Therefore, Malaviya became more active, and started collection for the establishment of the university.

It was decided that all the money collected on behalf of the university, should be delivered to the Raja Munshi Madho Lal of Banaras, who would deposited it in the Bank of Bengal at Banaras, till further advice by the committee. No money should be spent out of that till the university society was registered as an organized body and its rule and regulation were formulated. All expenditure in this respect should be met out of the funds of the Sanatan Dharma Mahasabha till then. This resolution was carried out commonly during Sanatan Dharma Mahasabha. Although the target to collect a crore of rupees by Hindu society was a difficult task but at the same time, the Pioneer was blessed for the scheme of Hindu University. It was said

> The most cardinal encouragement may be offered. Financial difficulties will fade way before the generosity of the distinguished and wealthy members of the great Hindu community. A crore of rupees does not seem to be an excessive sum to aim at for a purpose so clearly excellent and which, no doubts appeals to a very numerous class.[33]

Malaviya appreciated the paper editorial support.

Malaviya agreed with Sir Sundarlal who was recognized as leader of the Allahabad bar at that time and also acted as Vice-Chancellor of Allahabad University, Malaviya's choice therefore fell upon him. In spite of urging of Malaviya, Pt. Sunderlal did not accept the secretaryship. After getting failed in his attempt, Malaviya decided to bear the burden himself and started his mission of collection of funds for the Hindu University. Rs. 25 lakh were collected on 22 October, 1911 by the Hindu University Society.

33. *Ibid.*, p. 195.

> The name of the university was decided as Hindu University under the presence of Annie Besant, Rameshwar Singh, Bhagvan Das, Sir Sundarlal, Iswar Saran, including Malaviya, etc.[34]

During the absence of Mrs. Besant because of her Britain visit, from April to October 1911, Malaviya compiled a revised and more comprehensive scheme of the university's project in the form of a pamphlet entitled

> The Banaras Hindu University: Why it is wanted and what it aims at. This was circulated with the covering letter dated 15 June 1911 in the preparation for an appeal for the funds.[35]

He appealed the members of the Hindu society for the collection of 50 lacs which must be collected before the visit of prince in December. In his revised scheme Malaviya focused on technical education and dreamt that by achieving knowledge of various arts and sciences, our young men should make our country self-dependent and self-reliant. During his speech, before founding of Hindu University, he described the progress made by America and Europe during the past seventy-five years, particularly in producing articles of daily use, with the help of technology, and said that

> India has lagged much behind those countries where the study of science by experimentations is done for the good of the society and for the service of the county.[36]

Hence, it is clear from this declaration that Malaviya's main aim was to cultivate a nation which was economically rich and wanted to develop all necessary skills in Indians for earning money by their own occupation, with the help of people of the university who were the representative of India.

When the British Government came to the know that education which was to be imparted in proposed university through the medium of Hindi, they became alarmed greatly.

34. Dar, S.L. and Somaskandan, S., *History of the Banaras Hindu University*. Varanasi: Banaras Hindu University Press (1966), p. 193.
35. Parmanand, *op. cit.*, p. 198.
36. Chaturvedi., *op. cit.*, p. 61.

The education secretary, Sir Harcourt Butler, made it clear to Malaviya, during personal talks, that he should not expect any recognition from the government if education was not to be imparted through English, hence no permission would be given to any scheme of education in which provision was made for teaching through the mother-tongue. Malaviya never wanted to see his scheme getting failed, for this reason; he dropped the idea of imparting education through the mother-tongue. By that time, Sir Sundarlal had also agreed to take over the secretaryship of the University Society on the advice of Sir Harcout Butler. When Malaviya met Viceroy Lord Hardinge, in connection with establishment of Banaras Hindu University, the Viceroy told him,

> It has been complained to me that you oppose the Government silently.[37]

Malaviya at once answered,

> This is not a reality. You may get my writings and speeches scrutinized personally and if anyone finds any matter which may tend to propagate ill-will against the English people, I will at once lead pardon for the same.[38]

Lord Hardinge was influenced by his honesty and since then he always held great respect and faith in Malaviya. At a public meeting in Calcutta, the establishment of the Hindu University was formally declared, in which donations of rupees five lakhs were promised for the proposed university. Malaviya and his group of legislative body of Hindu society toured all important cities in northern India from Calcutta to Lahore. Within three months, promises were made for a sum of twenty-five lacs. Malaviya again met the Viceroy in Shimla, Lord Hardinge. When he returned from there, he informed his colleagues that the Viceroy had promised to give his agreement for the establishment of Banaras Hindu University.[39] The deputations returned back to Lahore from Shimla and enthusiastically attended public meetings.

37. *Ibid.*, p. 63.
38. *Ibid.*, p. 64.
39. *Ibid.*, p. 65.

Then Lala Lajpat Rai, declared:

> Charter or no charter, Hindu university must exist.[40]

Malaviya and Sir Sundarlal both were acting as complementary to each other to achieve the same objective that was Banaras Hindu University. Malaviya's work was to secure promises from rich citizens and Pt. Sundarlal worked for the implementation of the promises, i.e. to get promised amount. Sir Sundarlal himself donated a sum of one lakh to the Hindu University fund. The whole country was enough to achieve the collection to one crore and thirty-four lacs of rupees by January 1912, Mrs. Besant paid tributes to the sincerely and firmness of Malaviya for the cause of the Hindu University. She said

> He has sacrificed his worldly life his energies, his powerful art of speech, his whole self and health to the cause of this great Banaras Hindu University.[41]

Thus, this was the journey of struggle in Malaviya's life through which his educational philosophy came into action and is enjoyed today.

4.5.1 *Experiences Shared by the Contemporaries Regarding Malaviya's Dedication for Realization of Banaras Hindu University*

J.B. Kripalani gave a glowing illustration of how Malaviya influenced the people concerning the usefulness of Banaras Hindu University. He said

> I can never forget how Malaviya used to influence people to contribute for the Hindu University. Anywhere according to the need he used to keep the blueprints of the University ready with him to extend before his fellow travelers and explain the purpose of that great planned seat of learning where modern science was to be taught along with the Hindu religion and culture. He used to explain how he was going on to establish a university at Kashi holy place on the sacred bank of Ganga, in the city of Vishwanath, in the ancient seat or pilgrimage, where Maharaja Harish Chandra

40. *Ibid.*
41. *Ibid.*

> gave away his son and his wife, his all; where great sages used to perform penances since time immemorial: where every Hindu yearns to spend his last days: where innumerable Hindus have offered their ashes to the mother Ganga: which was a great seat of learning since time immemorial and where the students received free education with provision for free lodging and boarding and where now Physics, Modern Arts and Sciences shall be taught along with the ancient learning: that nothing was more sacred than donating for the purpose of spreading learning tribute magnanimously and obtain the blessings of Lord Shiva and immense spiritual virtues. He used to say all this in very simple language and I have marked many a fellow travelers pledging his support for the university. In frivolity I used to prefer pilfering for the noble cause.[42]

No doubt, Malaviya's dedication to establish his educational idea in the form of Banaras Hindu University is expressed by the university Kulgeet written by Shanti Swaroop Bhatnager as

> यह मालवीयजी की देशभक्ति, यह उनका सहस्र
> या उनकी शक्ति; प्रगति हुई है नवीन होकर, यह
> कर्मवीरों की राजधानी, मधुर मनोहर
> अति सुंदर, यह सर्व विद्या की राजधानी।

It meant that the Banaras Hindu University, the capital of knowledge, is a revised manifestation of his true dedication, courage, enthusiasm and patriotism.[43]

Malaviya's dedication is reflected from his indomitable enthusiasm, i.e. he did not take his day's meals till the targeted collection of money for that day, was not achieved. As for example one day it was the past noon, when he went to a local business man for university fund in Amritsar. Everyone in the company was feeling hungry and exhausted. The businessman arranged refreshments for the party but Malaviya refused to take anything. When he enquired the reason, it was expressed by party members to him, that it was Malaviya who promised not

42. Chaturvedi, *op. cit.*, p. 66.
43. Parmanand, *op. cit.*, p. 190.

to take anything till his target was reached. When the merchant came to the know about the target amount for the day, he immediately took out his cheque book and provided a cheque for the balance even though the amount was much more than what he was expected to donate.

Likewise, on one occasion he approached a Nawab who did not want to pay money for Banaras Hindu University and it was quite hard to make him agree. Malaviya accepted Nawab's shoe as a gift with great regard and announced in the paper that the particular Nawab had donated a shoe and that it would be put for sale on a certain day. When the Nawab heard this, he felt very much embarrassed and donated a handsome amount to get his shoe back. One day a millionaire, who faced a heavy financial loss, approached to Malaviya to seek his blessings and advice. Malaviya smiled and said,

> Donate five lakh rupees to Banaras Hindu University.

The millionaire looked at him amazingly because he had lost everything in business and was facing liquidation. But Malaviya consoled him and said,

> You came here to take my advice. Why don't you follow it?

The millionaire at once handed over a cheque of five lacs to Malaviya. The next day when the news was published about his donation, his credit rose, which saved him from bankruptcy.[44]

Malaviya's devotion, love and inner satisfaction were reflected from the following example as once a delegation of educationists from England came to visit Banaras Hindu University, Malaviya asked Professor Seshadri who was available at hand to take them around and showed them the Engineering College. As it was getting dusk, professor Seshadri expressed his doubt whether any college would be open by that time, But Malaviya encouraged him,

> Doesn't matter, some peons must be there.

Professor Seshadri had become apprehensive there was little possibility of any peon being there at that late hour. But Malaviya insisted,

44. *Ibid.*, p. 68.

> Doesn't matter. They will peep through the doors.

On this, one of the visitors remarked with a sense of admiration,

> Now I can understand how his university has come into the existence. It is this 'doesn't matter' spirit which has given birth to this great institution.[45]

And then Malaviya took the visitors around and attended his meeting very late at night. The first batch of examinees of the Banaras Hindu University appeared in 1918.

4.5.2 *Malaviya's Explanation on Issues Related to University*

On the issue of including the word 'Hindu' in the name of Banaras Hindu University, critics opposed it regarding communalism and sectarianism. Malaviya took great pain to clarify this point and he said the true purpose of the university will not be to promote narrow sectarianism but broad liberation of mind and religious spirit which will promote a feeling of brotherhood among Indians. He expressed,

> Unfortunately we are aware that the absences of any compulsory religious education in our state universities have not prevented the growth of sectarian feeling of the country. I believe that instruction in the truth of religion always positive, whether it will be Hindu or Musalmaan, whether it is imparted to the students of the Banaras Hindu University or to the Aligarh Muslim University, will tend to produce men, who, if they are true to their religion, will be true to their God, their kind and their country. And I look forward to the time when the students who will pass out of such universities, will meet each other in a closer embrace as the sons of the same motherland than they do at present.[46]

On the occasion of the final passing stage of the university bill, Malaviya made the following speech to explain the power of religion as

---

45. Chaturvedi, S., *op. cit.*, p. 71.
46. Dar, S.L. and Somaskandan, S., *op. cit.*, p. 286.

> I believe in the living power of religion. The want of religious education in our schools and colleges has long been felt. I believe that the absence of any provision for religious education in the otherwise excellent system which the government has introduced and has worked for the last sixty years in this country, has been accountable for many unfortunate results. I do not wish to dwell upon them. I am thankful to think that this acknowledged deficiency is going to be removed at the proposed important centre of education, which is happily going to be established at a place which many will be described as the most important centre of the religion and learning of the Hindus. I venture to hope that the good influence of Banaras Hindu University in the matter of religious instruction will be felt in other institutions far and dear, and that in the curse of a few years, religious instruction will become an integral part of the education imparted in schools and colleges supported by the Government and the people.[47]

Lastly Malaviya said,

> I conclude with the earnest hope and prayer, that this centre of life and light which is coming into existence, will not only be intellectually equal to the best of their fellow students in other parts of the world, but will also be trained to live a noble life, love their country and to be loyal to the crown.[48]

Thus, Malaviya clearly explained all the issues related to religious instruction, Hindu world, etc. and logically proved the need of such education.

4.5.3 *Banaras Hindu University under the Vice-Chancellorship of Malaviya*

Malaviya faced marked difficulties but, he bravely faced them. He was the Vice-Chancellor of Banaras Hindu University from 1919 to 1938. Often the university had faced financial crises but he always solved the problem with deep faith in

47. *Ibid.*, p. 291.
48. *Ibid.*

God and never lost his heart in critical situations. He remained optimistic in every crucial moments and kept a cheerful spirit in him which always motivated his co-workers also.

The Hindu University faced first trouble in 1920 when the students boycotted the Banaras Hindu University and joined the *Satyagraha* movement with Gandhi. Although there was much controversy between Gandhi and Malaviya but Malaviya neither hit Gandhi nor changed his view on the participation of university students in movement ever. Mrs. Annie Besant was the only Indian leader who stood by his side. Not only during Boycott but he faced opposition by society, when the Prince of Wales visited India in 1921.

Malaviya was very much loved by the university students and teachers as a Vice-Chancellor. When he was arrested in Bombay in 1931 while offering *Satyagraha,* a batch of 125 students and teachers started from Banaras to follow their *Kulpati*. In 1942, when the Congress passed its historic 'Quit India' resolution and all the leaders of the country were put behind the bars overnight, a number of students of the university, especially those belonged to the eastern districts of U.P. led the movement earnestly and held the reins of the government in their hands for days, together. The British Government had to send a special force to suppress this movement. Banaras Hindu University had actually become the thermopile of this movement. The British force entered in the university compound, broke the locks and open the doors of the university buildings and pulled out the students from the hostels mercilessly. Malaviya was also staying in the compound. He challenged the British Government but he was too infirm to move about to resist this invasion. He resigned from the post of the Vice-chancellorship in 1938 and was elected as Rector of the university. He was followed by Dr. Radhakrishnan as another distinguished Vice-Chancellor. Radhakrishnan handled all the situation of 1942 movement brightly.

When Malaviya was university's Rector, his health gradually went down and he passed away on 12 November 1946.

4.5.4 *Banaras Hindu University after Malaviya's Death*

In Banaras Hindu University many of the distinguished Vice-Chancellors paid their devotion and served it as a *Vidya Mandir* like Dr. Radhakrishnan, Dr. Amarnath Jha, Pt. Govind Malaviya, Acharya Narendra Deo and Dr. C.P. Ramaswami Aiyar, etc., presently being seen by Dr. Lal ji Singh. As long as Malaviya was alive the university kept its religious and national spirit alive but soon after his death the spirit died out and the university turned into an ordinary academic center.

Thus, Banaras Hindu University is essentially a national and cultural university and this character was maintained by Malaviya throughout his life. Once, someone asked Malaviya why his students were not selected for I.C.S. He quickly answered

> The University was not created to produce Government Servants. Our aim is to produce servants of the nation.[49]

In fact from the day of beginning till after 100 years the university made great servants of the nation, who contributed hugely for the best output of the motherland. Patriotism was the core of all his speeches and writings, therefore Malaviya always exhorted his students to become great patriots. No doubt Malaviya's vision for higher education is expressed in the form of Banaras Hindu University which is an extraordinary type of teaching-cum-residential university which developed into a full-fledged multi-disciplinary center of learning with various colleges, having a number of departments under departmental heads. The university is now growing larger and advanced day by day. The whole campus is now full of new established buildings for teaching and residential purposes.

Now university has two campus, four larger institutes, 16 faculties, 140 departments, four advanced centers, and four interdisciplinary schools (www.bhu.ac.in, 2012). The university is making its mark at the national and international levels in a number of frontier areas of science, technology, medicine, and agriculture, etc. Banaras Hindu University today had nearly 2500 research scholars and 650 foreign students from 34 nations under one roof who are pursuing different academic

49. *Ibid.*, p. 73.

programmes. A newly established Rajiv Gandhi South Campus, abbreviated as R.G.S.C., is situated about 75 kms. southwest of Varanasi on 2760 acres of land which is just the double area that of the main campus. Here the first academic session started in 2006-07. Rajiv Gandhi South Campus is emerging as potential hub for imparting education trainings and entrepreneurships, for development of skills in youth, women and marginalized sections of the society, covering the backward region of U.P. as well as adjacent states.

4.6 The Concept of Education

Etymologically education is derived from the Latin word *educere* which means "to bring up" and another word "educere" meant "bring forth". Some of the educationists give a different explanation of the word "*educare*", they say '*e*' means *out of* and *duco* means *to lead*, i.e. *to lead forth* or *to extract out*. This explanation presumes that all the knowledge inherent in children will automatically flow from inner to outer.

Mahatma Gandhi and Vivekananda both visionaries supported the above view, as Gandhi said,

> By education I mean all round drawing out of the best in the child and body, mind and spirit.[50]

Likewise Vivekananda defined

> Education as the manifestation of inherent capability of the child.[51]

So, education does not only mean the acquisition of knowledge or experience but it means the development of all those capacities in the individual which will enable him to control his environment and fulfill his possibilities. Shri Aurobindo believed that the chief aim of education should be to help the growing soul to draw out the best and make it perfect for a noble use.[52] Thus all the Indian philosophers whether Gandhi,

---

50. Sahu, Bhagirathi, *The New Educational Philosophy*, New Delhi: Sarup & Sons (2002), p. 170.
51. *Ibid.*, p. 214.
52. Sharma, R.A., *Shri Aurobindo*, New Delhi: Sarup & Sons (1972), p. 204.

Vivekanand, Tagore, Aurobindo approached education with almost similar meaning.

T.P. Nunn says the same thing in different words,

> Education is the complete development of the individual of the child so that he can make an original contribution to human life ascending to the best of his capacity.[53]

In Ancient India education was a means of self-discipline and self-purification. Its objective was to inculcate moral and spiritual values in human. Education is the process of socialization as it aims to train children in social life by acquiring those manners, customs, norms and ideals of the society. Sociological concept considers man as a social being and product of education. Education, in its sociological prospective, is considered as a process which informs and transforms man and society in accordance with some pre-conceived values and ideals. Education, as a sub-social system, acts as a conservative social agency and transmits the values, ideals, skills, knowledge, etc. to the younger generation. So sociological meaning reflects education as a tool which creates modification in thinking, feelings and actions, consequently developing human personality so that they might take proper place in society.

Malaviya wanted to develop a system of the education like the ancient times, which would qualify its members for the pursuit of the great aims of life—*Trivarga*—as laid down in the scriptures, viz. *Dharma*—discharge of religion duties, *Artha*—attainment of material prosperity, *Kama*—enjoyment of lawful pleasure. As regards the fourth great aim salvation or self-realization (*Moksha*),[54] were considered as an individual's supreme duty. Malaviya thought that it should be achieved by each individual by his own efforts under the guidance of religious faith and spiritual perception. While suggesting, such an ancient system of education, he was not averse to assimilate the light and spirit of the new scientific age. He felt that India cannot regain its wealth without studying modern science. He wanted a wide diffusion of science in India, as a tool for rescuing people

53. *Ibid.*, p. 14.
54. S. Somaskandan, "Malaviya ji's Contribution to Higher Education", *Pragya*, (2010), p. 285.

from their miserable conditions and poverty. Malaviya made it possible for each student by providing all facilities in university along with both theoretical and practical aspects of science in their own language. He considered essential to introduce an extensive system of technical and industrial education in the country. Thus, it was reflected from Malaviya's educational concept that it was based on the needs of the society. So as a social reformer, he always tried to preserve the best thoughts and culture of ancient India along with modern science and technology.

"Malaviya meant by education as the balanced training and development of the body, the intellect and the emotions of every individual." Accordingly, he prepared the prospectus of Hindu University with ample provisions for physical and cultural development of students. He, persistently, exhorted young men to build up health and strength of body and mind. For emotional expression, every student had been trained and was expected to master a minimum number of *ragas* and *raginis* and must able to play at least one musical instrument such as sitar, tabla, violin or harmonium.[55]

As Malaviya was not satisfied with the scheme of higher education so he exhorted,

> Life's best lessons are not learnt in the school room. Education has done and can still do much for India but it is hopeless to expect from it alone the higher type of character. I agree with those who think that education should from the beginning be combined with religious instruction.[56]

He also contended,

> Where the true religious spirit is inculcated, there must be an elevated feeling of humility and where there is love of God there will be greater love and less hatred of man.[57]

---

55. Parmanand, *op. cit.*, p. 448.
56. Malaviya first speech on BHU Bill. Oct. 1915 Dar, S. and Somaskandan, *op. cit.*, p. 115.
57. Convocation address March 8, 1899.

In Malaviya's educational scheme, first care was provided to the conservation and advancement of the cultural heritage of the Hindu Shastra and Sanskrit literature, generally as means of preserving and popularizing the best thoughts and culture of the Hinduism and all that was good and great in the ancient civilization of India. Secondly, he wanted to promote learning and research generally in Art and Science. Thirdly, he desired to diffuse scientific, technical and professional knowledge along with the necessary practical training for promotion of indigenous industries. Fourthly, he wanted to build up the character of youth through religion and ethics as an integral part of education.[58] Thus, Malaviya realized education as a single tool by which a nation attains prosperity. As in speech on financial statement in April 1904 in Allahabad—he said,

> It is now well understood that in all the countries, the happiness of the poor depends in a great measure on their education. It is by means of it alone that they can acquire those habits of prudence and self-respect from which all other good qualities spring: and if ever there was a country such habits are required. It is this.[59]

Therefore, Malaviya concept of education was based on Eclecticism, believing No school of thoughts, is able to meet the all requirements of various situations in life. So, the good ideas, concept picked up by him and blended together to make a complete philosophy. His educational concept revealed idealism, realism and pragmatism. As an idealist he believed immorality gained through education and wisdom. Education enlighten the total behavior of the individual and finally help in the realization of self and supreme. Education enables human mind to enjoy the contemplation of supreme Truth, Goodness and Beauty. He considered that the education should have a spiritual base. Along with *Satyamev Jayate Nanritum* i.e. it is the truth what triumphs, not false hood, he also had faith in *Shramev Jayate* i.e. it is the diligence that triumphs, not indolence, thus his educational ideas

58. *Malaviya first speech on the BHU Bill.* Oct. 1, 1915.
59. Panday, R, *The Making of Malaviya*, India: Kishore Vidya Niketan, (1956), p. 122.

reflected a pragmatic view. His educational ideas based on work philosophy along with idealistic objective. It should prepare the people to meet the challenges of the social environment and life. Thus, in his educational concept like other Indian philosopher, gave first priority to spiritual development of the learner and secondly he wanted to prepare them to learn new techniques to cope the problem of the material world. Malaviya stressed on legislative provision for education and said it is not because the people are unwilling to take education, but we have it as testimony of the Director of public institution that the people are crying everywhere for more and more schools, than statuary provision is needed to secure adequate funds for education, so he believed that it was the government's duty to provide education for whole school going population. Therefore, he realized the need of education as a prime one. He forced government to necessarily to take effective steps to secure education for the people and it seemed him that the best way to do it would be to have sufficient funds for education by legislation. Thus as a visionary he always realized the importance of education and its meaning for life.

4.6.1 *Malaviya's Views on Higher Education*

No doubt Malaviya's opinion on higher education was manifested in the form of Banaras Hindu University but when his speeches were analyzed, the goals of higher education and the role of government in developing higher education system got cleared.

In supporting the Nineteenth Indian National Congress held in Madras in 1903, Malaviya said on the University Bill

> Gentleman the one thing that we have to consider in connection with this question of university reforms is, what was it that let the enquiry being instituted? What was the state of things with which fault was found? What was the state of things which it was sought the remedy? And then consider what the remedies are which have been suggested and what the remedies are which the Government now purpose to apply. He focused as a

> complaint on the power and constitution of the senate and syndicate.[60]

So by asking much of the questions on role of senate, syndicate and members of such senate, he wanted to address the need of reformations in the higher education.

Malaviya said

> Gentleman when the Government of Lord Curzon appointed a commission, there was no doubt complaint was made by him, that the result of university education was not altogether satisfactory and were not satisfactory as they ought to be. Every speaker discussed the question of unsatisfactory character of the university education and has admitted that the university has produced eminent scholar of learning men who have distinguished themselves in the various walk of life into which they entered, men who have upheld the linking honour and intellect of the country and men who have sewed the Government with honour and credit. If there were some unfortunate young man who did not succeed in getting just the number of marks necessary to enable them to pass, that does not justify their being condemned as unworthy and dishonorable men who ought to be shunned like moral lepers.[61]

By this statement he wanted to express his sympathy for the students who were facing failures in attainment of higher education. Through higher education Malaviya wanted to enhance Nationalism. He focused on the growth of universities and realized the condition of university education during his time and said that

> University education has come to be regarded in every civilized country as the most important part of the National system of education and if the expenses incurred on university education in the West is compared with what British Government are expending on it here, it will be seen that Indian higher education are far below

60. *Ibid.*, p. 181.
61. *Ibid.*

> the standard of other civilized countries and have much be way to make up.[62]

So he recommended to establish such universities which act like powerhouse and eradicated the darkness of ignorance, poverty and misery which were hanging like a pall on the country. He thought that when large number of well-educated scholars would step into the society, the strength of the nation will increase and they would spread knowledge everywhere. So, Malaviya wanted every Indian to rejoice the growth of universities and their education. Thus, in Malaviya opinion, higher education should be provided adequate funds by government and should also meet national requirements. Through his many speeches he aware the British Government for their duty towards higher educational perspective. He suggested the model of higher education by combining learnings of scientific training with moral and religious education.

Malaviya's opinion on Pass and Failed Students—He said

> The line between a passed candidate and failed B.A. as has been, is a very short line and if the candidate has not succeeded, certainly we may be more charitable, then we are, and not condemn him as altogether an unworthy and undesirable person where existence ought to be provided against the legislature taking up the task of introducing a new performance.[63]

So, he did not mean higher education only as distribution of degrees, marking students as passed or failed but he understood it as a system making a person a complete personality, which enables men to control over every step of life and can make them self-reliant.

Malaviya's views on rights of University Act and Nomination of members of Senate and Syndicate—Malaviya wanted a proper nomination of knowledged, educated Indian in senate and syndicate, but at that time the situation was not good so he said,

62. *Ibid.*, p. 184.
63. *Ibid.*

> Gentlemen senates, which were the first body in which the principle of election was first introduced and worked are going to deprived of this power in the beginning of the 20th century. You cannot help feeling that hard of the clock is being put back forcibly. Gentleman nomination is going to make largely by government hardly say, can bring to the senate half of the men's ability and capacity expected to advise the government. And the public in matter of education that would come in through the channel of election.[64]

So, Malaviya wanted a proper representation of Indians in senate and syndicate.

Malaviya's view for the Member of Syndicate—Malaviya said,

> The senate, having power to appoint the syndicate which becomes practically dead, it is only to come to life practically when it is to appoint a syndicate new I do not pretend that I am familiar with the constitution of the senate's of many universities, but I have studied the constitution of some universities—in senate I want to exercise the privilege of electing such men as we consider to be best qualified to work on the syndicate.[65]

So, Malaviya's ideas were not only focused on academic excellence of higher education but also visualized the constitution of senate and syndicate.

Malaviya's view for the Academicians of the University: Malaviya said,

> I have the highest respect to the professors, under whom institution is being, imparted this country. I have never been disobedient to my professors and I can tell you that I consider it a high privilege to sitting the feet of learned men and imbibe the learning that they are able to impart. I think good and true are the men who are in the senate belong to all men connected with the

64. *Ibid.*, p. 182.
65. *Ibid.*, p. 183.

> educational department then they could take decision in right way.[66]

So, it revealed that he gave a proper regard to talented and knowledgeable person of university.

Malaviya favored residential system in higher education, establishment of the Hindu boarding house with the Muir College in Allahabad by the help of government for 200 students, and Banaras Hindu University was the first residential university which showed his vision of favouring residential system in higher education.

Regarding the Teaching Function of the University: Malaviya focused on quality teaching, facility to impart highest instruction in university system. He said,

> Viceroy complained that our universities did not produce men of high ability as it ought to, he forget that the young one of this country have aptitude enough to receive the benefits of highest kind of education. Those that have gone outside of the India prove it further. By citing example of Wood dispatch he focused educational condition of India. He also blamed to British Government that what steps were taken by government for advancing teaching, learning and to promote research. Again he blamed that five lacs would be set apart for 5 years of the purpose of giving instruction to the university and colleges you understand how this small sum will be distributed to different universities. By giving example of Sir Norman Lockyer who gave an estimate of expenditure of 60 lakhs for higher education, he said can we not ask the Government of India reasonably to give us at least one fourth of that sum, namely 15 lacs per year for higher education.[67]

So, Malaviya by citing all these example wanted to aware British Government that it was not acceptable to provide inadequate funds for achieving quality higher education. He said,

66. *Ibid.*, pp. 184-85.
67. *Ibid.*, p. 185.

> Give us universities and provide in them the facility to impart highest instruction, provide finance for developing the talents and for the cultivation of literatures, for the elevation of professional standards and provide also a place where learned men can find their calm and relax when they study in such seats of learning. Young men of their country have enough aptitude to receive the benefits of the highest kind of education imparted, in so it is the duty of Government, that it has been conscious for good university education.[68]

Lastly Malaviya said

> We Indian will see the reasonability of our claims and hoped for excellence & ample, liberal provisions for higher education, which will enable our young men to acquire something of that education which resend by the class universities of other countries.[69]

Thus, Malaviya demanded British Government for universities to be provided with ample resources, where much support was given to the scholars, thinkers, philosophers, researchers and acted as safeguard not only for those who live within their learned cloisters, but for all who come under their influence. Thus, Malaviya's ideology reflected that he was not only blamed British Government for the stunted advancement of higher education, but also explained the benefits of higher education. Malaviya visualized that higher education would be able to train the students to spread knowledge throughout the country with national spirit. So, he proposed the establishment of university which was to be learning and residential university, unlike the other five universities that existed in India at that time.

4.6.2 *Malaviya's Insight on Secondary Education*

Malaviya was not satisfied with the status of secondary education which existed at that period. After reviewing the last financial report in front of public he argued that,

---

68. *Ibid.*
69. *Ibid.*

> Government promised to increase the expenditure of 8 lakhs rupees per annum and non-recurring expenditure of 14½ lakhs rupees for secondary school scheme which was urgently needed but still local government was waiting for funds. It is regrettable that the Government of India has not thought it.[70]

So due to the lack of financial support secondary education had suffered a lot. In 1908 in Allahabad legislative council, he said that the provision for *teaching of science in secondary schools* is highly commendable.[71] Further he requested to the government to improve the quality of secondary education. But he also hoped that this improvement will not be brought about at the expense of any of the existing schools.

Malaviya admired,

> It is desirable that the number of secondary education schools should be increased rather than reduced. These schools are like little lamps which light up humble huts. It will be a great wrong to extinguish them or to let them die of inanition, in order that of few large lamps may be hung up in selected centers. Where the family is a large one, and the means for buying food are scanty, we must content ourselves with coarse food, so that all may share it and live, rather than spend it in such a way that a few should be well fed and the rest should starve and die. To bring about the desired improvement in the quality of secondary education, without cutting it down in extent, all that is necessary. Is the government should recognize its duty in the matter of such education, and make a substantial increase in its grants to strengthen existing aided secondary schools and to encourage the establishment of new ones.[72]

So such views of Malaviya showed that he was not only worried for the enhancement of higher education but also wanted to equal expansion of secondary schools in all places of India.

---

70. *Ibid.*
71. *Ibid.*, p. 136.
72. *Ibid.*, p. 165.

For the support of indigenous arts and industries Malaviya urged for the establishment of technical schools and colleges at secondary level. He pointed the main cause of the catastrophic condition of Indian famines and one of the greatest difficulties in the way of promoting relief, is because of the fact that the large masses of India depend on agriculture and there is lack of industry from which they can derive support. So, he visualized to revive indigenous vocations by secondary school teaching.

4.6.3 *Malaviya's Prospective on Primary/Elementary Education*

Historically, the demand for compulsory primary/elementary education in India emerged during the 18th century, which was a period of awareness and social change, and had considerably strengthened by the end of the 19th century. By this time, on one hand, the principle of compulsory education had been accepted in Britain, and on the other hand Indians had become aware for the role of education in the development of the other countries of the world. Perhaps, the first Indian to reinforce the demand for compulsory primary education for the Indian masses was Dadabhai Naoroji who pleaded before Indian Education Commission (1882) that steps should be taken to provide education to all children. Maharaja Sayajirao Gaekwad, the ruler of Baroda state introduced compulsory primary education in Amaravati division of India. This successful experiment gave support to the demand of compulsory primary education.

Malaviya by citing example Montagu Chelmsford proposal limitation focused on two dominating conditions responsible for poor and backward condition of Indians.

> One is that the immense masses of the people are poor, ignorant and helpless for beyond the standards of Europe; and the other is what there runs through Indian society a sense of cleavages of religion, race and caste. Which is constantly threatens its solidarity and wise political scheme must take serious need. Thus, he suggested government to take the educated classes of India, who are able to move with them and must do justice with them, recognized them with sympathy and allowed them as the representative of the Indian

> people's share in the administration. So, then they might co-operate with them to reduce the colossal poverty and illiteracy.[73]

Therefore, it is expressed that Malaviya understood that the lack of education was the root cause of the Indian poverty and backwardness in political scenario.

Malaviya by citing example of Australia, Germany and France said,

> In these countries there is principle of common qualification to read and write but in case of India we Indians would certainly desire that in any scheme of a recognized degree of education should entitle a person to vote without any other qualification. But I felt very much hurt on the lack of education among the Indians. In 1870 in England elementary education act was passed. English men began to say "we must educate our masses."[74]
>
> Similarly there is need in Indian government passed a reform bill based on the principle of 1868 in which education act will be passed and by which stigma of illiteracy from our land removed and India will reach the equal standard like other civilized countries.[75]

Further Malaviya cited example of England and Japan where 1871 act was introduced to establish and maintain schools in sufficient number and to admit all children of school going age in schools and he requested to follow the noble example of these countries.

Before Gokhale bill, Malaviya strongly recommended universal primary education during his speech on the united provinces district board bill, Malaviya in 1905 said,

> I refer to government for the promotion of primary education. How inadequately the district boards and the government have discharged their duties in this direction is shown by the fact that while in the year

73. *Ibid.*, p. 232.
74. *Ibid.*, p. 233.
75. *Ibid.*, p. 234.

> 1903-04 the proportion of scholars to the population of the school going age was in Bengal 30% for boys and 2.2% for girls, while in Madras 27.8% for boys and 4.8% for girls were going population in school. This is truly lamentable. These provinces were the pioneers in the matter of primary education. To ensure more satisfactory progress in the future, it is desirable now that the powers and duties of district boards are being clearly defined and I would suggest providing elementary education for all.[76]

In March 1912 during presentation of Gokhale Bill Malaviya supported him frequently for this purpose. He said,

> The present public system of education is one of the greatest gifts which the government has conferred on the people and the people feel deeply grateful for it. But this bill was failed due to some higher-class citizen of Indian who did not want to provide universal primary education to all castes and creeds.[77]

Malaviya in painful voice narrated the failure of this Bill in his own words as

> It is painful to recall how that modest Bill which sought only to give permission to certain local boards under certain conditions, to make elementary education free and compulsory was defeated by the votes of the government. Only 13 of us humble representatives of the people—voted for the motion to refer the Bill to a select committee and 38 persons at the head of whom stood his honors the lieutenant governor of Bengal—and which included all the officials and I am sorry to say, Certain Indian Members, voted against the motion and killed the bill.[78]

Malaviya found, Government of India has been pleased to say that the explanation of primary education is impeded due

76. Parmanand, *op. cit.*, p. 188.
77. *Malaviya Centenary Commemoration*, 1961, p. 2.
78. *Malaviya Speech in the Indian Legislative Assembly*, February 23, 1928.

to the indifference of the more advanced and ambitious classes. He said,

> I consider it is my duty to say that the remark is not true; it is not the indifference of the advanced ambitious classes but the unenthusiastic and cost-cutting policy. So, Government of India is responsible for this chronic want and consequently for the absence of hurting growth of education.[79]

Thus, Malaviya arose the issues like educational backwardness and accountability of the British Government for the welfare of the Indian people. The aforesaid analysis of Malaviya speech indicated that he was always worried due to the slow and steady progress of primary education and he wanted government always gave the highest priority to the compulsory primary education. Education, up to this stage, should be general and not specialized, and should give people a confident command over language and tool subjects.

4.6.4 *Malaviya's Arguments against British Policy of Education*

Malaviya always in his speeches criticized and blamed British Government about the rights and requirements of Indian people. He said,

> Government spends over one crore of rupees per year on the police, but it cannot find more than 43 lakhs on education.[80]

In his opinion the poor status of education was due to Macaulayism of education system and poor financial support of the government.

Malaviya advocated provision of agriculture, mechanical and commercial education at all levels from the primary to the university. He considered it necessary that the primary education should be made compulsory, if not free. During his dissent on the Indian Industrial Commission (1918), "he recommended mechanical training to be imparted in school attached to railway workshops. Malaviya feared that if such trainings were confined to railway works shops; it would not benefit Indians to any

79. Panday, R., op. cit., p. 122.
80. *Ibid.*, p. 165.

appreciable extent. He suggested the introduction of mechanical training in the ordinary school and recommended introduction of course of mechanical and electrical engineering in schools and colleges leading to an examination of the London B.Sc. standard. He expressed the hope that Calcutta and other universities would start such courses (as he himself did at the Banaras Hindu University), practical training being made available in railway and other workshops."[81]

He always alarmed British Government that it should be essential to give adequate financial support to the institutions providing such training and government should grant scholarships to trainees. He suggested immediate measure for starting first class electrical polytechnics, training in navigation and naval engineering and stressed the immediate need for starting commercial education in all universities. Therefore, his view on education system was much unambiguous at all levels.

If Malaviya was not agree with any policy of higher education then he opposed it logically by citing examples as he opposed the creation of an Imperial Industrial Service for carrying a scientific chemical research in aid of industries. He thought that by this way the future of Indian universities become in the hand of England like the existing imperial services.

> He referred indignantly to the services working such departments as agriculture, veterinary, metrological and geological survey, which were intended to be manned by Indian but having been initially recruited abroad by reason of Indian with requisite qualification not being available at that time, continued to be manned by European even after Indians have degree.[82]

So although he opposed Indian industrial commission report but at the same time he also realized that simple industrial advancement cannot restore Indian treasures to the position which it had at ancient times and also would not help India to occupy a rank among the civilized countries of the world. It reflected him as a visionary who served India for more than 100 years.

81. Parmanand, *op. cit.*, p. 293.
82. *Ibid.*

Malaviya opposed the Britishers' higher education system and administrative policies because he understood that Britishers' wrong education policies were accountable for the poor economic condition of India. During his presidential address on Lucknow in 1908 (in discontent in India and the reform proposal) he said

> One of the causes of increasing poverty of Indian people is the excursive costliness of the British administration in India. There is no Country on the earth which is poorer than India and none where official salaries of European are higher than who worked in India. This was the reason of poverty in India. The children of the Indian soil are practically excluded from all higher remunerated appointment. Indian are employed in a smaller appointment on the civil sides so the salary gained by European and Eurasians. No Indian soldier even above the post of Subedar major in military. So, if the salary which Indians were paid to Britishers indirectly in circulation the country, we will be able to feed many hungry mouths and to provide clothes to many necked bodies of India. So, Malaviya recommended for public service examination held simultaneously.[83]

Thus, Malaviya understood that the cause of British richness was the poor educational condition of India. Therefore by incorporating best model of higher education he tried to prepare soldiers, educated administrators who understood needs and real condition of the Indians and take action accordingly. The principle of education decided by Malaviya was different from Britishers' view.

4.7 On Goal of Education

The motive of Malaviya's life was expressed by his most used slogan "*Na twam kamay*" which means I neither aspire for kingdom, nor heaven, nor liberation (from life and death), I yearn for being able to remove the sufferings of the distressed. The purpose of education/aim of education, viewed by Malaviya were not much different because if Banaras Hindu University

83. Panday, R., *op. cit.*, p. 173.

would be like any other university having aim to produce graduate and provide degree, it would not have been fulfilled the goal of higher education which was visualized by Malaviya.

As Malaviya said,

> The purpose of Banaras Hindu University was not only to make doctor, engineer, advocate, bachelors having degree, etc. but also the men of high character, probity and honors, whose conduct through life will show that they bear the hall mark of a great university. Such character can be most securely built upon the solid foundation of religion.[84]

Therefore Malaviya's aim and purpose of education were same from all, broad and limited scopes. It has been described and discussed under separate heads. By establishment of Banaras Hindu University, his purpose was not to focus on community feeling, but to develop the spirit of nationalism. Malaviya wanted to develop a feeling of patriotism in the people who would then support humanity and society, promote peace on earth by choosing the path of righteousness and would understand and prove that every creature around them had its own importance, so they would never injure any fellow creatures.

4.7.1 *Education as Sole Tool to Make India once again Super Power*

Malaviya spent his whole life for building of nation it reflected in his message on the inauguration of Banaras Hindu University, he conveyed,

> It is my earnest hope and prayer that this centre of life and light which is coming into existence will produce students who will not only be intelligently equal to the best of their fellow student in outer parts of the world and who will strive to enable our country regain the glory of being a super knowledge society which once it was.[85]

84. Maine, S.K. et al., *Visionary of India Madan Mohan Malaviya*, New Delhi: Commonwealth Publication, p. 103.
85. Raju, P.K.N., "A Dream of Madan Mohan Malaviya", *Pragya,* Vol. 56, part 02 (2010), p. 262.

This statement reflected his vision and hope by education system of India.

Malaviya believed in great institutions of ancient India and their national solidity and prosperity. He wanted to establish such institutes by which ancient prosperity of India might be regained along with the need of a prosperous contemporary society. He wanted Indian youth to win in every field. They could compete at the global level. Malaviya dreamt of India to become knowledge-based society and not a society deteriorated by misuse of knowledge as is seen these days. Today students have information, which is mainly a superficial knowledge and such incompletely conceived knowledge harms the society. Thus, Malaviya's ideology of education was based on right meaning of education with practical sense. It was devoted not only for earning money but was more relevant in contemporary context also.

By education he wanted to make human resources which are educationally superior, philosophically perfect, culturally and materially rich and follows *Satyamev Jayate* in life. He said

> Mere industrial advancement cannot restore India to the position, which she once occupied among the civilized countries of the world and even industrial prosperity cannot be attained amongst all concerned, and these can only prevail and endure amongst those who are fair in all their delays strict in the observance of good faith and stead fast in their loyalty of truth.[86]

No doubt this statement is true even today. Today India has high intellectuals who migrated abroad because of the corrupt selection procedures, lack of job opportunities and difficult admission processes, etc. People feel cheated and exploited, so they migrate. Thus, there is a need to realize Malaviya's goal of education which produces knowledge-based society along with high moral intellect and values. Malaviya's goal of education was to re-establish the prosperity of Indian education system in the world and to regain it. No doubt India was once a one of the most powerful countries and if a peaceful and favorable climate

---

86. Maine, S.K., *loc. cit.*, p. 103.

is provided, it will regain its status. Therefore, if educationists and policy makers could understand India as a powerful nation not because of its power of arrows and army but because of being a knowledgeable and intellectual society, the future of India would have been started shining.

4.7.2 *Education as a Changing Agent in the Social Sector*

Society is composed by the vast and complex network of relationships, in which all humans participate. When a number of persons are engaged in activities that differ from those which are generally followed by the people, social change gets started. Education is the single most important factor responsible for the social change. In Malaviya's opinion, no system is more important or more urgent than to transform education, because education and social reforms are two sides of a coin.

If any society wants social, economic and cultural transformation, the realization of national goals related to the life, fulfillment of needs and aspiration of the people, this can only be done by education which is related to productivity, strengthens social and national integration, consolidates democracy as a form of government and helps the country to accept it as a way of life, hastens the process of modernization and strives to build character by cultivating social moral and spiritual power. Malaviya wanted to develop such a social environment in educational agencies like schools, colleges, universities, where customs, traditional values, norms, manners and morals are greatly enriched. During his childhood, he wanted to develop an ability in him to take interest in others, to share joys and sorrows, to work as a member of group.

About *Varna* system of Ancient India, i.e. *Brahmin, Kshatriya, Vaishya* and *Shudra*, he said that it is education that can transform the *Shudra* into Pandit. He promoted education which can give voice to the desires and feelings of the people who had been facing difficulties since centuries. He utilized education as a tool to promote reformations for the benefit of all the classes and communities of the population. His appeal in different council and other places reflected, in his views, that freedom and prosperity could only be gained, if Indian education system could be empowered. At presidential address during Indian National Congress Malaviya mentioned

> Five qualification which earn man the respect of others i.e. wealth, relation, age, time and knowledge. These five things entitle a man to respect of there each succeeding qualification and possession of wealth the lowest.[87]

He himself said

> वित्तं बन्धुर्वय कर्म विधा भवति पच्चमी।
> एतानी मान्यस्थानानि गरीयो यद्यदुत्तरम्।।

In Twelfth Indian National Congress in 1886 held at Calcutta, Malaviya said that there is a need of scientific, technical institutions for the people to overcome from poverty and famines of this country. Malaviya thought if Indian people got higher education, they would be able to compete in Indian civil services, own their positions and power. Then, they would help in correcting inappropriate in the rules of Britishers. So, Malaviya recognized education as a powerful tool for socio-economic transformation and social mobility and upgradation.

Malaviya wanted to create equality in the society for deprived classes not only by reserving seats in provincial politics but by providing them with equal educational opportunities. Basically, Malaviya wanted to develop a society where human resources' had high knowledge, skills and competencies. By implementing advanced and applied science and technical education, he wanted to accumulate human capital and its effective investment for development of the economy of nation. Therefore, he wanted to develop a sense of oneness, unity and belongingness in all the areas of thinking and behavior. He aimed at removing the obstacles being faced by Indians, which hindered the growth of nation and national integration, such as castism, communalism, diversity of language, lack of leadership and unsuitable education and regionalism. Thus, Malaviya regarded that there is a close link between education and national development and reconstruction. So according to him, educational plan should not be made in a vacuum, because

87. Report of the presidential Address, XXIV *Indian National Congress*, Lahore, Dec. 1909, The leader Office Allahabad, p. 13.

it has to be used as a powerful tool for socio-economic and political development and therefore it should to be related to the long-term national aspirations and to the national development, on which the country would step forward.

4.7.3 *Education as Key for Economic Growth of the Nation*

Malaviya believed that education is the crucial input for empowering people with skills and knowledge and for providing them with productive employment in future. According to him improvements in education only were not sufficient to enhance efficiency but essential also to improve the overall quality of life. It is a crucial instrument to enhance human consciousness for their rights and duties and also to enable them to enjoy the fruits of development in economy of India. Malaviya thought that higher education plays a very important role for the growth and development of human and so it is accountable for social, economic and scientific development of the country. He advocated, in his speeches, for the technological, scientific education and gave importance for industrial growth of indigenous industries for the rise of economy. He clearly expressed that lack of scientific and industrial education was the only cause of poverty and drought due to which Indians had been suffered. By educational expansion he wanted to develop indigenous factories and to motivate people to produce *Swadeshi* products by using their own resources of India. So basically, Malaviya emphasized on acceptance of scientific western technologies, because he thought that without accepting such technologies India could not fight at global level.

Malaviya in Allahabad legislative council held in April 1908 under the presidentship of Sir John (Prescott Hewett) said,

> Your honor's Government deserves the thanks of the public for having decided to carry out the scheme of Technical and Industrial education which was recommended by the industrial conferences. He said it is pleasing to note that ₹ 3,30,000 has been provided in the budget for technical and industrial education, partly under the heading of education and partly under civil works; and that ₹ 1,49,000 is set apart for introducing

> the teaching of science and manual training in schools. It is necessary, however, to point out that the whole provision for technical and scientific education which the government had decided to make is only satisfactory as the first installment of reforms. To provide the full measure of technical and scientific instruction and industrial training which are necessary to quality our people to make satisfactory progress in manufacturing industrial pursuit, a widespread system of technical and industrial education such as obtains in Japan is necessary, and I hope that the Government will steadily endeavor to build up a similar system here.[88]

So, he has vigorously advocated the industrial development. He thought that Indian industries had suffered discouragement and were neglected by the Britishers. Malaviya, for economic enhancement, advocated vocational teaching in secondary schools and recommended to provide an organized workshop to train the people. He motivated them to gain expertise for the establishment of *Swadashi* indigenous industries and prepare them to collect funds for organizing indigenous industries. So, Malaviya recognized education as an option to overcome the problems of unemployment as well as poor economic condition.

4.7.4 *Education as an Instrument for Political Freedom and Nationalism*

Malaviya wanted to make such citizens who are politically awared and devoted for the nation. In his speeches and statements there was core focus on expansion of educated class in India. During passing the proposal of Indian Constitutional reforms he urged,

> The proportion of the people who take interest in political question is very small, and said enormous country population poor, ignorant, non-political minded, immersed indeed in the struggle for existence. The rural classes have the greatest stake in the country, because they contributed most to its revenues, but they

88. Panday, R., *op. cit.*, p. 164.

> poorly equipped for politics and do not wish to take part in them.[89]

Therefore, it reflected that he believed that the main cause for the ignorance towards politics is the lack of education. Malaviya was worried due to unwillingness of people to participate in political issues. He cited the example of political backwardness of England and Canada and said at passing of reform bill 1867, in which all the Englishman began to realize that they must educate their masses, and they passed elementary education act in 1870 and making it universal. By citing these examples Malaviya wanted to attract the attention of British Government towards poor status of education system in India and he realized that illiteracy is main cause of political backwardness. As Mr. Foster stated

> Illiteracy and ignorance is pregnant with crime and misery, misfortune of an individual and danger to all community.[90]

Thus, he appealed to pass an "Education act" which will remove the stigma of illiteracy from our land and steadily raise the percentage of scholars in schools. He believed that by creating an educated class, it will be possible to prepare mass representatives who share in administration and bureaucracy.

He again argued to British Government that

> I would like to create attention of the Englishmen what passed in India from the period of 1897 to 1915. Education was not sufficiently spread, poverty was increasing, and racial inequality was kept between Europeans and Indians.[91]

Malaviya expressed the role of Indian National Congress for increasing the awareness in the Indians and said,

> let see the what educated Indians doing since 1885. They have been meeting regularly every year in Congress, at great personal sacrifice and earnestly pressing upon the bureaucracy measure after measure calculated to

89. *Ibid.*, p. 233.
90. *Ibid.*, p. 234.
91. *Ibid.*, p. 239.

> improve the lot of the rural population and the general mass of the people. So in his view Indian National Congress provided political stage to educated people who took interest in nation and worried for the rights of Indians. He said that it is Congress which forms its second session 1886, stated deepest sympathy for the vast number of population of India, and urged the representative institution. In 1888 urged to Britisher to foster and encourage education general as well as technical branches.[92]

Therefore, Malaviya appealed British Government for political awakening of Indians. He explained how the power of administration enhances nationalism. He said,

> Educated Indian feel that if the British electorate and parliament had agreed to admit them to share of power with them as they asked for in 1886, probably they too would have been able to achieve a considerable degree of similar progress in their country and they are naturally anxious that power should not be with held any longer form. The failure of the bureaucracy to do much of what it should have done to build up the national strength and prosperity of the Indian people during the last thirty-three years, in spite of the repeated representative of educated Indians. It has created a wide spread conviction among them that the healthy progress of the country will not be ensured unless power is given to them to promote it.[93]

So, Malaviya always suggested for satisfactory representations of Indians in the executive council, in lower provincial status and in higher councils. He forcefully said to British Government to arrange civil services exams simultaneously in India and England. He thought that if the educated class found place in politics as well as in civil services, in army, the zeal of nationalism will be improved automatically. Therefore, he always opposed communal award as he believed that by providing seats to the deprived classes, society could never achieve equality. Education

92. *Ibid.*
93. *Ibid.*, p. 240.

is the only means which provide equality in the society. Therefore, by education, he desired to develop such citizens in India, who are ready to participate in political process without selfish motive.

4.7.5 *Education for All*

Malaviya was supported the education for all without any distinction on the basis of caste, creed, religion and sex. This could be seen in the university during his vice-chancellorship. In 1925, when Malaviya had gone to Patna for the Mahasabha conference, he addressed a huge gathering in Arraha. When he was getting in the car someone brought a young boy, Jagjivan Ram and said to him

> The boy has matriculated but has difficulty in pursuing further studies.

Malaviya spontaneously told him,

> Please bring the boy with you to the university.

"He invited, Babu Jagjivan Ram to study with his own son and he stayed with his son in the hostel of the university. Malaviya paid his admission fee, hostel fees etc."[94] This incident proves that Malaviya was not only worried for the education of the elite classes but he gave importance to education for all.

Malaviya financially assisted hundreds of young *harijans* to receive higher education and raise their life in the university. Malaviya paid the fees of all poor bright students in the university. This may be because he himself suffered from poverty in his student life. He always expressed his faith in the education of deprived classes and poor students. He said

> You do not know how many Dhruv; how many Shivaji; and how many Ranapratap are there among the poor students.[95]

So he was always ready to help poor students. When Dr. Ambedkar expressed his wish to learn Sanskrit, no Brahmin Pandit came forward. It was Malaviya who asked Shri Nagappa

94. Maine, S.K. et al., *Visionary of Modern India Madan Mohan Malaviya* published by Commonwealth Publication, p. 151.
95. *Ibid.*

Shastri in Bombay (1932) to teach Sanskrit to Dr. Ambedkar.[96] All examples reflected Malaviya as unbiased personality who thought equally for all.

On 22 March 1915 at the time of passing of Hindu University Bill in the imperial legislative council against the objection of Sir Harcourt Butler, Malaviya replied,

> My lord, the university will be a denominational institute, but not a sectarian one. It will not promote narrow sectarianism but a broad liberty of mind and a religious spirit which will promote brotherly feeling between man and man.[97]

Therefore, Malaviya wanted to unify community by removing sectarian differences.

He always appreciated the efforts of Aligarh Muslim University for educational development. He thought if any community is educated, the nation will automatically be uplifted. Therefore, he was always favoured education for all. Along with this, Malaviya also gave importance to education of women. He said,

> Any scheme of education was incomplete as half is the portion of a community (The woman) is allowed to grow up in ignorance to be shut out from the light of knowledge.[98]

Therefore, Malaviya was dedicated for education of all.

4.7.6 Education Meant for the Inculcation of Tradition, Culture, Values and Religious Faith

The establishment of Banaras Hindu University in the form of residential university Kashi reflected that he believed Kashi as a place of ancient teaching and culture, and he wanted to inculcate tradition and culture of Ancient India. Malaviya thought that all the problem concern to human life was due to *Artha* and *Kaam* aspiration. Man has a lot of ambition, needs.

---

96. *Ibid.*
97. Somaskandan, S. "Malaviya contribution to Higher education", *Prajna,* vol. 56, part 02 (2010), p. 286.
98. Chandramauli K., "Malaviya ji's values and his relevance", *Prajna*, Vol. 56, Part 02 (2010), p. 300.

But man would attain peace in life only by deciding right goals by right means and this sense of righteousness would shape the values and strength in personality. This will be possible by inculcation of religious faith in man.

Malaviya's educational view reflected "Character-Industry Integrity", as he read in the first court meeting that

> These are the three cards to win the game of life. These will prove trumps every time before the game is ended; we cannot escape from our share in the game; we cannot be simple lookers. For good or evil, we are all here to play the game. How shall we do it? Shall we, if we think our hand a poor one, throw down our cards and make no effort to win? Surely not, that is the coward's way. Let us play like a true sports man like manner, making the best of every chance we get; doing always what is right even if it seems the losing game.[99]

Therefore, it reveals Malaviya vision. It is seen in the objective of Banaras Hindu University i.e. perfect the students in science and technology and industrial themes along with strong character. He wanted to prepare them to play these three cards successfully in their life.

Malaviya did not favour any moral education or value education as a discipline but by integration of religion he wanted to develop moral values, character and wholesome personality of the students. Therefore, he established Sanskrit Vidya Dharma vigyan faculty in Banaras Hindu University. As he always felt without religion the felling of righteousness, usefulness, patriotism, and self-realization could not be attained. Therefore Malaviya, came to the conclusion that in order to revitalize India as a nation it is essential to feed her youth with old spiritual and ethical food of culture. In the first court meeting Malaviya addressed

> I especially pleased to note that one of cardinal principle of the university is to train and bring up the alumni of

99. Dar, S.L. and Somaskandan, S., *op. cit.*, p. 381.

> the university in religion because all religion is based on the belief in one supreme being, the almighty God.[100]

This statement reflected that by inspiring religious faith in students, Malaviya wanted to have such citizens, who may be God fearing and God loving, and consequently imbibed with love for their fellow beings.

Thus, he wanted to develop such education system, which was founded on the Indian ideals, not dominated by the Western thought and culture. He thought religion must the part of education of every child. Then he will be able to fight any conflict and problem of materialistic world. So in Banaras Hindu University at *Ekadashi* or *Purnima* he delivered lectures on Gita and the Bhagvat, and tried to enhance religious faith and spirituality in the learners of the Banaras Hindu University, but there is no compulsion to attend this religious discourse. So through this way he wanted to develop the culture of religious faith, which inculcates the value and character in students.

4.7.7 *Education as Necessity*

He brought attention on the necessity of education, as it seems by his lecture during financial statement 1904 (April in Allahabad) he said,

> It is now well understood that in all countries the happiness of the poor depends in a great measure on their education. It is by means of it alone that they can acquire those habits of prudence and self respect from which all other good qualities spring: and if ever there was a country, where such habits are required, it is this. We have all often heard of the ills of early marriages and overflowing population; of the savings of a life squandered on some occasion of festivity; of the helplessness of the riots, which renders them a prey of money-lender; of their indifference to good clothes of houses, which have been urged on some occasions as an argument against lowering the public demands on them; and finally of the vanity of all laws to protect them, when no individual can be found who has courage enough to

100. Panday, R., *op. cit.*, p. 122.

> talk advantage of those educated in their favour; there is but one remedy for all this which is education. He wanted it by legislative support because he understood that it is more essential to provide statutory provision for adequate funds of education.[101]

If above speech analyzed, it can be concluded that Malaviya gave supreme importance to the need of education. For him education was something which ought to be brought within reach of everyone. He mostly advocated, in front of British Government, for providing sufficient funds for education. Presenting reform proposal in year 1908 he said,

> Education lies at the root of all reform.[102]

Consequently, he requested government to spend more and more funds upon education.

He said that the importance and necessity of education cannot be underestimated. He said

> No real economic and social development of people is possible without the education of the masses. Such education is the foundation and necessary antecedent of increased economic activity in all branches of national production in agriculture, small industries, manufactures and commerce, therefore it is the most solemn duty we owe to our people to promote education to the best extent we can. Along with this education, we have to promote industrial enterprise and indigenous manufactures.[103]

So, Malaviya realized sociological and economical role of education and he understood that Britishers were rich at the cost of Indians. Therefore, it was necessary that Indians should put our own shoulders, whole heartedly, to the wheel and defined a system of education which was technical, sensitive and industrial in all parts of provinces, which might be calculated along with the existing government system to meet the requirements of the country.

---

101. *Ibid.*, p. 123.
102. *Ibid.*, p. 53.
103. *Ibid.*, p. 54.

Therefore, it can be said that his educational goals were a blend of idealism and realism inspired by social, political and ancient tradition and culture. He had faith in the ideology that true happiness of the people could be promoted and secured not only by material advancement but all these material advancement are worthless if man does not realize his eternal duties towards mankind as described in our religion.

Malaviya's educational philosophy reflected that for him nothing is more desirable than to perform duty with religious sprit. Thus, Malaviya's purpose of education was to develop humanity, nationalism and true religiosity in the people of India. He wanted to develop such educational schemes where Indians learn scientific, technical, industrial education along with the study of best culture of ancient India. In his opinion, the real purpose of education was to develop the sense of duty towards God, Motherland, to our fellow people and to promote sacrificing tendency in the citizens for the nation and for the sake of Motherland.

4.8 Objectives of Education

The aims and objectives of education are one of the most important aspects of education philosophy. Generally, education emerges from experience and aims and is constantly reshaped to achieve the purpose of education. Purpose of education is the matter of foresightedness while objective of education is hind sighted. Malaviya's education philosophy opposite to metaphysical view believed in flexible educational aim. He framed realistic educational objectives which arose due to social and political experiences of his life. So, his educational objectives were based on social origin rather than metaphysical view. He recommended only those objectives of education that were rationally relevant for human being and their social development. His aims of education had been critically examined by his actions throughout his life and his socio-economical, political and religious ideas. After analyzing his speeches and writings following objectives are framed out.

4.8.1 *Character Building*

The development of character is an important aim of education. But the educators generally do not achieve unanimity about the qualities to be developed, in students, for this purpose. As Aristole attributed the qualities of an ideal character to his "magnanimous man", who possessed all the mental virtues, who maintained his proper pride, who did not undervalue his demerits and who despised whoever deserved to be despised. His "magnanimous" man belonged to the class of "*haves*", had no sympathy for the underdogs and pursued values which had little relevance to common man. While Platonic citizen have four cardinal virtues like temperance, courage, wisdom and justice. Malaviya educational philosophy has aimed for achieving ideal character like ancient Indians, who possessed religious virtues. It was his believe that peace and prosperity would prevail in society if all humans fulfilled their religious obligations.

Malaviya said,

> A teaching university would half perform its function, if it does not seek to develop the heart power of its scholars with the same solicitude with which it would develop their brain power. Hence the proposed university has placed the formation of character in youth as one of its principle objective.[104]

Therefore, Malaviya's motive was not only to enhance mental knowledge of the students of Banaras Hindu University but by education he wanted to develop a sound mind, controlled senses with full of balance between emotional and mental sphere.

Malaviya focused on "character-industry integrity" for achieving success in life. Malaviya coded it as the supreme priority than any other desires. He appealed the students to follow *Brahmcharya,* look younger girls like sisters, elders like mother and respect to women, be aware about your character because once it is lost would never come again as it was. Therefore in Banaras Hindu University formation of character of youth is one of the prime objectives. As he said

104. Dar, S.L. and Somaskandan, *op. cit.*, p. 136.

> University will not seek merely to turn out men as engineers, scientist, doctors, merchants, and theologian but also as men of high character, probity and humor whose conduct through life will show that they bear the hall mark of a great university.[105]

For character formation, he cultivated a solid foundation of religious culture in university. For development of ethical and civil sense of their duties in the students, he realized it was necessary to integrate religion in education system. He wanted to develop characteristics in students such as truthfulness, integrity, fortitude, self-help, self-respect, self-control, hospitality, unselfish public action for good and all the above which shown friendliness to whole creation.

> Many times during evening visit in hostels of Banaras Hindu University Malaviya, by telling anecdotes, solemn injections, eloquent discourses, developed good will among students and men, and tried to elevate all the virtues in their character. (*History of Banaras Hindu University*, p. 158)

For character building Malaviya envisioned realization and practice of higher values, training of mind or ill power; discipline of instincts, changing instinctive behavior to moral behavior. Thus, he thought a spirituality guided person does not show false pride and ego but smoothly behaves with others and he realized about his existence, soul consciousness and understood the nature of his duty thus became successful.

By citing a lot of examples of *Vedas*, *Upanisads*, *Gita* and *Bhagavata,* Malaviya always tried to change the mindset of the notorious students into good ones and sublimate their beastly desires and instincts. As Sanskrit *Subhashitani*, motivated students for attainment of good character as follows.

> वृत्तं यत्नेन सरक्षेत् वित्तमायाति याति च।
> अक्षीणो वित्ततः क्षीणों वृत्तस्तु हतोहतः।।

सुभाषितानि

---

105. *Ibid.*, p. 138.

One shall protect his 'sheela' (good character) with efforts (not his wealth), money can be earned and lost (i.e. money is not stable, you have it today tomorrow you may lose it). A wealthy person without a good character is as good as dead.[106] Another one mostly said by him as—

यथा हि मलिनैः वस्त्रैः यत्र कुत्र उपविष्यते।
वृततः चलितोपि एवं शेषं वृत्तं न रक्षति।।

सुभाषितानि

As a person with dirty cloth does not hesitate to sit anywhere, a person whose character is spoiled, will not hesitate to do bad.[107] As everyone must have experienced this particularly in rainy days, when you come out of your home, you will take all care to protect yourself from the mud etc. but once somebody splashes some of it on you, you are tension free. You will not be bothered by the mud there after. Similarly to save your character, you have to take care only at first time. Thus Malaviya, by education, wanted to make a person a complete man having all attributes, whose character shines like a sun.

4.8.2 *On Integrated Education*

Dr. S. Radhakrishnan said about Malaviya that he did not want to follow India of 5,000 years ago. Radhakrishnan said,

> On his foe thought: he adjusted himself to the spirit of modern times and did his level best to inspire his countrymen with progressive impulses and utilize science for the service of man. While preserving the imperishable treasures of our past, we moved forward with the times.[108]

This zeal was also appeared when Malaviya opposed Bhagvan Das and Annie Besant against their forced idea, i.e. establishment of the university should be based on Theosophy and muddy buildings. He promoted an education which could have acted as a bridge between best of ancient culture of East and science and technology of the West.

---

106. From http://sa.wiktionary.org/wiki/ schlok 277. retrieved July 14/2012
107. From http://sa.wiktionary.org/wiki/schlok 52. retrieved July 14/2012
108. Maine., et al., p. 103.

Although Malaviya believed in industrial development but he did not have blind faith on unjustified, materialistic industrial advancement. He said,

> Industrial advancement cannot restore India in number position which she once occupied among the civilized centered of the world, but it can be attained by the citizens who are fair in all there dealing strict in their decisions, loyal for truth.[109]

In his views that type of citizen could be developed only by abiding influence of religion in education. So, Malaviya focused on integrated education.

4.8.3 *On Scientific and Technical Education*

During drafting the scheme of education for Banaras Hindu University, Malaviya was pressurized by orthodox Hindus to follow theosophical education and traditional education of Vedas and Sanskrit. After analyzing what is the best for nation he gave revised scheme of education. His proposal reflected modern syllabus along with teaching and research in many subjects by which economic and social condition of country could be improved.[110]

Before the foundation of university Malaviya focused on the relevance of technical education in his speeches. As in 1907 in his financial statement, at Allahabad legislative Council, he said,

> Such a system should provide necessary instructions for all the different classes of persons who may desire to be engaged in productive industry, namely, as mechanical engineers, workmen, foremen, or overseers and mangers or masters. The industries in which they are likely to be employed may conveniently be referred to as manufacturers, handicrafts art industries and agriculture, I have already dealt with agriculture and leave aside art industries for the present. I would confine my remarks now to manufacturers and handicrafts and I submit that there should be at least one institution in these provinces for giving instruction in the former, and

109. Dar, S.L. and Somaskandan, S., *op. cit.*, p. 138.
110. Parmanand, *op. cit.*, p. 221.

> one school in every district for giving instruction in the latter. I am willing that for the present attention may be mainly directed to the textile, industries, and the sugar industry, while in what I may call the secondary technical schools which I wish to see started in every district, teaching may be restricted to those handicrafts which are as it were native to the district, special provision being made for instruction in handloom weaving in nearly every one of the schools. In the superior institution for the teaching of manufacturing industries. Which I have mentioned, provision should be made for training managers and foremen, and instruction should be imparted at least in industrial chemistry, mechanical engineering, textile manufacture and sugar refining.[111]

So Malaviya, by citing examples of technical schools, wanted to develop a such model education system which could act as a guide and harbinger for those people who suffered from poverty and illiteracy.

Thus, it was visualized that he wanted to upgrade the economic condition of the country by dealing with the problem of unemployment through technical institutions. At the time of Famine commission in 1878 Malaviya said,

> At the root of the poverty of Indian people and the risk to which they exposed in seasons of the scarcity lies the unfortunate circumstance that agriculture forms almost the sole occupation of the mass of the people, and that no remedy for the present evils can be complete which does not include introduction of a diversity of the occupations is only the mean through which the surplus population may be drawn from agriculture pursuit and led to earn the means of subsistence in manufactures and employments.[112]

Therefore, Malaviya's goal was to promote indigenous industry, technological education to overcome from poverty and from those conditions which people faced during famine.

111. Panday, R., *op. cit.*, p. 234.
112. Dar, S.L. and Somaskandan, S., *op. cit.*, p. 118.

So, accordingly he formulated the objectives of the university to advance and diffuse such scientific, technical and professional knowledge combined with the necessary practical training. He wanted to promote researches in advanced and applied sciences. During 1935-36 Malaviya's dedication to persuade the legend personality in the fields of science and society, i.e. Albert Einstein to visit Banaras Hindu University for research guidance. Thus, he believed that the fusion of the country's ageless sublimity with modern science and technology could make India a prosper and contented Nation.[113]

C.M. Sogani was the third recipient of D.Sc. from Banaras Hindu University in 1928 under the supervision of Raman. While conferring the degree to Raman on 11 February 1932, Malaviya exhorted,

> By your achievement in the field of science, you have already won the worldwide distinction and have raised the glory of the motherland. I pray to God that you may continue to do your work for a long number of years, and with higher and higher distinction in the world of science for the benefit of the mankind and for the glory of the motherland. During providing Honorary D.Sc. degree to J.C. Bose and P.C. Ray he proclaimed, I am establishing a University, which will combine ancient wisdom with the knowledge of the physical sciences and technology.[114]

Bhatnagar and Narlikar described the dedication of Malaviya for the excellence of science and technology. Narlikar wrote in his article, while searching talents of India, he had heard about me I was pursuing research as an Isaac Newton student at the University of Cambridge under Sir Arthur Eddington, one of the most prominent and important astrophysicists of his time. While on visit to the UK for a round table conference, he visited to him in Cambridge in 1931 and invited him to join Banaras Hindu University.

Narlikar also described how he was welcomed and respected by Malaviya first time in 1932 in Banaras Hindu University

113. *Ibid.*, 364.
114. *Ibid.*, p. 641.

Campus in the New physics lecture theatre and at 7.30 in evening when he walked in the campus in moonlight, the hostels, the college building and beyond it love of Malaviya and holy Ganga was sufficient to set his mind to reside in India, although he had the return ticket of passage to Landon.[115] The Banaras Hindu University Kulgeet was composed by S.S. Bhatnagar (in the summer in 1924 at Gangotri, first time sung at the science Congress session in Banaras Hindu University in 1925), one of the most renowned scientists, who was a professor in Chemistry for three years during 1921-24.[116] Malaviya used to attend popular lectures on science organized by S.S. Joshi of Science College and other professors of the university.

For the first time in India, he established departments for mechanical and electrical engineering, glass technology, pharmaceutical chemistry, mining and metallurgy, chemical engineering as well as Sanskrit and Ayurveda, apart from many other courses which existed in other institutions in India. He attracted the brilliant scholars such as U.C. Nag, Charles A. King, A.B. Dhruva, Ganesh Prasad, Birbal Sahni, S.S. Bhatnagar, V.V. Narlikar, R.K. Asundi, Sir J.C. Bose and many others to guide the students at any cost. So all his action for enhancement of science and technology reflects that he tried to establish modern Takshashila in Kashi with a blend of the best of the East and West. While he was appreciated Oxford and Cambridge with their centuries old traditions, he was also proud of his university. It is no wonder that the Banaras Hindu University graduates played a pivotal role in shaping modern India—Devendra Lal, U.R. Rao, V.V. Narlikar, C.N.R. Rao, T.V. Ramakrishnan, to name a few. C.N.R. Rao's shared his educational and spiritual experiences as; no honor is greater than the one from one's own Alma Mater,

> When I entered this capital of learning in 1951 to pursue M.Sc. In Chemistry, the first thing I did was to take off

115. Narlikar, V.V., "*Manestay Mahdastu ch*" in *Prajna*, Vol. 21, Part 2 special issue of silver jubilee (1976), p. 1.
116. Gairola, S.S, "More than half a century at the Banaras Hindu University", *Prajna*, Vol. 21, Part 2, special issue of silver jubilee (1976), p. 58.

> my shoes at the main entrance and walked bare-foot to pay my respects to the Mahamana.

The faculty of Science College or Engineering College who ever worked at the time of Malaviya, were much devoted for their duties and they joined the university for the cost of money but on the cost of faith of Malaviya. As R.K. Asundi said how he approached to Malaviya when he was drawing salary in Aligarh. Malaviya said,

> Have I not seen you sufficiently and heard about you? You will not call for interview. You send a formal application that is enough for me.[117]

Therefore, it was Malaviya's devotion that made university enriched with eminent professors and teachers of science.

Malaviya had a global view with regard to invite persons of outstanding ability. To achieve this goal, he had correspondence with eminent scientists including Ernest Rutherford, Sir Arthur Eddington and others. In his cherished ambition, Malaviya not only invited great lectures on science and technology but also motivated many science projects.

> He was extremely anxious to start postgraduate level courses in sugar technology by taking advantage of agriculture and industrial chemistry department. He also encouraged nuclear physics section in science department.[118]

Therefore, Malaviya thought scientifically about every aspect of national development. He tried to enrich both religious and scientific environments in the university. Malaviya's knew that when the immediate supports would appear dim then, for the realization of goals, one should work hard. Thus in British period, to achieve his noble goal, he worked hard to save the Nation not only for the revival of religious spirit but also for the revival of scientific spirit of Indians.

---

117. Asundi, R.K., "The never to be forgotten personality of Madan Mohan Malaviya ji", *Prajna*, Vol. 21, Part 2, special issue of silver jubilee (1976), p. 27.
118. Tiwari, U.D., *Inspiring Episode of Mahamana Pt. Madan Mohan Malaviya,* Varanasi: BHU Press, 1984, p. 164.

4.8.4 *On Physical Development*

Malaviya always emphasized on proper physical development of children. He delivered his views on the importance of deterioration of physique among the people of India. As he said,

> We do not meet with the strongly built broad shouldered man as often now as we used to twenty-five years ago. There has been a regrettable abandonment of the useful practice of physical culture which was handed down to us by our forefather. In my own time I have noticed a great unwillingness on the part of many a young to take physical exercise, so it is important that the Govt. has provided facility for the physical exercise in schools and colleges.

Malaviya vigorously said,

> It is important because as taste for physical exercise perceptibly diminished the people are not as strong as they used to be and succumb to disease much more easily. So it is essential, that we should do something to revive at least as much interest, and taste for physical exercise as was generally to be seen long years ago. There is need to organize school and college tournaments and student might be encouraged by their parents, guardians and friends to devoted little attention to do physical exercise. But even those who passed out from schools and colleges devoted little more time and attention to the reservation of promotion of a healthy and strong physique. It is pleasing to see English gentlemen of the age of sixty taking part every day in tennis, badminton or some other exercise. Let us adopt a similar good practice.[119]

So, Malaviya exhorted to build up physical health and strength. Malaviya on numerous occasions, during addressing students' gathering in Banaras Hindu University or elsewhere, always tried to inculcate the value of physical stamina amongst the youth.[120] Dr. S.S. Joshi (Staff of the chemistry department

---

119. Panday, R., *op. cit.*, p. 56.
120. Dar, S.L. and Somaskandan, S., *op. cit.*, p. 493.

since 1928 and retired as head the of the department and the principal of college of sciences) was presented his simple recipe as

> Drink milk, take exercise, repeated God's name every day concentrate on your studies and your desires are sure to be fulfilled.

Joshi in his article "Pt. Madan Mohan Malaviya a Tribute and reminiscences, wrote that Malaviya always addressed the Banaras Hindu University students for the importance of the value of physical stamina."[121]

Malaviya arranged proper facility for physical exercises/ playing games in the university. The extensive playgrounds were laying between rows of hostels, abundance space was left for team games such as football, hockey and cricket. When Malaviya was opposed by Bhagvan Das in 1921 for providing unnecessarily greater facility to physical education, Malaviya said, "If my friend wants to go to Nagva site, he will found students who will be advised to play Kabaddi which gives them as much exercise as cricket or tennis."[122] In 1921 a playground for cricket, hockey and tennis was laid out in the Nagwa campus. An akhara was also made. A riding school was also planned by Malaviya which would provide physical training to high order princes who were the chief patron of the university. The Maharaja of Bikaner had given ₹ 20,000/- for the purpose. But this would not suffice because larger amount of money required.[123]

Arrangement were made for physical exercises in Indian style which could be taken individually in the student's own room or in the hostel's compound with relatively inexpensive equipment. *Shivaji hall* was (spacious gymnasium hall) made in 1929. During his address to guest in Dec. 1929—Malaviya said,

> His last desire is that the university teaches for degrees in physical culture.[124]

---

121. Singh, Nandlal, *Mahamana Malaviya ji Birth Centenary Commemoration*, Varanasi, 1961, p. 101.
122. Malaviya address to the court Dec. 1921.
123. Parmanand, *op. cit.*, p. 639.
124. Dar, S.L. and Somaskandan, S., *op. cit.*, p. 506.

So in university the importance of physical culture was being more keenly appreciated, there was an appreciable rise in the number of students taking part in physical exercises and outdoor games. In 1936 famous athlete Prof. Ram Murti (Indian's sandow) instructed Banaras Hindu University students for body building by indigenous method. His guidance stimulated interest among the students in physical culture.

Malaviya regularly visited the hostels, met students in the Shiva ji hall and in the playgrounds and talked to the young men, praising those who had developed their muscles, exhorting and encouraging those that were beginning to do so. He would recall his own fondness for wrestling by which he had greatly benefited and that he still continued to take exercise at home and maintained agility unusual for his age. So, Malaviya realized the body as the first requirement for any kind of austerity (*Sadhana*)

शरीर माद्य खलु धर्म साधनमं[125]

it is the instrument for all good deeds and is the tabernacle of soul. The existence of spirit cannot be imagined without a body. So according to him, sound physical health is essential for struggle of existence. It is the principle and most valuable asset of the individual. According to him a diseased body produces a diseased mind and diseased thoughts.

In 1925 when Akbar Shah Khan Najibabadi challenged Malaviya to fight a fourth battle of Panipat to which he would bring no more than 700 Indian Muslims (not Afghans or Pathans) to fight 2500 Hindus, when he would vanquish, Malaviya painfully aware Hindus for the deterioration of physique of the average Hindus and encouraged physical culture as a prominent item in the programme of *Hindu Sangathan* which he launched in 1923.[126] Therefore, in Banaras Hindu University, Malaviya started many types of physical activities like gymnastics, games, sports and yogasans, meditation, besides all these he gave more emphasis to maintenance of Celibacy (*Brahamcharya*) by the students and said it is the self-killing

125. *Ibid.*, p. 508.
126. *Times of India,* 6 June 1925, quoted in Indraprakash founder of Hindu Mahasabha, p. 119.

to waste the valuable energy and one should be sustaining to preserve it, as said in *Shivsamhita* ("मरणं बिन्दु पातेन, जीवनं बिन्दु ध्यारणत्" शिव संहिता). Therefore, Malaviya's prime objective was to produce good physical health of the students full of 3 v's as vim, vigor and vitality.

4.8.5 *On Vocational Development*

Malaviya believed in the words, "*Ann chinta chamtkar, kateray kavita kuth*", means a hungry man cannot achieve anything great and good in his life. He understood education as a process of making oneself reliant so it should be productive. He advocated for vocational base of education and laid importance of commercial education. During his speech on the reform proposal in 1908 he said,

> The important causes of widespread poverty in the country are the decline of indigenous arts and industries,

and he urged for the establishment of technical schools and colleges as important educational centers throughout the country and for the encouragement of indigenous arts and industries. During Famine commission of 1898 he forcibly drew attention of the Government of India for promoting industrial pursuits. He said,

> In India such unfortunate circumstances obtained because, agriculture is the sole occupation of the mass of the people and there is no remedy for the evils can be completed until the introduction of the diversity of occupation. Through which the surpluses population may be drawn from agriculture pursuits and led to earn the means of subsistence in manufactures and some such employments.[127]

So, he recommended to integrate vocations like agriculture, wood work, spinning, weaving, tailoring, mechanical works, horticulture, bee keeping, rural handicrafts, and cottage industries in curriculum; he wanted that vocational guidance should be given to equip the students with skills and enterprise of vocations. He understood that this type of self-supporting

127. Panday, R., *op. cit.*, p. 36.

education will help a student to maintain his livelihood in future, and it would act as an insurance against the unemployment. Therefore, Malaviya's aim was to provide better opportunity to those young students who were after getting university's degree and run after either the government jobs or fell into devious ways and felt frustration and unrest due to lack of jobs. They were not ashamed to ask for job to others. So in Malaviya's view to overcome from such dilemma, i.e. lack of vocational opportunity, it was important that the university education must be coordinated with the needs of life and should prepare an individual to earn their bread and butter.

4.8.6 *On Research*

Malaviya viewed that the prime aim of higher education was to do research for generation of knowledge. He was eagerly aware for the vital progress of research in the university and took great pains to provide the resources for the encouragement for the research. In December 1991 during address to University Court, Malaviya highly appreciated and congratulate

> Dr. Ganesh Prasad for notable increase in the number of research students in mathematics. Not only he appreciated Dr. Ganesh but also he prevailed Ganesh Prasad to miss his chance of election as pro vice-chancellor in order that his scholarly work might not suffer because of involvement in administrative duties.[128]

Malaviya helped researchers by enlisting the services of teachers who had received training in research or obtained research degrees at reputed universities of abroad in university. By providing adequate funds liberally, for the equipment and the maintenance of laboratories, he facilitated students to do their research with full dedication. In December 1922, he coded

> Hindu university laboratories were among the best equipped in India in his address. To the university court he discussed about the amount spent on the various laboratories.[129]

128. *Ibid.*, p. 482.
129. *Ibid.*, p. 483.

In the beginning of 1931 D.Litt. D.Sc. and LL.D high standard research degree were provided to the research scholars. He was keen to promote the research and frequently visited in science laboratories to see what work was in progress and to determine the needs of the researchers. Even after working for hours at the time of evening walk, he would drop it to see the work being done in the laboratory by electric light after nightfall. He would always ask to the young researchers about their unfulfilled needs and problems, he might express frequently their zest for researches. He was interested to meet with distinguished scholars who came to see the university and tried to introduce them to university students for motivation. Besides this

> he gave inspiring talks on various occasions such as when welcoming distinguished visitors to the university, presiding over meeting or functions at a college, hostel or gymnasium and during Gita Lecture and Kathas.[130]

Malaviya was interested in inviting eminent scholars whom he met or heard of.

> He extended pressing invitation even to Einstein and Max Mullar to come out only for a year.[131] Likewise Acharya Vishwa Bandhu was invited to be the head of an independent department of Vedic.[132]

B.M. Ghosal was serving on a salary of ₹ 450 in the Allahabad Boys School, an institution for the education of European and Anglo Indian students, and was the first Indian on the staff of that college to attain this pay, was persuaded by Malaviya who was looking for a teacher of Physics at the teacher training college, to take that post on ₹ 200 in 1920, similarly Joytish Chandra Mukherji, an expert auditor was persuaded to take up the professorship in commerce at the training college, has impressed Malaviya with his ability in auditing the account of Central Hindu School, in which irregularities were determined. So, Malaviya was always impressed by the performance of such persons, and he invited to well knowledgeable professors to

130. *Ibid.*, p. 482.
131. S.S. Joshi in CCV. p. 105.
132. *Vishwa Jyoti*, January, 1962 p. 4.

work in the university besides looking other approaches. Thus, it is concluded that he understood that the success of university depends upon quality faculty and quality research work, so he always enforced quality laboratory, quality teachers, quality research work to achieve this objective. The revised scheme of Banaras Hindu University, to promote learning and research generally in arts and science in all branches, reflected his dedication to develop research environment in the university.

4.8.7 *On Developing the Sense of Dutifulness*

Malaviya's lifestyle justified the following noble ideas:

> Actions speak louder than words. Words are dreams but actions are reality. Example is more inspiring than precept.

He said

> The thing which I like the most on earth is righteousness: it is our eternal duty. Righteousness is the straight path for character building and worldly happiness. It instills a high degree of selfless service in human being, which leads to the welfare of society and nation.

By citing Gita's *shlok* he tried to make people understand many important things as "*Sakal Padarath Hai Jagmahi, Karmhin Nar Pavet Nahi.*" He always respected to those people who were dedicated for their works. It was his dutifulness that even in his old age, he said that he had no time to death. In his ill condition he was devoted for work of country and visited to different parts of India for political awareness.

It was Malaviya's dedication for work that he founded Banaras Hindu University as first residential university in adverse situation by begging money and land. He was regarded as a man of action because of his sense of duty. He visualized work as worship and did not care much for immediate *moksha* than *karma*. This expressed by Shri Jyoti Bhushan Gupta who written about him as

> About 10 or 12 days prior to his death, Malaviya, though ill and with fever was on his way to village outside the limits of Kashi for addressing some religious gathering. It was then that Malaviya told Shri Joyti

> Bhushan that in case he was seriously ill on the way, he should not be carried back to Kashi; and when asked why, his answer was that he did not wish to die in Kashi and thus attain *moksha* immediately, as he wished to be reborn to complete his unfinished work in the university, and his other work outside.[133]

Through education, he wanted to develop the sense of responsibility in elders towards younger generations. He thought that nothing great can be achieved without collective efforts of group of people. He believed that people work in harmony only when they have sense of mutual trust. The mutual trust is infested when every single individual follows the footsteps of truth. Therefore, along with the sense of duty in individual, he gave importance to the path of truth. He admired that the Banaras Hindu University had been established to forward a special message to the world. As he said

> We have lit the lamp of knowledge in the temple of learning. It is the duty of those men who possess great courage and patience and who have developed themselves as a constant spirit of self-sacrifice, who passes devotion to the cause which they understood to be glorious and who are torchbearers of the future, serve an institution like the Banaras Hindu University.

Lord Hardinge replied to him and defined his dedication of work in such words as

> "Heaven helps those who help themselves." "I watched the dedication of Malaviya and other member of deputation how they spent time for collection of funds, enlisting the sympathy and generosity of their countrymen for their scheme. I watched how they were wandering from door to door, city to city and got welcome by the people and the result is that they were getting success to collect the sound financial footing for the establishment of the university."[134]

133. Rane, M.B., "Malaviyaji a symbol of ancient Indian culture", Varanasi, Mahamana Birth Century Commemoration, Vol. 25, December 1961, p. 74.
134. Dar, S.L. and Somaskandan, S., *op. cit.*, p. 348.

No doubt these words of Lord Hardinge show his salute to Malaviya's dutiful personality. Therefore, in form of education he wanted to make such a person who understood first his duty then his rights.

4.8.8 *Upliftment of the Hindu Civilization*

Malaviya and many of his collaborators had an abiding faith in religious instruction. The scheme of university was dreamt by Malaviya and his supporters because all were realized disorganized and disintegrated and deprived condition of Hindu religion. Malaviya as an orthodox metaphysical thinker realized it could only be remedied by a wide diffusion of real knowledge of *Sanatan Dharma*. So Malaviya and a number of distinguished Indians who having same mind set banded themselves establish a Banaras Hindu University at Banaras. The selection of place was clarified by the Maharaja of Bikaner as

> Kashi has always been regarded as the sanctum sanctorum of pious Hindu. In Malaviya's own inimitable words 'It is one of the most ancient cities of the world. It is hoary with scared memories' (of Harischandra, Buddha, Vyasa, Tulsidas, and Kabir) let us build this place as a great seat of learning for the Hindus.[135] (p. 119 why at Kashi purpose of Hindu University A.B. Mishra)

So, the basic cornerstone of his educational philosophy was the upliftment of Hindu religion. On the foundation ceremony of Banaras Hindu University in 1916 Malaviya said,

> We cannot divest ourselves of the consciousness that we have inherited a culture and civilization of our own, which reaches further back in time than that of any other people, and which possesses, as we believe, in a special degree of elements of social stability as well as the fundamental principle of physical, moral, and spiritual progress and welfare. Amidst all the vicissitudes through which Hindu Society has passed, it has all essentials, clung to that civilization and has

135. Mishra, A.B., "Purpose of Hindu University", Varanasi, BHU Press, p. 119.

> ever been governed by it. There was naturally a wide spread desire of our community that we should have a central educational institution of our own, to preserve and promote our distinctive civilization and culture and instructed in the prospect of our religion.[136]

Thus all his life action and speeches reflected Malaviya as a religious instructor who wanted to save the tradition and culture of *Sanatan Dharma* and developed perfect understanding in Hindus for their religion which was one of the objective of Banaras Hindu University also.

4.8.9 *On Women Education*

Malaviya realized that women status has been lower than that of men in India due to conservative traditionalism. He agreed with the fact that during the later Vedic period the Aryans had sealed the fate of women culturally and socially by denying them to study Vedas and thus half of our population was deprived of most fundamental human rights. He obelized that their condition also deteriorated due to the execution of the "purdah". Women were regarded as the bond slaves of men. Their position got further awful due to their economic dependence on men. This condition has been persisting for ages so illiteracy and ignorance was more prevalent in women folk than in men folk. During his speech he said if we make an historical survey of women education prior to 19th century, women folk lay under a confuse educational environment. No constructive and organized efforts had been made in this direction. According to the investigation made by Mr. Adam Smith himself there were only four women literate in Bengal district out of a population of half a million of them. In the presidencies of Bombay and Madras, the condition was however, not depressing. So, women education was suffering setback owing to the strict observation of Purdah system in Muslim community and prevalence of child marriage and other social customs of the Hindus. Women education was erroneously regarded as a serious breach of morals. The East India Company did not make any effort to promote women education. During

136. Dar, S.L. and Somaskandan, S., *op. cit.*, p. 343.

the term of Lord William Bentinck and Dalhousie, the situation showed some improvement. In the year 1854, some provision was made for the education of the girls. During 1905-21, women education received much impetus and it made considerable progress.

In view of Malaviya, women education should be regarded as inseparable part of our entire education system and should be considered as important as men education.

> Malaviya in the year 1907 in an essay on women education elaborated this fact, that India will not get progress unless female education was expended like male education. He laid emphasis on women education like western country.[137] (*Abuyadaya* 8 July, 1907)

He obliged the role of women in building the character of would be citizens, economic reconstruction of the country and in social reform. He said it remains undeniable and unchallengeable. So, Malaviya focused on the issue of women education and said it is very essential that they should be mentally well-equipped to avail equal responsibilities like men.

The principles decided by Malaviya for women education was that it should have practical values and separated from the boys. He wanted that special attention should be paid towards their health. He wanted to change the attitude of men for women. By citing the example of *Manu Smriti* saying Malaviya tried to understood man the power of women respect as Manu says where women are respected, there the Gods delight, and where they are not all work and effort come to naught. There is no hope of rise for the family or country where women are neglected disrespected and where they live in sadness. So, he realized that there was need to raise opportunities for the female education. Accordingly, he arranged opportunities of women education in Banaras Hindu University. Malaviya said

> 'No teacher like mother.' In comparison to men education, women education is more important. They are the first teachers of our politician, philosopher, industrialist, and

137. *Ibid.*, p. 342.

> leader. So, especially women education affects future citizen of India[138] *(Aaj,* 14 December 1929).

Like Gandhi, Malaviya wanted men regarded women as their helpmates and better halves instead of regarding them as domestic drudge and instruments of pleasure. Otherwise, the society became semi paralyzed. So, it is important to understand that men and women are supplementary pair of one another. Malaviya wanted to make women like Sita, Savitri, Gargi, Apala, etc. because in many of his lectures he expressed great attribute for these women. In relation to women education curriculum Malaviya accepted that knowledge should not be divided into compartments or closed separately for men and women, but he also wanted to educate women in domestic affairs for helping the upbringing of child. So, he obliged that if future mother of the society is educated, society will become shaped.

Malaviya's attitude for women students was strict as cited by Dr. Smt. Durga Bai Deshmukh who was distinguished alumnus of the university; in her article Homage to a great soul she wrote that

> she wanted to continue her education Banaras Hindu University B.A. Hons. In political science but Malaviya strongly disapproved and said that women students should not go to the men's college and the women college had no subject of the political science. At that time, therefore, she went to the Andhra University.

She also wrote

> She felt proud that she was not educated from BHU and remembered every day to Malaviya ji when she saw the building of Andhra Mahila Sabha which she founded by raised 80 lakhs of rupees like Malaviya, to spread the women education.[139]

Lastly, she admired it that she can do only due to the inspiration of Mahamana in her article. So no doubt, Malaviya always appreciated women education. Malaviya wanted to

---

138. *Aaj*, 14, December, 1929.
139. "*Durgabai Deshmukh Homage to Great Soul*", *Prajna*, Vols. 21-22, dimond jublee (1971), p. 31.

provide training of self defense, child care, mothering, religious, moral and character education, along with vocational courses to make them self-sufficient and self-reliant. Therefore, it can be said that Malaviya wanted awakening of consciousness in women through education. His vision is not only awaken the women, but also made conscious to men folk for realizing that by providing proper education and care, proper dignity to women they lead country and family on the path of progress.

4.9 Malaviya and Curriculum

Malaviya considered curriculum as the mirror of the national needs. He wanted to include social, political, economic needs along with the culture, history, civilization and tradition of the country during curriculum construction. Malaviya was not satisfied with the universities established on the basis of London University. He realized that the curriculum of these universities were not fulfilling the Indian needs, it creates slaves of Britishers. So many times his anger burst in the form of what Indians desired from education system. Therefore his approach about curriculum based on utilitarian philosophy. He advocated to integer at all such subjects which will be useful for daily life. After analyzing his thoughts it inferred that his attitude is dynamic, flexible and activity based when he decided educational scheme of Banaras Hindu University. Through curriculum he wanted to promote physical, mental and spiritual dimension of the learner. So in his scheme of curriculum there was provision of physical, religious and all those entire educational subjects as science and technology occurred which raised the economic condition of the country by making self-reliant citizens.

He favored 'integrated curriculum' which facilitated all necessary disciplines which are helpful in the development of wholesome personality of human being. He was against the pure rigid and traditional curriculum as it was seen when he faced much controversy by theosophist to give importance to theosophy in university then he negotiated their thoughts and propagated modern educational scheme in Banaras Hindu University. Malaviya's metaphysics believed in the existence of materialistic world along with spiritual world so in educational curriculum he wanted to create a balance between both the aspects. Consequently learners will be satisfied their materialistic as well as spiritual need. Therefore, Malaviya after analyzing the situation of the country and people's need thought that for a balanced development of youth scientific and spiritual education are necessary. Therefore, Malaviya appreciated non formal religious education in the form of Gita lectures and Bhagavat Katha in curriculum.

Through Katha and Gita lectures Malaviya wanted to upgrade the spiritual sense in the learners and preserve the Hindu Sanatan rituals. For expansion of Hindu Shastra and Sanatan Dharma, Malaviya incorporated Sanskrit learning to teach *Vedas*, *Smiritis*, *Darsanas*, *Itihasas* and *Puran*. Astronomical and meteorological taught in Jyotisha section of the *Vedang*. All of these subjects fulfill the first objective of Banaras Hindu University, i.e. to promote the study of the Hindu Shastra and of Sanskrit literature generally as a means of preserving and popularizing for the benefit of the Hindus in particular and of the world at large in general, the best thought and culture of the Hindus, and all that was good and great in the ancient civilization of India.[140]

Malaviya dreamt of to develop nationalism in the students through education so he gave priority to the social science subjects like history, geography, political science, economics, philosophy, comparative studies, literature and language.[141] All these subjects were taught in college of arts and literature in Banaras Hindu University. Seeing the economic condition of the country, Malaviya desired to develop the scientific temperament in Indians and less dependency on agriculture. So, he built up the college of science and technology which reflects him as a visionary. Looking the demands of the country he introduced the curriculum of the Mining Engineering, Geology, Metallurgical science, Industrial chemistry, Mechanical engineering, physics, life science, nuclear physics, etc.

140. Dar, S.L. and Somaskandan, S., *op. cit.*, p. 340.
141. *Ibid.*, p. 67.

> All science subjects were taught in Banaras Hindu University by renowned professors (Cambridge and London educated) up to 1923.[142]

> Malaviya also started courses of Ceramic and glass technology in 1924 for manufacturing of Soaps, Cosmetics, inks, glassware, and porcelain etc.[143]

"Teaching of Pharmaceutical chemistry began in 1932. The degree of B.Sc. and M.Sc. in pharmacy instituted in 1935. Later on electro chemistry began to be taught by the S.S. Joshi, the Engineering college of Banaras Hindu University set up machinery to generate electric energy which was sufficient not only for the university use but also for the population of related towns."[144] "It also started manufacture of electric fans."[145] Malaviya not only proposed these subjects but also worried for the proper arrangement of laboratories and required equipments. Time to time he communicated with the teachers of concerning departments and request them to provide the list of their requirement. "Although Malaviya faced opposition by the orthodox group but he provided staunch support to such discipline for the industrial development by citing the example of fast rising countries as Japan, U.S.A. and Germany where universities played a vital role to solve the problems of the society."[146]

Malaviya wanted to make India self-dependent country where people were skilled in agriculture farming by using right technology of agriculture earns more than their expenditure. So to fulfill this objective he started agricultural education in Banaras Hindu University in the year 1920.

> For realizing his dream, he met to the Maharaja Saheb of Banaras to grant about 2100 acres of land on lease which was finally settled and sum of 11,600 was paid by university as an advance for the annual rent. College

142. *Ibid.*, p. 69.
143. *Ibid.*, p. 463.
144. Parmanand, *op. cit.*, p. 461.
145. *Ibid.*, p. 461.
146. *Ibid.*, p. 462.

> of Agriculture scheme was prepared by the three invited professors, principals as Dr. Mann, Prof. Sam Higginbottom, and Rai Ganga Ram Bahadur.[147]

A canal construction was also proposed. Therefore not only science, industrial and religious education, Malaviya also had scientific vision on the agricultural education. Plant pathology and agriculture botany, plant physiology were also started in 1931.[148]

> Malaviya was interested to promote Indian system of medicines even he hardly accepted the treatment of the allopathic system, though he had many allopathic friends and admirers.[149]

He desired to make Banaras Hindu University as a leading center of Ayurvedic Studies in the country.

> Teaching of Ayurveda began in the faculty of oriental learning in 1918 with eminent professor Triambak Shastri, Umacharan Sen, Arjun Mishra.[150]
>
> Later on Pharmacy department was also established. Along with this Ayurvedic Garden, hospital on the name of Sir Sundar Lal was started in 1924 in which one half of the bed was provided for Ayurvedic treatment while rest was given for allopathic treatment. Malaviya for the practical purpose focused on arranging dissecting Hall and study of Anatomy.[151]

He liked Ayurvedic medicine but he had no prejudice mind set for the allopath.

> In Malaviya's curriculum scheme, dairy department adjunct to the animal husbandry was founded, because his purpose was to prepare best mental and physical health of the students. He established Goshala in the university.[152]

147. J.B. Gupta (Treasurer, BHU) in BHU Gazette, Dec. 23, 1961.
148. Dar, S.L. and Somaskandan, S., *op. cit.*, p. 464.
149. Parmanand, *op. cit.*, p. 464.
150. *Ibid.*, p. 451.
151. *Ibid.*, p. 452.
152. *Ibid.*, p. 453.

A college for training graduates for the teaching profession was started in August 1918. Course of L.L.B. started in Law faculty was inaugurated in August 1923. Along with ideological studies, Malaviya also laid stress on the study of classical and modern languages.

> He promoted women education in 1929 in Banaras Hindu University, but he opposed coeducation and built separate women college and hostel facility. He would however be satisfied with teaching them similar subjects which were prescribed for men but wanted them to learn those fine arts, music and painting and also useful domestic art and science.[153]

In the women college with the starting of intermediate classes followed two years later by B.A. classes of the subjects like English, Sanskrit, Hindi, History, Economics, Domestic Science, Philosophy, Logic, Music and Painting were taught regularly. 25% girls students were donated scholarship by Birla family. Malaviya provided ample provision for the physical development of the students.

> He facilitates Akhara to wrestle, at the Nagva site students, plated Kabaddi which gives much exercise than cricket. Facilities of physical education training increased rapidly in the year 1929. The construction of Gymnasium was started in 1929. Wide place for play provided in front of each hostel. Malaviya appreciated inter hostel/inter faculty competition of play.[154]

Malaviya realized that it was highly desirable that students should have taken military training along with cultural, scientific and vocational training. He attempted for the formation of university training crops, in 1921 government sectioned it. After this he formed university training crops, but only two platoons were sectioned by the government. In 1924, he wrote to the government for military training facility to all university students who were interested in joining the university training crops. This reflects Malaviya nationalist sentiments.

153. *Ibid.*, p. 464.
154. *Ibid.*, p. 466.

> As he understood the key of Swaraj was the control over military.[155]

He wanted to start this training at the school age. By military training Malaviya wanted to train Indian people for the defense of the motherland. Therefore, from the above discussion it concluded that Malaviya as a pragmatic philosopher wanted to integrate the best of the Western education, i.e. science and technology in best Indian tradition and culture. But the core of curriculum approach was based on the ideals of *Sanatan* virtues. So, Malaviya through his curriculum scheme wanted to develop the sense of *sataymav jaytay and shramev jaytay* in the students. By former his intension is to enhance moral values but by later he wanted to upgrade importance of activity and work experience in educational process.

4.10 Malaviya and Teaching Methods

Although Malaviya's personality was multifaceted, but one thing is common in all his chosen multi occupations i.e. his elocution power which benefitted him in leadership, advocacy, teaching and journalism. He realized that the success of his life was depended on logical ability, reasoning and power of observation. Therefore, he hoped that teacher should adopt such teaching methods which help in development of the mental qualities of the learner. In relation to adopting teaching methods, his view were idealist and pragmatic both. He believed in the statement "*Shardavan labhatay gyanum*" so he emphasized on the development of the interest, will power in learner by using appropriate teaching methods. In order to make teaching more lively, appealing and interesting Malaviya focused on four techniques as question, illustration, dialogue and quotation, which was also reflected in his speeches. In his opinion the basic principle to teach any subject is that the motivation of the child should be awakened by making the subject matter more interesting. Malaviya considered science and religion parallel to each other, so he focused on both deductive and inductive methods to analyze any thought scientifically. So, he liked informal dialectic method, i.e. questioning and cross

155. Dar, S.L. and Somaskandan, S., *op. cit.*, p. 556.

questioning. His pragmatic sense was reflected as he paid attention for the construction of well-equipped laboratory and library. So, he did not like old, worn out traditional methods of teaching. He gave emphasis on laboratory work. He forced teacher to teach through learning by doing, experience and practical. He wanted theoretical conceptualization by practical. Malaviya gave importance to self-study methods, chanting of *Gayatri mantra* for the enhancement of right concentration and intellect. He wanted that teacher should stimulate the natural aptitude of the child and channelize them into useful work. For primary education Malaviya focused on reading method, repetition of sayings of teachers by citing his own example that he learned most of the *shlok* in his Sanskrit pathshala by recitation. At secondary level, he insisted the learner and teacher for vocational training in workshop and science practical for the understanding of concepts. For the post graduate students his view was different than undergraduate students. He wanted that P.G. students should be trained in hard intellectual endeavor. University should provide training and research opportunities to deserving students.

He was not, as such, against the use of English in teaching but he was aware about the potential of Indians, so at primary and secondary levels he emphasized that the use of foreign language on the budding children tantamount would destroy their developing personality. After British opposition he agreed for using English as a medium of instruction in the university. Malaviya knew that India was a vast country where different languages were spoken in far-off regions, each region has also a specific culture, ways and tradition but the main stem of what is called Indian culture is common to all of them. So, he said diversity of our language should not be allowed to frighten us and at the same time to accept any foreign language as a unity factor.

> It was Malaviya who did magnanimous task for the promotion of the Hindi language. He tried for the revival of Hindi and encouraged the production of Hindi books. He presented data in front of the government as the number of pupil who read Hindi was six times

> more than that of the pupils who elected to read Urdu, so he requested government to adopt right policy for conducting the teaching in Hindi except to use Urdu for the teaching purpose in elementary school in North provinces.[156]

Malaviya also advocated the adverse effects of Persian script on education. In the course of which he blamed for the slow progress of primary education in the upper provinces due to lack of instruction in vernacular languages.

He claimed that the secret of the rapid progress of education in Bengal was use of Bengali for the education and court. Again he cited the example of Oudh and northwest provinces where primary education was given in Hindi but villagers felt much ignorance when they were not able to read a warrant and summon which were given in Persian language.[157] Thus, Malaviya favoured the use of Hindi not only because of interest of Hindu community, but on the basis of ratio of the population spoke Hindi and difficulty faced by them he favoured it.

Along with the formal classroom activity Malaviya preferred to non-formal activities executed by teachers. So mostly he preferred religious, vocational, ordinary social activities, and activities concerned with language and hygiene etc. in university.

Malaviya considered knowledge cannot be generated from outside, it is inner but he had faith on the better environment of educational institutes. He preferred that knowledge could be obtained through one's own senses, own understanding and by reasoning ability, so many times in university he motivated teachers to arrange group discussions on relevant topics. Like Plato he had a firmly believed that the progress of the country depends on the development of the youth. He agreed with the fact, visualized by Plato that it was the duty of state or nation to regulate education. Education for Plato means acquisition of virtues. Similar to him he also gave more importance to character formation and moral values. So, he focused on choosing the

---

156. Gajrani, S. and Ram, S., *Pandit Madan Mohan Malaviya in Political Philosophy,* New Delhi, 1922, p. 65.
157. Parmanand, *op. cit.*, p. 96.

teaching methods which motivate the desires, courage and wisdom in the learner.

4.11 Malaviya and Teacher

Malaviya considered teachers as role models for their students. He agreed by the fact that upbringing of child greatly depends on the teacher's personality. In most of his speeches he cited the examples of his own teachers who influenced him. As an idealist he advocated teachers as a man of character and integrity. He was himself an ideal example in front of the students. He considered teachers as an elderly person or superior who were followed by younger people. As Lord Krishna said in Gita Malaviya had faith in Indian tradition in which teacher was considered equal to God (Tridev). So, he wanted students to give proper respect to their teachers. He focused on qualities which were necessary for the teachers as strong character, lofty knowledge of his subject, sweet communication, high moral values, discipline, economic sense in spending time and caring like parents etc. He believed that no knowledge can be gained without teacher. A true teacher removes all the darkness i.e. ignorance. During his Vice-Chancellor ship he was fond of going round to see the teaching department's work, even took the liberty of entering in classroom when lectures were in progress and taking a seat in the rear. In some cases he did it to hear the lectures of Hindi, Sanskrit and English literature but in other case to make sure that teacher was up to mark or not. The total effect of this exercise was beneficial; it was a salutary check on drones and shirkers. Malaviya's first priority was teachers have deep knowledge of their subject and strong character. He also communicated to overseas for the availability of the best teacher at any cost and gave proper respect to them.

Teachers appointed by Malaviya were so qualityful that no one would be able to say whether they were selected by three face interview or by written test. Most of the teachers were selected on the basis of his own observation, his name and fame. In most of the cases, Malaviya appointed them by formal application. But he was keen to look the merit of the teacher before his appointment.

As Chandra Bali Tripathi illustrates how Malaviya put the interest of the university foremost in the choice of teachers for it. Tripathi was a son in law of the eminent Hindi scholar Ram Chandra Shukla an alumnus of the Banaras Hindu University. He wished that he was appointed as lecture in the Banaras Hindu University after M.A. Degree but Malaviya was unable to comply because of the fact that his masters degree was of the third class and the teacher with the same qualification had been lastly removed from the service.[158]

Teachers of Banaras Hindu University as C.V. Raman got Nobel Prize, many teachers as Dr. J.C. Bose, Dr. P.C. Roy, Prof. P. Geddes, Sir Prafulla Chandra Roy, Ram Chandra Shukla, Dr. A.B. Dhruv, Iswar Saran, Dr. S.S. Bhatnagar, Dr. S.S. Joshi and Dr. S. Radhakrishnan Vice-Chancellor of Banaras Hindu University were the search of Malaviya. Thus if these personalities were analyzed from quality point of view, it would be cleared automatically what Malaviya meant by a teacher.

Therefore, Malaviya hoped an impressive personality in the teacher. He wanted the residence of the teacher should be in the vicinity of the campus. Consequently, students are able to follow their ideal living style. Malaviya not only appointed the best teacher in university but he requested to stay and serve the Banaras Hindu University. "As, 'Bal Krishna Mishra a versatile scholar, versed alike in logic, Veda, Vyakaran, and literature, in which he was daily consulted by learned pundits of Kashi, got a higher paid appointment in another university then Malaviya successfully dissuaded him by saying' susansathan na parityajatam 'Don't leave a good place' if money was consideration what could he say, but his university afforded opportunities of acquiring and advancing learning which he would miss elsewhere. Many instances are recorded by teachers of how his affectionate treatment bound them, him and his university."[159]

---

158. *Court character and primary education into the north west provinces and oudh*, p. 16.
159. Chandra Bali Tripathi, *Mahamana Madan Mohan Malaviya*, p. 56.

He wanted teacher and student interact frequently, save and enhance prosperity of each other. In teacher he preferred leadership ability, initiative quality, devotion, and dedication, determination towards their profession, democratic, cooperative, positive attitude, honesty and truth. Malaviya wanted that teacher should be friend, guide and mentor of the learner and free from any biasness of cast, creed, and religion of the students. Malaviya considered teacher as a strong pole who made the nation and society. He understood him as a hero of young children who not only by delivering good lecture increases the knowledge of the students but by his ideal conduct, behavior, draws a permanent effect on the students.

4.12 Malaviya's View on Students

Malaviya visualized students in idealistic way. He focused on the development of high ideals among the children because with high ideals the chances misconduct is likely to be rare. He wanted all round development of the child by providing needful education and training. He considered child as citizen of the nation. So, he preferred for them military training as the part of education along with science, math, and high technological and physical education. Malaviya realized that parents and teacher were not only responsible factor for all round development of the child but it's the duty of government to provide best culture, educational environment and facility in the educational institutions. Thus many times in his speech he appealed to British Government for educational reforms. In relation to child conduct and life action, he wanted that students should follow code and conduct of Ancient time. Some time he cited the example of *Subhashitani* as

आलस्य कुतो विद्या विद्यस्य कुतो धनम्।
धनस्य कुतो मित्रम् मित्रस्य कुतो सुखम्।

How can a lazy person acquire knowledge?

Without knowledge how will one get wealth? Without wealth who will become friends? And without friends how will anyone become happy? So, he said to students to do labor concentrate on your studies and be aware about your physical strength.

He was anxious for the formation of hostels and providing residential accommodation to all enrolled students. The living room of the hostels was decently furnished and lighted with electricity although he was criticized by the Bhagvan Das and Gandhi for the costly buildings. Malaviya never thought for kachha houses or muddy buildings in university campus. Formation of residential Banaras Hindu University and Hindu Boarding house were the result of his realization of residential problems of students.

Malaviya always cared for the poor students and said,

> Who knows there may be a Vyasa or Kalidas among them.[160]

He appreciated the moral stamina of the poor students. Sir Muthuswami Iyer, acting chief justice of the Madras High Court rose question to Malaviya related to his position and his poor condition of the family. He accepted that it was his poverty due to which he reached to the Vice-Chancellor position's and top leader.[161]

> When someone asked what happened when he was born in wealthy family then he answered that then I would not have been here.[162]

Many teachers and old boys of the university have paid great tribute to Malaviya due to his kindness for poor students. Malaviya as a vice chancellor provided free studentship in excess and during his time in department of theology, oriental learning and teacher training institute there was no fees charged by students. He also gave ad hoc remission of dues to the conditional students.

> He would recommend some of his friends for the payment of fees of needy students. When no other expedient was available, he would supply the rupees from his own purse.[163]

160. Parmanand, *op. cit.*, p. 476.
161. T. Pant, Malaviya Centenary Supplement, *Leader*, Dec. 1961.
162. Address to the BHU court, December 1921.
163. Parmanand, p. 486.

When Malaviya had no balance in his account, he asked his servant to get some money, but did not send empty handed to any student.

> Many students of depressed class as Girdhari Lal wrote about him that he went regularly to the Malaviya's residence to see him and get inspiration by him. He speaks Malaviya as the greatest man of his age. The tuition fees and hostel fees of harijan students were remitted and their other expenses also were found by Malaviya's. Another example as Sri Dharma Prakash, M.P. prominent Harijan leader testifies that Malaviya's financially assisted hundred of young Harijans to receive higher education and their life. Jagjivan Ram also acknowledges gratefully to Malaviya's kind support for his education.[164]

Therefore, it was found that in Malaviya's Saraswati temple there was no discrimination between the students of high and low cast and creed.

For the needy students, student aid library and self-help societies should be made at departmental level. Malaviya like naturalist philosopher did not consider that child is free from evil, at that time when he will not come in the contact with community customs. It is society and bad atmosphere which corrupted the natural goodness of the child. Child has its own natural disposition. Malaviya worried very much in case of illness of students. He immediately summoned the doctors and homeopathic Vaidya both. Malaviya took accountability of any mistake done by the Banaras Hindu University Students.

> He himself apologized for such mistake as it was narrated by Tripathi in case of Harihar BaBa.[165]

Similarly in case of boatman Ganga Putra, when he came to abuse Banaras Hindu University's students in residence of Malaviya, then he came out and touched his feet and asked him to forgive his students for such incident and said,

---

164. *Ibid.*, p. 488.
165. Tripathi, p. 208.

I shall have your boat mended.[166]

During two decades of his vice-chancellorship he easily controlled students' unrest due to his technique of gentle persuasion. Malaviya told students "Forget the world altogether or lay it wholly aside when engaged in study" along with this he always narrated a slogan "Drink milk, take exercise, repeat God name every day; concentrate on your studies and your desires are sure to be fulfilled." Therefore, Malaviya exhorted students to build up the physical health and strength. Malaviya, on numerous occasions of student gathering, addressed on the importance of Physical strength. As cited in *Subhashitani* shlok

व्यायामात् लभ्यते स्वास्थ्यं दीर्घायुष्यं बलं सुखम्।
आरोग्यं परमं भाग्यं स्वास्थ्यं सर्वार्थसाधनम्।

संस्कृत सुभाषितानि-05

One gets health, strength, long life and happiness by (body) exercise. Good health is the greatest blessing, health is means of everything. In university, Malaviya provides ample provision which facilitated students for physical fitness.

He would admonish any student who appeared before him unshaved, or with uncombed hair and carelessly buttoned shirt, unpolished shoes and would tell him that this was not the Aryan style. He wanted students to be worthy Aryans: to be honest and straight forward, to lead clean life of high purpose and continence, to be helpful to all living creature, not human being alone to serve the poor and the afflicted, to speak no ill of any body and to be loyal to their work and motherland. Malaviya prominently disliked misbehaves of the boys with girls and punished them. When a professor arranged a function in which a dance performance was given by a women's college student, he issued strict orders prohibiting women students' participation in the programme. Malaviya never appreciated students' participation in politics which disturbed their minds, even his own son revolted against him during non-cooperation movement. Malaviya always gave oath to the Banaras Hindu University students to follow Brahmcharya principle in student's life and look girls of younger age as sister and elder as mother.

166. *Ibid.*

He always addressed ladies as daughters. By providing examples of Lakshman, Meghnath, etc. in religious discourses he tried to create atmosphere of code and conduct in the minds of students. In *Dikshant* speech he gave oath to the students

> Speak truth, behave as Dharma dictates (Dharmacharan), and do not miss swaadhyay (Literally, swadhyay means self-study). After paying Gurudakshina (fees) to the Guru (teacher), do not stop family propagation.

Therefore from his early career to end his life he served the students and dedicated to provide them facilitation to go forward. Malaviya realized student centered education will solve only the immediate problem. But the real problem begins when one enters in life and faces the world. So in such situations it matters little, how someone behave in school days but matters more how one behave afterwards. So, it is essential to keep the students in touch of reality of the world and their minds ready to face the situation. In his view such thoughts can only be generated by religious education, which socially and morally justified the needs of life.

4.13 On Student-Teacher Relationship

Malaviya was very much influenced by the teacher-taught relationship of ancient education system. As in ancient time at the time of orientation the Upanishadic Guru and Shishya prayed to God.

> सह नाववतु सहनौ भुनत्तु सह वीर्यं करवाव है।
> तेजस्विनावधीतमस्तु मा विद्विषाव है। शान्तिः शान्तिः शान्तिः।।

"May we both be protected equally well. May our learning be equally fruitful for both of us? May we both remain competent and vigorous. May the knowledge acquired by us illumine our lives. May there be no hostility between us" (*Yajur Veda*/*Kathopanishad*). Malaviya dreamt of the same relationship between student and teacher as discussed in above *shlok*. Thus, he established a residential university where teacher considered as mentor or guardian of the students. He motivated teachers to consider their students as their family members and sons and daughters.

Malaviya frequently visited to hostels and interacted with the students about their problems and studies and advised right solutions. As cited by S.S. Joshi (Alumnus of BHU) in his article, Malaviya's relation with students was like father, friend, and counsellor in Banaras Hindu University. His door was freely opened to all and vast gathering of the students was addressed by Malaviya. Students were influenced by his such attitude and valuable advices. Malaviya always inspired the students to give proper respect to their teachers as discussed in Upanishad

> Knowledge (is acquired) by serving the teacher, or by a lot of money or by (exchange of) knowledge. A fourth (path) is not available. Again the relationship between teacher and student expressed in following words as just as a person gets water after digging earth with a spade, so a student who serves his guru gets knowledge. Thus, Malaviya considered teacher as first and last friend for students to guide them with light of knowledge.[167]

4.14 Malaviya's View on Discipline and Educational Administration

Malaviya practiced discipline during his studies and religious discourses since his childhood. His primary education was done in Sanskrit Pathshala where Pt. Hardeo Guruji laid emphasis on the preaching of Sanskrit *shlok* and disciplinary action. So during his early life, Malaviya was grown up in an orthodox family and Pathshala, but later on he was admitted in the European disciplined school, where he felt difficulty to mange between orthodox religious and social prejudices and European disciplines. Malaviya was much disciplined in his orthodox practices, so he would not drink the water provided at school and he had to come home to quench thirst. Thus, this dedication and self-controlling power of Malaviya presented him as a self-disciplined personality. Another action of his life, as not taking food before the achievement of targeted collection during collection of funds for Banaras Hindu University, chanting of *Gayatri mantra*, all exhibited his firm determination for actions and goals. His dressing sense, his turban, scarf, etc. expressed

167. Amba Dutta Bhatt, Sahityacharya in Jhalkian, p. 107.

his disciplined lifestyle. Thus, Malaviya was a person motivated by internal environment.

Although most of the time Malaviya did not reach the station at the time of arrival of the train and caught train in running way but it was not due to his insincerity but because of his busyness. Any philosopher's thoughts were based on his own life's action so before discussing his views on discipline, some examples of his life are needed to be cited. Malaviya did not agree to provide limited freedom to students. He liked disciplined student but criticized to impose disciplinarian strategy from outside by punishment etc. He liked to grow discipline in students from inner side or self-control. He disliked to create fear of discipline in the child's mind but many times by providing freedom to students he inspired inner voice or conscience. So, Malaviya did not believe that discipline meant external compulsion. In his opinion true discipline comes from within. So, he told students to balance between external and internal environment. A proper balance between mind, body and soul is important for achieving success. Malaviya forgave the students of the Banaras Hindu University on any undisciplined issue but on issues related to the character, he did not tolerate. As for example when one of the students of the Banaras Hindu University had thrown a flower at the group of the girl students at a university function, Malaviya peremptorily ordered,

> Stand out or you are a coward.

The young man stood up; he confessed his guilt and apologized.[168] Another incident, when he came to know that a dancing women had been invited by inmates to give a performance in the hostels, he pounced on the organizer and stopped the entertainment.[169] Thus for him the real discipline means to discharge unpleasant duties and obligation and not only performing acts of choice. From the social point of view he suggested students to perform the duties which are not harmful and according to social code and conduct. He said *atamvat sarvebhutahshu* which meant "Regard every one as testimony

168. *Malaviya addressed in court* in December 1929.
169. Awasthi, Girja Shanker, Jhalkian, p. 102.

of God." So in Malaviya's view the problem of indiscipline and maladjustment was growing due to authoritarian discipline strategy. He agreed with the fact that authoritarian approach of discipline, unable to touch the inner core of life, breeds obstinacy, impudence, antagonism and fear. In such manner morality justified by force. So those who trained under this system will not enjoy freedom or peace. They will try to escape from it. So in his opinion the formation of habits from childhood may be the most suitable method for developing desirable behavior. As Malaviya from childhood practiced orthodox *Sanatan* living style, so whole of his life his habit help him to select right choice spontaneously and he was not confused.

Malaviya denied to arrange All India Congress Session in Banaras, and also he has taken stand against Gandhi view for closing the university in support of non-cooperation movement. His such actions reflect that he did not like the political atmosphere and any nonsense in university. For the disciplined environment Malaviya had the best administration policy and provided better duties to the teacher for the management of the disciplinary action in the university.

> Under the Banaras Hindu University act and statutes, discipline of students was a function of the senate (or academic council) and the executive council was barred from interfering in it. The senate, a body of over sixty teacher members drew up a set of rules of conduct for resident as well as non-resident students, by which a fine of four annas per day was imposed for absence from classes without leave: a metal badge with the name of the university engraved on it was to be worn by every student for the purpose of identification when moving out of doors. Rules of conduct for students residing in hostels were displayed in the premises but are stated not to have been enforced with any degree of strictness.[170]

The duty of enforcing the rules was laid on the provosts and wardens of the hostels and loges and in the case of day scholars on the secretary of the city student's supervisory committee.

170. Parmanand, *op. cit.*, p. 498.

Discipline in the college and classroom was to be enforced by the principal of the college concerned. The pro-vice-chancellor was the highest functionary in the disciplinary hierarchy but punishment exceeding a fine or expulsion from residential unit could be awarded by the vice-chancellor of the Banaras Hindu University.

> A proctorial system was inaugurated in November 1927 at the instance of Malaviya. Five senior teachers Prof. P.K. Dutt, N.P. Gandhi, T.N. Sen, R.S. Jain and Gurmukh Nihal Singh were appointed as Proctor each with three able bodied men, called Bull-Dogs to help in tackling rowdy delinquents. The weak point of this disciplinary arrangement was that the Vice-Chancellor in whom ultimate power vested had no time to perform it effectively.[171]

So Malaviya disciplinary action reflected from the administrative structure of the Banaras Hindu University during his vice-chancellorship. Malaviya wanted to promote patriotism, public spirit, citizenship, and disciplined corporate life in the university students. He wanted to attain discipline in the students by promoting the sense of responsibility among the students. In Malaviya's time

> No rules and regulation forcefully pushed but it was the spirit of obedience to the rules that played the most important part in the matter of discipline.[172]

Therefore in Banaras Hindu University, Malaviya, before the formation of rules of discipline, kept this ideal in the mind. Thus, Malaviya wanted self-discipline in the students. Through religious discourses he wished to generate humanistic discipline in the mind of the learner consequently the student's respect for all the individuals irrespective to the cast, creed and genders, colour, obtained and they never create any harm for the others. So the purpose of discipline according to Malaviya should not to make student submissive. It should be free from the punishment and forced rule. It should develop character; train their intelligence enable the students to deal good life

171. *Ibid.*
172. *Ibid.*, p. 503.

by developing sense of responsibility. Thus through discipline Malaviya aim was to equip children with all such qualities which are needed for the success of life because he knew all the achievement dependent on disciplined behavior.

4.15 Malaviya and his Views on the School Environment

Malaviya was criticized by Gandhi, Bhagvan Das, Annie Besant, etc. for spending high expenditure on the university buildings, not only during the formation of Banaras Hindu University but also at the time of formation of Hindu Boarding House. But Malaviya's conception about the school building, hostel, playgrounds, garden, library building, and about the architectural plan of the university was clear and not alter after any contradiction. In Malaviya's educational plan true picture of culture and tradition of the country may be seen. If the campus is looked, it will be realized what Malaviya wanted natural setting in the university along with well-equipped buildings. Broad roads, having big trees on both sides, sufficient space in classrooms, good sanitation and ventilation facility, adequate space in front of all hostels except playgrounds, calm places for yoga, special facility for swimming, exercise, gardening and beautification of the campus, enriched library, glorious Vishwanath temple all expressed Malaviya's vision about university/school environment and infrastructure.

The layout of Banaras Hindu University was made by the "Patrick Geddes, who learned more Hindu Shastra and fully united Eastern passivism and western activism in his own life and transferred it into the architectural plan of Banaras Hindu University."[173] Malaviya was influenced by *Sanatan Dharma* and ancient Gurukul system so he desired that

> The university students in morning to see the Ganga and performed Gayatri mantra as said in Rig Veda (iii.62.10).[174] "Let us obtain the adorable splendor of the sun; May he arouse our minds."

The holistic plan of Banaras Hindu University concluded mesocosmic reflection of several niches and layers of Hindu

173. Dar, S.L. and Somaskandan, S., *op. cit.*, p. 559.
174. *Ibid.*, p. 886.

cosmogony where lies the harmonious interdependency and interaction between Nature and man: Divinity and Humanity: a way which has been mentioned in the Rig Veda (ii.23.3). Therefore after properly analyzing his epitome, Banaras Hindu University, it was concluded that he recognized Gurukul system as the best system for Higher education and by blending the best of west he presented modern concept of Gurukul in the form of first residential university i.e. Banaras Hindu University. Various times in his speeches he coded his dream to provide food, residence, and valuable study material for about 10000 students in the university.

Malaviya's dedication about academic atmosphere of the university was reflected when he got worried about the establishment of the library. He said,

> I want 1000 students to sit together for the study in the library of the university, play together in the evening in the playground as dazzling stars in the sky.

In library a slogan was written over there "*Kavya shastravinoden kalo gachhati dhimtam*" means scholars should spend their time in study and gaining knowledge to express their vision. He wanted to develop such a culture in the university which could make people think that *Tapsawees* lived there.

For the academic enhancement he was not only ready to make building, laboratory, etc. but also worried for arranging the best needed equipment, he would visit science laboratories to see what work in progress and also interact to students for their needs and motivated them to speedy steps of research. It was his motivation to the students when Ganesh Prasad went over the Calcutta to join the professorship then Banaras Hindu University students were independently ready to run the mathematical society of the Banaras. Thus although Malaviya interested to make palatial building but he better understood that bricks and mortar do not make school and university, its university teaching staff, spirit, and devotion which make university system. He appreciated teachers who establish departmental Library, self-help society for the poor students. In University extra affection provided to deprived students it create such environment that people understood them as the representative of this great alma mater. Thus Malaviya regards School/University as the temple of Saraswati, goddess of Vidya, as on foundation stone it was written that

> May Saraswati, incarnate in the *shurti* (heart) of wisdom, ever bloom and shine with worship from her human children; may they ever assiduously imbibe the vital milk of knowledge flowing from her sweet breasts of science and philosophy; may all minds turn to acts of good alone; and may all hearts be filled with love of supreme.[175]

Thus for Malaviya any educational institute may become like a temple of goddess Saraswati.

Conclusion

Thus after analyzing the educational ideas of Malaviya it can be concluded that he was an eclectic Indian philosopher who had chosen and picked up valuable theories and principles from different schools of thoughts. Then he blended them together to meet all the requirements of education system and society. His eclectic behavior was somewhat inspired by "*Nabhagunjar*" philosophy. *Nabhagunjar* is an incognito, given shape by *Shri Krishna* to draw attention of the *Arjun,* who was engrossed in sharpening his arrow. It is peculiar type of animal which was a combination of the beautiful organs of various animals and birds. Thus, Eclecticism is found in his educational philosophy which was expressed from his idealistic, pragmatic and realistic approach in sociological, scientific and psychological prospective of education. His educational thoughts are a comprehensive mixture of intellect, vision and curiosity. So Malaviya's educational philosophy is comprised of the cumulative experiences of whole human race. He tried to prepare a perfect base for modern education by selecting the best aim, best curriculum and the best teaching method. He took great pain to remove crudeness and angularities of the educational system of that time.

175. *Ibid*., p. 887.

It was found that his educational ideas were not only enriched with the idea of higher education but also provided a real vision for primary and secondary education. Malaviya foresighted hundred years ago that why India alone was denied to the great advantages which were accrued from a system of free and compulsory elementary education,[176] which was implemented completely in 2009 by the *right to education act*, so it can be said that Malaviya was a keen visionary who realized the educational needs 100 years before we implemented them. His educational thoughts were interwoven with idealistic and pragmatic threads which took origin from the social welfare concept. It was found that as an experimentalist he experimented about the modern concept of *Gurukul* system by blending the best of modern western sciences and technology with Indian culture and tradition. He dreamt of an integrated curriculum so he introduced engineering, industrial agricultural and vocational studies in his scheme of education to fulfill the objective of preparing the students as self-reliant people. Malaviya's realistic attention is expressed by his scheme of curriculum that was urgently based on the economic and social needs of India. In relation to discipline it was found that the aim of Malaviya was to train students in the art of self-discipline. He believed that no worthwhile achievement could be made in life in absence of self-discipline. It is required for the achievement of knowledge, formation of good habits and development of scientific temperament of mind and is a quality of civilized people to save one's energy. On the contrary self-discipline is the utilization of energy for mastering the self to achieve higher output. Malaviya was against the use of punishment. The core concept of his whole educational philosophy was the preservation of *Sanatan Dharma* for future generations. Thus, accordingly, through integration of religious education in the form of non-formal Gita lectures and by formal classes in faculty of *Sanskrit Vidya Dharma Sansathan*, he tried to achieve his fundamental goal, i.e. upliftment of the Hindu scripture and uniting the disintegrated Hindu society.

---

176. *Ibid.*, p. 353.

His educational philosophy expressed him as Nationalist who wanted to develop patriotism in the youth. He also felt that without integration of religious education it might be impossible to generate nationalism and spiritualism in India. He realized the importance of ethical discipline as told in Ancient teachings. By education, Malaviya wanted to develop such social consciousness in an individual that one could understand another individual as needy as oneself is. So Malaviya, through educational imperatives, wanted to establish a society in which all enjoy happiness, all are the source of happiness to others, all see auspicious days and no one suffers any injury.[177] As before beginning of his speeches he coded

सर्वे भवन्तु सुखिनः सर्वे सन्तु निरामयः।
सर्वे भद्राणि पश्यन्तु मा कश्चिद् दुखः भाव भवेत्।।

Malaviya's educational ideas had some ideological difference from Gandhi's educational view. He had realized the needs of future India so he never denied the idea to adopt machines, technologies and industrial courses in higher education. He was worried to prepare skilled youth, who would be accountable to remove poverty from India. In his convocation address on 14th December 1929, he said,

> The responsibility to make the future of India lies largely upon you. I wish to play you an honorable part in producing natural confidence, harmony and goodwill among persons and parties, agreement among whom is essential, to establish self Government in India. Let us be determined to be just doing all and fear nothing. If you do this you will deserve well of the motherland.[178]

Thus Malaviya's educational thoughts were based on the concept of Nationalism, religion, science and technology.

Malaviya favoured social equality and equity in relation to education. He wanted to revive the old social stratification of society which prevented certain castes from getting educated. Malaviya wanted a functional division of Labour which could be

177. *Report of the presidential address xxiv Indian National Congress* (1909), the leader office Allahabad, p. 19.
178. Lahore, Dec. 1909; *The Leader*, office, Allahabad, p. 28.

fit according to abilities and aptitudes of individual irrespective of any particularistic norm. In relation to educational boundary, he had a broad mind because he was also communicated to international academicians for betterment of the university and requested to provide their valuable lectures to the students. So, it can be clearly expressed that Malaviya's educational ideas believed in the "*Vasudhaiv Kutumbkam*" which conceived a global social order where everybody interacted to each other with brotherhood, love and affection irrespective of their differentiation in socio-cultural backgrounds.

He was a rational idealist and at the same time he was also a pragmatic visionary; as it was reflected in his speeches and scheme of Banaras Hindu University. He was an outstanding and contemporary thinker and was familiar with the view that only by large scale production; the needs of the masses of Indians can be fulfilled. The realization, that the science and technology of the *sin-qua-non* for the national development, was firstly realized in India by him only. It is noteworthy to remark that he realized the needs and the problems of both domains, material as well as metaphysical.

5

An Evaluation of Madan Mohan Malaviya's Educational Philosophy in Contemporary Comparative Setting

5.1 Introduction

This chapter probes the link between different Indian educational philosophers' approaches in a comparative setting with Malaviya's educational views. Using comparative methodology, Malaviya's educational philosophy was compared with Tagore, Gandhi, and Sir Syed Ahmed Khan. Researcher tried to focus on the key thoughts of these contemporary visionaries, especially in relation to higher education. Tagore, Gandhi, Malaviya, and Sir Syed Ahmed Khan were products of the same Indian culture and tradition, but divergent views of these philosophers on the same problems of the country, might be because of their different upbringing, home environment, and working in different conditions. However, they were one from heart in terms of love for nation. Through critical analysis, researcher tried to look at the educational philosophy of these philosophers and compared them on several aspects, namely originality, principles, aims, medium of learning, way of distribution of knowledge, and harmonization of National views. The campaign launched by Malaviya, Dr. Annie Besant, Tagore, and Sir Syed brought about evolution and development of Banaras Hindu University, Shantiniketan, and Aligarh Muslim University, respectively, which is a saga of Romance and adventure. It seems that in 19th century India produced intellectual giants in every field which contributed to various facets of renaissance, viz. political, cultural, literary, and educational. The Indian University Act, 1904, permitting establishment of universities through private funding, was a challenge to the national genius of the country. It was the period when many charismatic personalities arose on the social political horizon of the country, excelling the different areas of life, not only made India politically independent and economically vibrant but also enhanced productivity, socially cohesiveness and unity.

5.2 Malaviya and Tagore

The two bright stars that dominated the educational and political firmament of the country with a strong touch of spirituality in the first half of the twentieth century were indeed Tagore and Malaviya, endearingly called by millions of people as Gurudev and Mahamana. Though they belong to different ideologies, but they had common fiber of love for ancient Indian culture. Both the visionary faced different controversies, problems but their common aspirations were aimed at one objective, i.e. freedom from political slavery, emancipation of masses through education and prosperity of the country through upliftment of the scientific literacy and technological advancement. Their thinking was traditional and indigenous. But they did not ignore the best treasures of the Western culture. Both wanted that the scientific and technological breeze from the West should flow freely towards India and for the same, country should keep the windows open.

Tagore was a prominent poet and profound thinker. He was born in the same year as Malaviya, in an aristocratic Brahmin family of zamindars in Calcutta on 7 May 1861. Like Malaviya's birthplace Prayag, Calcutta also played a pivotal role in Tagore's educational philosophy. As K.R. Kriplani remarks,

> If ever there was truth in the Bengalis boast that what Bengal thinks today, the rest of India think tomorrow.[1]

Although he was not educated from any university, he was a man of learning. He had his own original ideas about education, which led him to establish an educational institution named

1. Kriplani, K.R., *Gandhi, Tagore and Nehru*. Bombay: Hind Kitab Limited, 1947, p. 23.

Shantiniketan, with the intention of re-opening the channels of communication between the East and the West and blending humans in the indigenous ideals. He travelled extensively to different countries of the world and was a successful mediator between the Eastern and Western cultures. The profound social and cultural involvement of his family later played a strong role in the formulation of Tagore's educational priorities. His grandfather, Dwarkanath, was involved in supporting medical facilities, educational institutions, and the arts. He also fought for the religious and social reforms. Within the joint family, Tagore's thirteen brothers and sisters were mathematicians, journalists, novelists, musicians, and artists. His cousins, who shared the family mansion, were leaders in theatres, science, and art. Tagore was thus, born in a family where the atmosphere was charged with deep religious feelings but was free from adherence to forms and rituals.[2] Like him Malaviya's family background, which discussed in chapter second, also played a pivotal role in genesis of his educational thoughts.

5.2.1 *Inspiring Factors for Building of Banaras Hindu University and School of Shantiniketan*

Thoughts are mostly generated in crisis and sufferings. If both of the visionaries are observed one by one, it is detected that Malaviya's upbringing, his family background, his political activities, his faith in *Sanatan Dharma* were the accountable factors for the genesis of his education philosophy. It was recognized that Malaviya practically analyzed the need of the nation and observed the distressful conditions of Hindus and their religion. He realized that religion was being neglected everywhere. So he was worried to regain status of Hindu religion. Malaviya observed missionary activities were expanded in country everywhere. Propagation of the Christian faith was the primary aim of these institution as Dr. Duff put it:

> One great object was to convey, as largely as possible, a knowledge of our ordinary improved literature and science to the young person: but another, and a more

2. Salkar, K.R., *Rabindranath Tagore: His Impact on Indian Education*. New Delhi: Sterling Publisher, 1990, p. 4.

> vital object was to convey a thorough knowledge of Christianity with its evidences and doctrines. Our purpose was therefore to combine in close, inspirable and harmonious union, what has been called a useful secular with a decidedly religious education.[3]

Students of other faith coming to these institutions for acquisition of modern knowledge had to put up with compulsory religious instructions of Christianity. So the objective of Indian education system in British period was to diffuse improved arts, science, philosophy, and literature of Europe. Its primary aim was to prepare indigenous clerks to handle local administration and to prepare a class of persons, who act as interpreter between Britishers and millions of Indian people whom they govern. As Lord Macaulay said,

> We must do our best to form a class who are Indians in blood and color, but English in taste, in opinion, in morals and intellect.[4]

National universities Calcutta, Bombay and Madras were established in 1857. But the administration and policy of these universities were governed by only involvement of Britishers. Chancellors of these university were the Governors of the respective states and the Indians in senate and administration were in few numbers, as in Calcutta University out of 38 members six were Indians, in the Bombay University five Indians in a senate consisting of 29 members. In the Madras University, there were three Indians out of forty members. During 1857-82, although there were rapid growth in number of colleges and enrollment of students but English was the official language and medium of instructions and very little attention was paid towards Indians. In 1844, English was declared as a compulsory requirement to apply to government all civil services. Due to this Indian traditional education system gradually vanished due to the lack of governmental support. All these conditions of education alarmed Malaviya who began his social life in 1880

3. Dar, S.L. and Somaskandan, S., *History of the Banaras Hindu University*. Varanasi: Banaras Hindu University Press, 1966, p. 29.
4. *Ibid.*, p. 30.

by joining Prayag Hindu Samaj.[5] In politics, the incidents like birth of the Indian National Congress (1885) and All India Muslim Conference (1886) were knocking on Malaviya's mind to think what he would do for the nation and for his belonging community. After this, his much of the political activities pushed him to do task for the sake of the nation and Hindu religion. So Malaviya was critical to British philosophy of education in India. He clearly realized the aim and objective of British education was against the Indian interest. Along with this the upliftment of Muslims through educational activities also inspired him to do something same for Hindus. Consequently his conscious allowed him to shake hands with great Hindu emperors, and Annie Besant for completing the noble cause, i.e. upgrading Hindu Shastra and Hindus and Hindustan. Annie Besant also had the same idea. According to her,

> Development of the national spirit through an education founded on Indian ideals and enriched, not dominated by the thought and culture of the west.[6]

On the aspect of incorporation of science and technology, she was agreed that without it India could not attain prosperity. The same view was endorsed by Malaviya. So his idea of forming a university was supported by Annie Besant and Hindu emperors who aspired for the kind of education system from where they were educated, i.e. Gurukul system. While the idea was generated by a group of people but it was planned and nourished by Malaviya in future.

On the other hand, Shantiniketan was the experiment of the Tagore. Before beginning of his dream institution Tagore brought his family over to Shelaidah a village in his family estate and arranged private education there for his children. The dreams were made in Tagore's mind in 1898. His father Debendranath Tagore had felt the presence of God and divine exhilaration in this place after a long search of peace. Shantiniketan was the repose of his life and last pilgrimage of life's journey. In order to

5. Chaturvedi, S., *Madan Mohan Malaviya*. New Delhi: Publication division Ministry of Information and Broadcasting Government of India, 1984, p. 35.
6. Dar, S.L. and Somaskandan, S., *op. cit.*, p. 42.

give practical shape to his educational ideas Tagore established a school in his father's Ashram. Here, primarily a two-storied building existed which was transformed in an educational institution in 1901. Tagore named it Shantiniketan—an abode of Peace. While starting this school he had in mind the forest hermitage of India. It was a Tapoban School.

> In Shantiniketan Tagore has sought to develop the idea of a house of peace, a boy's Republic, a school house without task master, to serve as a model to young India.[7]

Tagore wrote in his memoirs:

> At Shelaidah we lived entirely different life and determine we should not go through the grind of stereotyped school teaching prevails in our country.[8]

Thus, Tagore embarked his novel experiment in the field of education by bringing out an educational programme at Bolpur, about 100 miles from Calcutta, away from the din and noise of the city environment. Actually, Tagore institution arose

> Not out of any theory of education but he says, it is the memory of my school days. Therefore people naturally thought that as a school it might not be one of the best kind; but it was sure to be something outrageously new, being the product of daring experience.[9]

In the genesis of Shantiniketan, he wrote,

> Education divorced from Nature has brought untold harm to young children. The sense of isolation that is generated through such separation has caused great evil to mankind. This misfortune has beset the world since a long time ago. That is why this institution came to be founded.[10]

---

7. Rhys, E., *Rabindranath Tagore—A Biographical Study*. New York: MacMillan Publisher, 1916, p. 107.
8. Salkar, K.R., *Rabindranath Tagore: His Impact on Indian Education*. New Delhi: Sterling Publisher, 1990, p. 81.
9. Salkar, K.R., Educational Concepts in the Thinking of Rabindranath Tagore, M.Ed. Dissertation (unpublished), 1968.
10. Sahu, B., *The New Educational Philosophy*. New Delhi: Sarup & Sons, 2002, p. 200.

Tagore idea of Shantiniketan was supported by many foreigners such as Leonard Elmhirst, whose name is almost synonymous with Shantiniketan and who was a co-sharer of Tagore's ideology of rural reconstruction, was the most dynamic personality involved in fulfilling the many dreams of Tagore. His deep ideals motivated him to do such noble task reflect in his saying

> We went a place where the beauty of Nature and the noblest pursuits of man are in a pleasant harmon.[11]

In his own words, he admired it as

> It seems that the subconscious remembrance of some primeval dwelling—place where in our ancestors minds were figured and voiced the mysteries of the inarticulate rocks, the rushing water and the dark whispers of the forest, was constantly stirring my blood with its call. Some shadow-hunted living reminiscence in me seemed to ache for the prenatal or cradle and playground it once shared with the primal life in the illimitable magic of land, water and air.[12]

Therefore, unpleasant experiences of his school days, deep love for children and desire that children's might feel as happy as possible and train them to use gifts of their mind, body, and spirit. His interests to provide freedom, life inspiring, life-centered and natural education, Upanishadic ideas, Ashramas, Gurukul ideals, simple living and high thinking, love of mother tongue, music, culture and poetic sense, etc. appealed him very much. Consequently, Tagore became inspired to open school at Bolpur which became known as Shantiniketan and in 1921 it was recognized as Viswa Bharati.

5.2.2 *Approaches of Malaviya and Tagore*

Tagore was a leading Indian thinker, a prominent figure due to his poetic brilliance. He was the first non-westerner to be honored by Nobel Prize in 1913 for his English version

---

11. Ernest Rhys, *Rabindranath Tagore—A Biographical Study*. New York: MacMillan & Co. Publisher, 1915, p. 134.
12. A Poet School—Rabindranath Tagore, Bulletin No. 9, Viswa Bharati, July 1946, p. 5.

literature *Gitanjali*. He was recognized as international face while Malaviya was basically a philosopher of Hindu *Sanatan Dharma* who had nationalist approach. National service was the prime goal of Malaviya, it was evident from his multifaceted personality when he was a teacher in government high school, he left it. Likewise, when he was in a top editorship, left it, at prime of his legal practice at the district court of Allahabad, he left advocacy and lastly when he was recognized as well-known politician in Indian National Congress, he took interest in university establishment. So Malaviya, while seeking the kind of service wanted to perform for the sake of nation and his search ended with the establishment of Banaras Hindu University. After analyzing all the event of Malaviya's life it can be said about him that wealth and luxury were not important for him. He was always fond of working for service of mother land. Malaviya was the champion of truth. His thoughts and actions spoke for themselves in this regard. Malaviya enriched in economic crisis, nourished by very rich *sanskar* of Hindu *Sanatan* rituals.

On one side where Malaviya took active part in Congress sessions from 1886 to 1938. Almost in all sessions his image emerged as thinker and unflagging fighter for politico-intellectual and cultural emancipation. He used all energy for the sake of nation as selfless personality who never believed in recognition. Tagore had not taken keen interest in politics as his taste was much poetic and so literary. Tagore belonged to rich status family and nurtured in servocracy (servant parenting). He visited England at the age of seventeen as this was aristocratic tradition in those days of rich families. He came back in 1880 after one and half year without any university degree. Tagore's family was recognized as amongst the leaders of Calcutta's new aristocracy also one of the pioneers of Western education and Western way of life in India. Tagore has many Western friends like Sir W. Rothenstein, an artist, judicious critic and writer who was responsible to introduce him to W.B. Yeats and to other literary giants of England. He visited abroad 17 times spanning five continents. On 24 May 1912, he met William Rothenstien over dinner and expressed his views as

> The mansoon clouds generate in the bank of the Nile, fertilize the far distant shores of the Ganga, ideas may have to cross from the east to the western shores to find welcome in men's heart and fulfill their promise. East is East, West is West. God forbid that it should be otherwise—but the main twain must meet in amity, peace and understanding, their meeting will be more fruitful because of their differences.[13]

Tagore's exclamation after getting Nobel award was

> I shall never have peace again. The bird in the nest had found his sky.[14]

These statements expressed Tagore's inclination towards internationalism.

In 1916, he wrote from America,

> The school at Shantiniketan must find a center of humanistic culture for all the races of the world.[15]

During post-1919 period, Tagore toured England and America, continued tour to Switzerland, Germany, Copenhagen, and Sweden which brought him success in terms of fame and money for fulfilling his educational ideals. Therefore, it can be concluded that Tagore was influenced by the Western culture while Malaviya's exposure to the Western countries was less compared to Tagore and his deep faith of *Sanatan Dharma* motivated him to study the best of Indian thoughts. Malaviya's significant place in Indian politics never allowed him to think beyond the nation. His eloquent speeches on Sanskrit, Hindi, and English, moderate personality, progressive, and modern thoughts had respectful place in Indian politics and in the heart of Indian people. His dream to "shape Indians by Indians for Indians" made him the dearest face of India. His negotiating tendency, logics, suggestions further influenced Britishers.

---

13. Salkar, K.R., *Rabindranath Tagore: His Impact on Indian Education*. New Delhi: Sterling Publisher, 1990, p. 8.
14. Ghose, S., *Rabindranath Tagore*. Delhi: Sahitya Academy, 1986, p. 34.
15. Mukherji, P., *Life of Tagore*. Translated by Sisirkumar Ghose, New Delhi: Indira Book, 1975, p. 15.

Malaviya reviewed imperial policies in a constructive manner and presented a correct nationalistic perspective as an active member of various committees. During his long political career, his influence never waned. So the soul of Malaviya worked as tolerant and liberal Hindu who worked for nation.

Malaviya as an eclectic philosopher welcomed only the best of Western science and technology for economic enhancement but did not like the incorporation of Western culture. While Tagore not only liked the scientific ideas of Western countries but tried to integrate Western culture also. The vision of Visva Bharati was two folded as Tagore wanted it to become a guiding center of Indian studies and at the same time a focal point of Asian studies. He was interested in Asian studies because it was the aim of Tagore to strengthen the Asian unity. Tagore's aim was to make Visva Bharati as a cultural center where scholars from all over the world would gather to study the world culture. He was influenced by the dazzling progress of mind and matter achieved by the soviet society. Being as an experimentalist he said

> The Russian experiment has provided me with much food for thought. Sound education may automatically solve many problems of human society. He compared the situations with Indian context, In Russia wherever I look I see no one else but workers. Only a decade ago, the masses in Russia were literate, helpless and hungry as our own masses; equally blindly religious, equally stupidly superstitious...who could be more astonished than an unfortunate Indian like me to see that how in these few years they had removed the mountains of ignorance and helplessness, it is due to the education system.[16]

Thus, Tagore's visits of Russia, Peru, Japan and other Western countries in early and later ages influenced his educational scheme and approach. Therefore, it is concluded that Tagore believed in ideals of universal culture. It maybe

16. Sinha, S., *Social Thinking of Rabindranath Tagore*. Bombay: Asia Publishing House, 1962, p. 17.

the outcome of his extensive travels to different countries of the world and his wide outlook on life. Tagore considered the coordination of all cultural resources was necessary for the perfection of mental life. Thus, he noticed good points in his own culture but never denounced others. In his educational approach he focused on judicious synthesis of contributions of Eastern and Western cultures and wanted to develop the beautiful conglomerate of the world culture. Malaviya's socio-economic, political and educational ideas hovered around a central theme *Sanatan*, i.e. everlasting, unchangeable, ever fresh, perennial truth. In metaphysical tradition, philosophers believed on some eternity. Malaviya also belonged to this group of *traditional philosophers*. He was in favour of cultivating virtues rather than adopting values.

Tagore's pattern of education reflected independence, perfection, and universality. When dark clouds of the second world war were hovering over the horizon. Tagore was distressed and said

> I do not wish to open the papers, or listen to radio. The endless history of tyranny is unbearable.... I have lost all desire to live any longer.[17]

These words of Tagore reflected him as a person who understood whole world as two hemisphere of the brain of mankind. If one is paralyzed, the whole body degenerates. So he had universal brotherhood feeling. In his poetic approach

> He thought poet should not borrow his medium ready-made from shop of orthodox respectability. He should have his own seeds and prepare his own soil.[18]

He recognized the greatness of all religions and emphasized the need of comparative study of all religions. Thus, rather than belonging to an orthodox religious philosopher he was humanist. As he said,

---

17. Salkar, K.R., *op. cit.*, p. 13.
18. Tagore, R., *My Reminiscences*, New York: MacMillan Company, 1917, p. 9.

> Reality is human and Truth is human. Human being is true over and above all and of all His manifestations men is incomparable.[19]

Thus, Tagore was a *humanist and a universalist in his approach* and his love for nature, poetic sense and his family background was accountable for his *naturalistic approach*.

Therefore, Malaviya and Tagore although faced same politico-socio-economic situation in country, but their different upbringing, thinking way, belief system forced them to apply different approach to solve the problems of country and their own. Consequently, their approaches developed but each of them seeker to make his educational system on the vehicle of his philosophy of life. The one thing is common in both the visionaries approach is they tried to fulfill the promise of preservation of Ancient culture Malaviya love of *Sanatan Dharma* were akin to, almost identical with Tagore's message of love and universal brotherhood, but still they were marked off as two distinct attitudes towards life. Thus, it is clear that the educational systems they envisaged are thoroughly imbued with their respective life philosophies and through their creative activity they expressed themselves. Therefore, Malaviya's political business and Tagore's poetic interest directed them to behave as nationalist and internationalist respectively. Consequently, their approach towards education, culture, nation, and religion, were somewhat different to each other.

5.2.3 *Malaviya and Tagore on Religion, Morality and Spirituality*

Malaviya was the follower of the *Sanatan Dharma*. He understood *Dharma* is not merely a set of belief but set of principles of healthy and beneficial life. Therefore, he suggested people to know those principles and act like a true Aryan (or follower of *Vaidika Dharma*. Malaviya meant by *Sanatan Dharma* as the religion of perfect knowledge, eternity, and endlessness. Yet he believed *Sanatan Dharma* is based on six philosophies, but it was governed by one idea and leading to

19. Lectures and addresses—Rabindranath Tagore (selected by Anthony X. Soars), MacMillan & Co., Ltd., Landon, 1950, p. 21.

one goal. According to him, it is the *Dharma* which makes us realize the unity of all the knowledge, makes no distinction between science, philosophy, and religion. He said that all are alike and based on the Veda. The science were the Vedangas, and the philosophies were Vedopangas, remaining other limbs of the Veda culminating in the Vedanta. Finally, all summed up together as the knowledge of alone that is supreme and invisible. He believed in one only without second. Malaviya was the follower of *Gita* and *Upanishad*, so he believed in the *Gita* saying which manifested human being right is to work only, but never with its fruits; do not let the fruits of action be the purpose of one's action.[20]

He said when a man understands this law, he can watch over his desires, and do not allow them to attach themselves towards fruits of action. He believed in the thought that nothing can be sprout forward without sowing a seed. Likewise no one can obtain happiness without having accomplished acts capable of leading to happiness. So he concluded if a man spreads happiness around him, he will reap happiness, if he spreads misery, he will reap misery and thus after knowing this law, one can prepare herself/himself for favorable or unfavorable circumstances. So for Malaviya religion is the way of living and supreme goal of life.

While Tagore considered

> Religion as religion of men and advocated that God manifests Himself in men in the sense through human activity that he realizes in the universe.[21]

In Tagore view, religion includes sense of humanity. It is the spiritual truth. Spirituality is the core of religion. Religion for Tagore is not Asceticism. Tagore asserted that institutional religion was false and dogmatic. So his conception of religion is the essence of human beings. In his view, even an atheist can be a spiritual person. So he focused on two aspect, i.e. humanization of God and divinization of human beings.[22]

20. *Gita*, Ch. 2, verse 47.
21. Salkar, K.R., *op. cit.*, p. 38.
22. Joyti, I.T., Rabindranath Tagore's vision of religion retrieved at 1.30. am from snphilosophers2005.tripod.com /jyoti 2005. at 14/05/2014.

Tagore and Malaviya both were same on the point, i.e. possibility of human beings to be united with God. Both agreed on the fact that reason and logic are insufficient to reach the God. So Malaviya was considered as an orthodox *Sanatani* while Tagore, sometimes, seemed to be more Christian than the Christian as cited by Dr. Aronson in his book, *Rabindranath Through Western Eyes*. As Tagore says,

> Nobody has exalted man more in every sphere than Jesus.[23]

One thing observed in Tagore's religious view that he was attracted to Christian theism it is because it confirms the ideas which he had already absorbed from the Upanishads. So if Malaviya was considered as an oriental philosopher then Tagore belonged to oriental occidentals in his religious approach.

Malaviya and Tagore's approaches were different on incorporation of religion in education. Malaviya laid emphasis on the need of religious education in universities and schools respectively. He appreciated a number of denominational institutions which had been steadily growing as temple of religious education like Muhammadan Anglo-Oriental College at Aligarh and many other colleges and schools such as Dayanand Anglo Vedic College, Hewett Kshatriya High School at Banaras, etc. Because he thought that a system of education which makes no provision for religious teaching is essentially imperfect and incomplete.[24] His first and foremost desire was that the culture and religion should not be divorced. Malaviya's approach to integrate religion in education was neither narrow nor sectarian but much broad. As by this way he wanted to promote peace on earth and good will among humans, and leading mankind into the path of righteousness. Malaviya did not like

> The resolution of education that took place in 1904, i.e. extension of the education upon European principles. He said these institutions provided education but beyond this we regarded something as advantageous education

23. Salkar, K.R., *op. cit.*, p. 8.
24. Chitkara, M.G., *Rashtriya Swayamsevak Sangh: National Upsurge*, New Delhi: APH Publication, 2004, p. 133.

> which awaken thoughts and formed characters of youth.[25]

This could be only possible by integration of religion in education. He said

> Every Nation cherishes its own religion. The Hindus were no exception to the rule. On the contrary, probably no other people on the earth are more deeply attached to their religion than the Hindus themselves. If they were asked what blessings they did not enjoy under British rule, they would probably unhesitatingly name religious freedom. Again he logically defended for religious education by citing example of America and England that followed church/missionary affiliated education. If it was essential to make suitable provision for satisfying the religion requirement of that countries, it would also be essential for Indian education system.[26]

So he recognized that mode of providing religious education was not dangerous one. But he followed the freedom of attending religious lectures. By integration of religion in education he wanted to create a personality which reflected truthfulness, fortitude, self-help, self-respect, self-control and unselfish love for the nation. Malaviya hoped that the academic content should provide a right balance between the material life and spiritual life. So he emphasized on the need of religious education along with all modern subjects, which also seen in one of the objectives of Banaras Hindu University.

For moral progress he wanted teachers and students should get trained about religion and rituals. He believed if no provision is made for providing education of religion then we will generate ill-educated and incomplete men even if they have degrees. While Tagore thought religion could never be taught as a set of lessons. He believed that a person, who makes it profession to teach about God and Goodness to others, merely confuses and does not guide the aspirants of truth. Religion to

25. Dar, S.L. and Somaskandan, S., *History of the Banaras Hindu University*. Varanasi: Banaras Hindu University Press, 1966, p. 32.
26. *Ibid*., p. 145.

him is thus to be lived not taught.[27] Tagore was strongly against the idea of imparting moral instruction by teachers in schools. For him it is pure wastage of time and efforts as he said:

> It is as religion futile as it is disagreeable and I cannot think of anything that does more harm for the society.[28]

While Tagore's had firm conviction about religion that

> It is not a fractional thing that can be doled out in fixed weekly or daily measures as one among the various subjects in the school syllabus. It is the truth of our complete being, the consciousness of our personal relationship with the infinite. It is the true center of gravity of our life. This can be attain during our childhood by daily living in place where the truth of the spiritual world is not obscured by a crowed of necessities assuming artificial importance, where life is simple, surrounded by fullness of leisure, by ample space and pure air and profound peace of Nature and where men live with a perfect faith in the eternal life before them.[29]

Thus, Tagore by providing education in the lap of Nature, beneath the shade of overhanging trees and under the open sky, at the festival of complete moon and through the music of rains wanted to develop unison with God's marvelous creation and men.[30] Therefore, through the idea of forest school he desired to develop the spirituality in the students.

The preference of place for the establishment of their respective universities are also reflected their approaches. Malaviya selected Kashi which was regarded as representing city of the Aryans and known as city of religion and knowledge in India. This city showed rich association with Hindu's faith and culture, and so was eminently fitted to attract the Hindu

27. Salkar, K.R., *Rabindranath Tagore: His Impact on Education*. New Delhi: Sterling Publication, 1990, p. 38.
28. *Ibid.*
29. Rabindranath Tagore—My School, Viswa Bharati, Pamphlet No. 1, p. 7.
30. Mani, R.S., *Educational Ideas & Ideals of Gandhi and Tagore*. New Delhi: New Book Society of India, 1964, p. 189.

world for achieving salvation at the end of life. In this city Lord Buddha directed his wondering steps and he stayed for years to preach his new message to mankind. Great Shankaracharya the founder of the Advaita philosophy also came here to preach his doctrines. Through centuries of political disturbance and against the onslaught of rival faiths, Kashi had ever maintained its position as the citadel of the Hindu faith and the torch of Hindu learning and Hindu culture. So Malaviya chose this place and expressed,

> When such University was fully developed, it would become a shrine of learning, both oriental and western, to which students from all parts of the Hindu world will be attracted for the purpose of education in the same way as the Ganga attracts pilgrims from all over India.[31]

While Tagore was selected the place Bolpur in West Bengal totally in natural surroundings not inspired by any religious motive, although this place was not famous for any kind of religious doctrines, but this place exhibited sight of forest or *Tapovana* where life of the students were lived in its full natural school rooms, underneath the shadowy trees and in the thatched mud cottages outwardly the sign of poverty but inwardly, some of the highest flights of human thoughts which mankind had ever attained, were reached—the ideal of Brahmachari Ashram.[32] So Tagore believed in a universal religion aiming the unification of the mankind. At Shantiniketan no religion was taught or practiced. Here the idea of universal religion was propagated. At Shantiniketan no actual stress on moral and religious education was given, since Tagore believed that these two cannot be a part of the school syllabus but the whole Shantiniketan curriculum was so devised that one could imbibe these values naturally in an atmosphere of freedom and social environment.[33]

Malaviya said:

---

31. Dar, S.L. and Somaskandan, S., *History of the Banaras Hindu University*. Varanasi: Banaras Hindu University Press, 1966, p. 131.
32. Kriplani, K.R., *Gandhi, Tagore and Nehru*, Bombay, Hinds Kitab Ltd., 1947.
33. Salkar, K.R., *Rabindranath Tagore: His Impact on Education*. New Delhi: Sterling Publication, 1990, p. 39.

> A Teaching University would but half perform its function if it does not seek to develop the heart power of its scholars with the same solicitude with which it would develop the brain power.[34]

This statement reflected that Malaviya gave importance to affective domain of the students. His vision is not only to train the youth in professional degrees but to make them a citizen who has high moral character. Malaviya stated that such character can only be built upon the solid foundation of religion. Malaviya's thoughts were forcing him to experiment on the issue, i.e. character formation. He said,

> How to train character to create moral ideals, and to give to them a vital compelling force in the creation of the character and to conduct daily life without basing them on religious section. He accepted the fact that without the dominating and ennobling influence of religion, character lacks its best protection and support, and is more likely to be shaken by difficulties and to succumb to temptation than it would be, if the roots of its strength lay deep in the immutable principles taught by religion.[35]

Malaviya visualized that moral progress is necessary than material progress of the nation. He said:

> Mere industrial development cannot ensure happiness and prosperity to any people; nor can it raise them in the scale of nations. Moral upliftment was necessary because this quality prevails and endures only those amongst who are upright in their dealings, strict in faith, and loyal for the truth. And such men can be generally met with in society only when the society is under the abiding influence of a great religion acting as a living force.[36]

34. Dar, S.L. and Somaskandan, S., *op. cit.*, p. 136.
35. *Ibid.*, p. 137.
36. Salkar, K.R., *op. cit.*, p. 37.

While in Tagore's opinion religious education was not the teaching of some rules of morality and dogmas. Writing on religious education in the year 1912 he pointed out that

> The best way to achieve this could be through the unity of life and sensitivity then by the rule of sanctified dogma.[37]

In his own school, he felt that student could enjoy and realize their reunion of delight in the midst of nature. In his opinion religious feeling is not external imposition but an internal development and it definitely leads you to sublimity of thoughts. Tagore's ideas on religious education are based on the educational program in which he laid emphasis upon the harmony between nature and men. They are derived from consciousness of the unity that underlies in all beings. He regarded that human personality flourishes by spiritual development rather than artificial dogmas and rules.

Therefore, ideas of Malaviya and Tagore about religion and its integration were much different from each other. One wanted religious instruction widely by study of scriptures of Veda, Gita and Upanishad while other wanted to develop religious faith, love to all creature by study of Nature and by realization of internal soul. Malaviya's concept of religion regarded the best way to make an individual personality more sound was integration of religion in education, it acted as safeguard for Indian culture, tradition, and religion, i.e. visualized in Banaras Hindu University. While Tagore's concept acted as ideal of one world it regarded as mean for unity of the entire human or his concept clears religion of man. It was based on monism. He was a universal man who stood for one world, one order, one religion and unity of cultures. This was reflected in his dream epitome, i.e. Visva-Bharati. Tagore was impressed by Rousseau, Russell, Montessori, Froebel, John Dewey, etc. so he incorporated their ideas also with his innovation in Shantiniketan. Like Frobel he took education to a metaphysical level. He stressed the idea of unity in diversity; in his sense whole universe is viewed as a single great organization in which an eternal uniformity expresses

37. *Ibid.*, p. 38.

itself. This principle of uniformity expresses itself as much in external nature as in spirit. So his vision was to unite Man, Nature, and God, developing faith in universal religion aiming at the unification of the mankind. Therefore, both Malaviya and Tagore believed in Humanism and love of Universe, but the manner to express their love is different. Malaviya by preaching Vedas, Upanishad, etc. wanted to disperse the feelings of Vasudhaiva Kutumbakam while Tagore by uniting diversity of Nature and unity of God in all creatures wanted to unite Man, Nature, and God.

5.2.4 *Views of Malaviya and Tagore on Science and Religion*

The scientific discoveries have challenged the authority of religion; the method of science is observational, empirical, inductive, rational, and experimental. Science relies only on evidence and nothing else. Religion believes in the testimony of the prophets and saints and on the authority of the scriptures. Rationality and experimentation have no place in the religion. Scientific method is objective but religion enforced on subjective revelation. Science stands for the freedom of thoughts, religion on the contrary leads to the mental slavery. Science promotes the spirit of enquiry; religion leads to the blind acceptance of dogma. In his views, the scientist and the religious person have different attitude. But on this aspect Malaviya's and Tagore's view were differed. Malaviya considered science and religion were not antagonistic to each other but they are parallel. He wanted to create lawful balance between religion and science. He cited many examples of religious rituals which have scientific logic. He wanted a wide diffusion of science in India as a means of rescuing the people from the abject poverty into which they have fallen, which is not possible until science, both practical and theoretical, can be learnt by Indians in their own country and vernaculars.[38] So Malaviya came to the conclusion that in order to revitalize India it was necessary to feed her youth with the old spiritual and moral food and enriched with science and technology of the West. Consequently in Banaras Hindu University Malaviya proposed all science branches as agriculture

38. Dar, S.L. and Somaskandan, S., *op. cit.*, p. 118.

science, physics, chemistry, mining, metallurgy, Ayurveda, along with this Sanskrit, philosophy, Veda studies.

He said,

> No enlighten Hindu can fail to be removed by a reflection on the achievements of his ancestors in the field of religion, philosophy and science; nor can blind to know the features of the new cycle in which Human destiny now revolves amidst influence of the western civilization. So While his patriotism fixes his eyes on the rapid changes taking place in the world, his national bias attaches him to the rich legacy he has inherited, which he values and cherishes all the more as it is threatened to be absorbed by the commercial spirit of Europe.[39]

So his goal was to modernize Hindus, in the best of Western culture with learning of religion and tradition of his Nation. While Tagore admired religion would hardly serve any useful purpose in education. In his opinion scientific spirit and religious creed were two different things. He agreed with the fact that scientific theories are tentative it can be testified and modified if there were sufficient reasons. But religious principles are not open for the verification, rationality, and explanations.

5.2.5 *Views of Malaviya and Tagore on Medium of Instruction*

When Malaviya developed his educational idea for university he desired Sanskrit to be used as a medium of instruction for those who wished to qualify themselves as the teachers of religion and for the highest degree of medicine. Rest of the instructions will be imparted through the medium of the Indian vernaculars. But after realizing practical problems in implementation of educational plan Malaviya gave revised scheme. He felt that this could not be possible in science because of absence of suitable textbook in the vernaculars. Malaviya recognized that the adoption of one vernacular as the medium of instruction would raise several difficulties to draw its alumni from all parts of India. Thus, Malaviya considered that it would be wise to avoid this difficulty in the beginning of the university. Malaviya was also pressurized by the Britishers to

39. *Ibid.*, p. 237.

impart instruction in English Language. So Malaviya negotiated his vision of instruction in vernacular language and agreed that instruction shall be imparted through the medium of English. But he was agreed by the fact that as the vernaculars are gradually developed, it will be the power of the university to allow any one or more of them to be used vernaculars as the medium of instruction in subject and courses in which they may consider it practicable and useful to do so.

While Tagore's view was somewhat different. He was in favor of providing education through mother tongue not only at school but even at the higher level of education also. As Tagore said,

> I know what the counter argument will be, 'You want to give higher education through Indian language, but where are the textbooks?' I am aware that there are none. But unless the higher education is given in our own languages, how are textbook to come into existence.[40]

He beautifully described the effects when learning is not through the mother tongue.

> Learning should as far as possible follow the process of eating when the taste begins from the fiber bite, the stomach is awakened to its function before it is loaded, so that its digestive juices get full play. Nothing like this happens, however, when the Bengali boy is taught in English. While one is choking and spluttering over the spelling and grammar, the inside remains starved, and when at length the taste is felt, the appetite has vanished.[41]

Thus, in respect to elementary education Tagore believed no elementary education could be said to be creative unless it was given to the child in his or her mother tongue. Tagore in article "Siksher-Her-Pher" ("Confusion in Education") points out the folly of imparting education through an alien language

40. Salkar, K.R., *Rabindranath Tagore: His Impact on Education*. New Delhi: Sterling Publication, 1990, p. 70.
41. *Ibid.*, p. 65.

and how inadequate such an education is. By citing example of *Encyclopedia Britannica* he commented

> Too much of the students time and energy was absorbed in the effort to master a foreign language, i.e. English. Only lip service paid by this popular education system. And after a century of British rule India remained a predominantly illiterate country.[42]

He said

> Education in English language may be compared to rainfall in a spot that is a long way from our roots. Not enough moisture seeps through the intervening barrier of the earth to quench our thrust.[43]

So it reflected that Tagore realized by such education system education becomes limited to small privileged group of societies. He says,

> If I want my son to grow into a man, I should see that he grows up like a man right from his childhood. Otherwise he would always remain a child. He should be told not to rely entirely on memory, be given planet of opportunity to think for him and use of imagination. This cannot be achieved by reading book in foreign language.[44]

Thus, even though Tagore liked western culture, English and English people but he loved Indian children and realized their problem in understanding English language.

5.2.6 *Malaviya and Tagore on Model of Education*

Tagore's model of education reflected his poetic sense in which freedom, love of art, culture, and music were the master keys. Shantiniketan really reveals cosmopolitan outlook of Tagore. As an experimentalist he never thought that his institute would fulfill all his dreams. He was impressed by Soviet education model, and their revolutionary ideas. He saw that Russian had made and said:

42. *Ibid.*, p. 67.
43. *Ibid.*
44. *Ibid.*, p. 70.

> A module system of education in which character, cast never endure.[45]

He also did not prefer the standardization of children's mind and repulsive uniformity in their thinking, in relation to religion. It was his desire that children should be allowed to live a life of their own amidst extreme freedom and develop a verity of interest to participate in activities which could stimulate their faculties and strengthen their own self into complete person. While Malaviya's model of education supplies trained Indians, capable of carrying out scientific research and taking art as leaders not merely as laborers in industrial and commercial enterprise. His model of education was based on *Sanatan Dharma* faith, science, and culture of India.

Tagore viewed

> Education as a vehicle for appreciating the richest aspects of other cultures, while maintaining one's own cultural specificity.[46]

For Tagore education is the process of development of whole man, not merely the intellectual development of the individual. Tagore advocated wholeness of the life and education. He states,

> Education is a permanent part of the adventure of life. It is not like a painful, hospital treatment for curing them of the congenital malady of their ignorance, but is a function of the health, the natural expression of their minds vitality.[47]

According to Tagore, education leads to freedom from ignorance which is one of the root causes of our poverty. His belief is that if education is life in itself, it cannot be divorced from the economic life of the people. Tagore fulfilled this aim in the institution by rural upliftment objective. In Shantiniketan, there was crafts leading centers where different activities were introduced for the earning purposes. His educational philosophy was based on the three principles: Freedom and joy for the child;

45. *Ibid.*, p. 39.
46. *Ibid.*, p. 41.
47. *Ibid.*, p. 21.

creative self-expression and active communion with man and nature. Tagore admits that an education,

> Divorced from the streams of life and confined within the four walls of the classroom becomes artificial and loses its value.[48]

Tagore's aim of education was comprehensive. Tagore beautifully describes

> We adorned the cage but the parrot lay starving.

Because aim of education was to develop intellectual side much and to some extent the physical aspects of child's personality. It merely touched the external dimension of persona, ignoring the fact that child had a soul, inner urge and full of potentials.[49]

Tagore by education wanted to cultivate the power of acquiring ideas through independent efforts and ability to learn directly from nature and life. He told that the storage of knowledge gained from the books was not as important as the ability to use what is learnt. He wanted to develop constant curiosity and alertness in mind of children. Malaviya also wanted such education which made self-reliant citizen accordingly in his educational scheme he provided all facility and training.

5.2.7 *View on Nationalism*

Tagore realized that nationalism by itself was not adequate for a world unified by modern science and technology. Nationalism for Tagore did not mean enhancement of our nation at the cost of the others, by exploiting it through all ignoble means. He proclaimed,

> The interdependence of people and countries rather than independence must be the principle for life and progress, today and tomorrow.[50]

While for Malaviya Hindu/Indus Valley Civilization was considered as Indian Nation. His roots were firmly attached

48. Taneja, V.R., *Educational Thought and Practice*. New Delhi: Sterling Publishers, 1983, p. 15.
49. Salkar, K.R., *op. cit.*, p. 19.
50. *Ibid.*, p. 87.

with Indian culture and civilization, so for him India, Indian, and Indianization were the prime objectives. Although he did not deny the amalgamation of his thoughts with Western culture and he said that problem is not only to wipe away differences, but also know how to unite while keeping the differences intact a difficult task. Malaviya wanted sure guarantee on issue of communal unity, Malaviya visualized that single way to win freedom was inter-communal unity. So he wanted Indian to make such a law and constitution that no body may be afraid of anyone else in the country in whatever circumstances are there. He thought strength of each community is important for the overall growth of the nation, as the growth and strength of each limb of the body is important for a good healthy body. So he preferred the schools and colleges run on the basis of community and religious faith. His originality lies in the fact that he preferred the best of all thinking, and never favored a rigid secretion view of life. He never opposed any idea only because it came from some other culture or country, but he preferred to choose the best out of everything.

Thus, it concluded that both were a silent educationist who did their duty towards country in a dignified and humble way without expecting name and fame in reverse. Both of the visionaries believed that the lack of education and ignorance is the root cause of the poverty, so both were devoted to spread education as national mass movement. Tagore was not socialist, nor had he any love for communism. But he was understood the feeling of Malaviya and respect his ideas. He said about Banaras Hindu University that it is the example of real Hindu.

5.3 Malaviya and Gandhi

5.3.1 *Comparison between Malaviya and Gandhi on Political and Educational Issues (Journey after 1915 till Malaviya's Death)*

Gandhi and Malaviya were primarily known as politician, statesman, and social reformer in Indian History. Both of visionaries' life and career were so rich that volumes required for comparing their philosophies. One is known as Bapu, Mahatma and other is called as Mahamana or *Devata Purush* due to their sacrifices for the country. Both had similarity in their views on same interest issues such as removal of untouchability, national language, provincial language, use of Swadeshi goods (as Khaddar hand-made cloth), development of indigenous industries, communal unity, struggle for peasantry, economic equality, education of health and hygiene, labor, women, political freedom from British slavery by non-violence way, practice of truth in life, Gita, love of nation, etc. But they were differed on some issues of education.

Gandhi's upbringing was quite different than Malaviya. Malaviya faced poor circumstances in family and his whole education was completed in poor condition by paying fee barely in Indian schools. He did not take any degree from abroad, but Gandhi belonged to upper middle class and took education of barrister ship in England. He spent 20 years in South Africa (Durban), where he saw a series of insulting events of disgracing Indians which awakened Gandhi's political feelings. He founded there the Natal Indian Congress in 1894. In 1903, he shifted to Transvaal and acquired educational experiences in the Tolstoy farm. His philosophy of education took shape here. In 1904, Gandhi started the phoenix settlement in South Africa which proved a symbol of an ideal school-cum-workshop where the students not only gained the literary training but also took practical training on agriculture and printing.[51]

In January 1915, Gandhi when returned to India he first met first to Tagore, Malaviya and Gopal Krishna Gokhale whom he considered his political Guru. On the advice of Andrew, he settled his phoenix party at Shantiniketan Ashram of Tagore where phoenix boys and Shantiniketan boys learned with one another and introduced reforms. On May 25, 1915 at Kochrab Ahmedabad, a Satyagraha Ashrama (Sabarmati Ashram) was formed by Gandhi, where he tried to experiment his views on education which he learned from Tolstoy Farm. Here he was called Bapu by students.[52] In this Ashram, pupils were trained in physical labour, using Swadeshi goods, truth, non-violence,

51. Mani, R.S., *Educational Ideas and Ideals of Gandhi and Tagore*. New Delhi: New Book Society of India, 1986, p. 38.
52. *Ibid*., p. 73.

non-stealing, sanitary services, spinning, agriculture, dairy, tannery, and national education. In April 1937, Gandhi founded the Sewagram Ashram at Wardha. He generated the idea of basic education.[53] So his educational ideas was influenced by the phoenix experiment of South Africa and his dissatisfaction with the prevailing system of education.

Malaviya was eight years elder than Mahatma Gandhi. Gandhi was much influenced by his experiences, lifestyle, knowledge of Hindu *Sanatan Dharma*, and zeal to attain freedom. He said for him,

> I do not consider anybody greater patriot than Malaviyaji. There is no one in sight amongst all living Indians who has rendered more services of India than him.[54]

Mahatma Gandhi considered him as a *Devata Purush* and elder brother. Malaviya started his political carrier in 1886 earlier than Gandhi in India but Gandhi begun his movement in South Africa before India. He had his own experiences of Africa of foundation of the Natal Indian Congress (1894)[55] and movements which he launched in Africa.

Both were worked together in many political movements for the same goal and with the same spirit, but on certain issues they were ant responsive to each other. As during the years 1920 and 1921 Gandhi led Non-Cooperation Movement with the objective of paralyzing government. He wanted to clear the way of *Swaraj* and avenging the Punjab along with Khilafat wrongs. Malaviya had the difference from him on Khilafat issues. Malaviya detected Khilafat as danger for Hinduism as already occurred in the previous years in India. He had reported a large scale of apostasy of Hinduism to Islam in the North-West Frontier Province[56] (letter from *Frontier* in Abhyudaya, February 2, 1920). It reflected that he was not against the Hindu-Muslim unity, but he was not the supporter of pen-

53. *Ibid.*
54. Tiwari, U.D., *A Short Biography Mahamana Malaviya*. Varanasi: Mahamana Malaviya Foundation, 2007, p. 55.
55. Mani, R.S., *op. cit.*, p. 54.
56. Abhyudaya, February 2, 1920.

Islamic movement. He observed that Khilafat movement was taken by Ali brother not as movement for the freedom but regarded as good fight for Islam[57] (*Leader*, 23 April 1921). On the other hand, Gandhi considered Non-Cooperation as the weapon for obtaining redress of the wrong that was being done in Turkey[58] (*Azad: India Wins Freedom*). After differences Gandhi was going to make an important pronouncement about his own position in politics. He said:

> If I am in minority, I may not pursue my policy in the name of the Congress.[59]

Nehru, Mrs. Besant, Tej Bahadur Sapru, Motilal, Malaviya, Tilak all were opposed this idea. Despite strenuous opposition, they approved the comprehensive programme of Non-Cooperation, comprising boycott of the legislative councils, the law courts, and the government added educational institutions, establishment of national schools and colleges.

Malaviya yet supported Gandhi during Non-Cooperation, and co-operated him, but on the task to boycott of the educational institution, he did not join his hands with Gandhi. When one audience told him why he did not strengthen Gandhi's hand by joining him, Malaviya's answer was,

> Gandhi is after all a man and I think he is mistaken. I follow my Conscience.[60]

Malaviya opposed Gandhi's view by delivering his speech. He said,

> Boycott of education was suicidal, and the funds which government maintained for some educational institute grant in aid to others were our own and it was unwise to deny ourselves services.[61]

57. *Leader*, 23 April 1921.
58. *Azad: India Wins Freedom,* p. 25.
59. Dar, S.L. and Somaskandan, S., *op. cit.*, p. 535.
60. Chaturvedi, S., p. 136.
61. Dar, S.L. and Somaskandan, S., *History of the Banaras Hindu University*. Varanasi: Banaras Hindu University Press, 1966, p. 562.

Malaviya proclaimed that the government control did not affect the university freedom in matters of academic, also did not hamper the aspiration of *Swaraj*. He declared

> To sacrifice a hundred Hindu University if they stood in the way of the country for attaining freedom. Malaviya alarmed Swaraj could not be won without education, education was impossible without aid. He appealed the students not to surrender their individual judgment and to remember that boycott of educational institutes would amount to intellectual suicide which was not the way of Swaraj.[62]

At the same time Gandhi addressed students in the Kashi Naresh Hall of the central Hindu college at Kamachha. He said:

> I never undertook anything without him. From the time I returned to the country it has been my intention to live my life with him. I wish to tell you that there is a great difference of opinion between me and my brother; but my fraternal regard for him is not the least affected by it. My prayer to you also is that even if you are of the same opinion as I; please do not allow your reverence for him to be lessened. I am sure whatever Malaviya ji is doing is because he considers it to be his duty.

In presidential remark Malaviya said

> I do not believe in keeping birds in cage. Malaviya told students for you it is yet time for study let not the fate of the immature Sanyasi befall you. It is our duty to establish self-government; it is to devote yourselves to study. Consult your parents if you consider it your duty to act against their wishes, touch their feet and go; but remember one who does not satisfy his parents and teachers can satisfy no body.[63]

Thus, though Gandhi and Malaviya were different to each other on Non-Cooperation issue. They acquired responsive cooperation in their opposition way. Even Malaviya opposed the students to participate in the politics but on the cause of

62. *Ibid*.
63. *Ibid*., p. 564.

social welfare, he always appreciated students to provide their services for poor and needy people as at the time of earthquake on 14 January 1934 in Northern India. He appealed for the relief funds and provided relief to victims in Banaras Hindu University in the form of free scholarship and fee.[64] After forty years, Malaviya was recognized by Shiv Prakash who became agreed with Malaviyan view and said:

> Right for the great leaders of that day to utilize students in their political agitation and interference with their studies and to disturb the even tenor of educational institution[65] (August 12, 1962 Shiv Prakash in the weekly of India). Gandhi also supported him in *Young India*.

Even Malaviya faced the opposition by Indians but he was not deterred by the Congress resolution, i.e. boycott of the visit of the Prince of Wales who was invited in Banaras Hindu University and Malaviya was conferring an honorary degree to him.[66] He accepted the membership of the committee set up by the government and opposed the motive of All India Congress Committee (July 1921) for boycotting the Prince visit. All these actions may be part of his strategy to save future of higher education in the country.

So Gandhi's action in relation to establishment of national universities, schools, colleges in country without help of British Government, reflects his willpower which allowed Indians to do this courageous task of Non-Cooperation in a peaceful manner. By this activity, Gandhi wanted to show the type of Indian education system and mode of instruction needed. As a Chancellor he inaugurated, Gujarat Vidyapith and opened the National College in Calcutta, Bihar Vidya Pith, and Kashi Vidya Pith at Banaras.[67] He tried to make attempts to run the Banaras and Aligarh Universities as national institution meant free from

---

64. Parmanand, *Madan Mohan Malaviya: An Historical Biography*. Varanasi: Malaviya Adhyan Sansthan, 1967, p. 911.
65. August 12, 1962 (Sri Prakash in the weekly of India).
66. *Aj*, August 1921.
67. Rawat, P.L., *History of Indian Education*. Agra: Ram Prasad and Sons, 1994, p. 225.

governmental control and run entirely without government grants. But when he was unsuccessful to attain this objective, his vision was visualized in the form of Kashi Vidya Pith and the Jamia Millia as alternatives.[68] Hindi was used as medium of instruction and any fund from British Government would not be received by this university Gandhi did not give more weight to higher education prospective then the need of freedom. His dream was to prepare youth first to fight against British domain by boycott the government at all places and effectively withdraw the Indian youth from all educational institutions which were governed by British Government. While Malaviya's view was different. He wanted to educate the youth of the country and made them eligible and skilled for acquiring the best post in civil services, military, etc. then to make them leaders to fight for freedom.

After the prince visit in Banaras Hindu University, Malaviya started herculean efforts to bring peace between Gandhi and government. On Gandhi's imprisonment Malaviya was considered as All-India leader. Sarala Devi Chaundhurani said:

> In my opinion Malaviya is the best fitted to lead the country after Gandhi.[69] (Jayakar, Vol. I, p. 500)

He undertook an extensive tour covering northern India from extreme West to the extreme East to restore the drooping morale of Congress workers. He followed the four main aims of Gandhi's programme as maintenance of peace, communal harmony, assimilation of six crore harijans and khaddar. During his tour, he delivered speech on communal harmony, participate in Shuddi movement and strengthen Hindus. When Muslim suggested to stoppage of Shuddi, Malaviya referred refuse and said if Muslims did not attack Hindus these would automatically cease. During this duration, he did much for the Sikhs also. In his address Malaviya had paid tribute to the Sikhs and their gurus and suggested that Hindus should celebrate anniversary of Sikh guru. Gandhi's opinion was different, he respected all communities and religion but he did not believe in the society based on communal differences. While Malaviya

68. *Ibid.*
69. Jayakar, Vol. I, p. 500.

tried to strengthen Hindus first, although he respected harmony between different communities.

Gandhi was interested to push Hindu-Muslim unity, Malaviya also wanted, but his action to establish Hindu Mahasabha, Mahabirdal, programme of Shuddi, statement and reaction on Hindu-Muslim riot, strengthen Sikhs, establishment of Hindu University, upliftment of harijan to prevent their conversion into other religion, Satyagraha for Ganga's bathing, establishing Hindu Society, speeches on *Sanatan Dharma* always motivated Muslim to consider him most communal. Sometimes on the name of Malaviya they started telling Gandhi as Ali brother said:

> If Malaviya all, that Bapu says where am I to place you (for Nehru).

In another letter he says:

> If Bapu believes in all that he says about Malaviya—and there can be little doubt of it—then I must despair in near future at any rate.[70]

Thus, Malaviya's figure was not like Gandhi in politics. Former was perceived by the people as communal leader while later was considered as a leader who always tried for Hindu-Muslim unity till his death.

When Gandhi visited Banaras Hindu University, he met Malaviya and shared his feeling to achieve the goal to promote Harijans. Both participated in *Mantra Diksha* on the bank of the Ganga and Hugli.[71] It reflected they had strong bonding of relationship to achieve the same goal. In the year of 1929, Malaviya toured to country for the removal of Untouchability.

In 1929, Gandhi and Malaviya were with each other for three months in England on the issue of demand of full independence in round table conference. Both delivered the same views on issue like demand of separate electorate almost in same temperament. But Malaviya was failed, when Ambedkar offered him to sip a water from the same glass of Ambedkar

70. Dar, S.L. and Somaskandan, S., *History of the Banaras Hindu University*. Varanasi: Banaras Hindu University Press, 1966, p. 654.
71. *Ibid*., p. 771.

to prove it that he did not regard Ambedkar as untouchable.[72] By this one example it could not be said that he did not regard untouchables but due to his orthodox habit formation he was not able to do this. Both said,

> We do not want to expel Englishmen from India but do not want them as Masters.[73]

Both opposed separate representation other than Muslims and Sikhs. Gandhi said to Birla to persuade Malaviya, to support him on the subject of Muslim representation but Malaviya was unhappy because of undue concession to the Muslims and thereby weaken the Sikhs and Hindus. Malaviya was always determined himself as individual personality as When King Geroge V asked him, as follower of Gandhi he told that he was a fellow worker, not a follower of Gandhi.[74] When Ambedkar started hard bargaining in conference going at Puna during communal award. Gandhi satisfied Ambedkar by saying not only 71 out of 148 seats reserved for Harijan by the separate electorates and rest was filled by the election of mixed electorates. Malaviya was the first signatory on this decision.[75]

For the sake of university discipline and education, Malaviya always negotiated his political interest as when A.I.C.C. held a session at Malaviya's residence in the campus of Banaras Hindu University in Feb. 1933, Malaviya opposed the proposal of holding the next session of the Congress at Banaras,

> On the ground that students of the Banaras Hindu University would attend it in large and damage the position of the University.[76]

Both were agreed to open temples for Harijan. Although there were some differences on the temple entry bill between Malaviya and Gandhi. But soon Malaviya repeatedly declared in his speeches that there was no section for Untouchability in

72. The water tumbler part of the story is not reported in the proceedings but appeared in the press, p. 815.
73. Parmanand, *Madan Mohan Malaviya: An Historical Biography*. Varanasi: Malaviya Adhyan Sansthan, 1967, p. 815.
74. *Ibid.*, p. 817.
75. *Ibid.*, p. 880.
76. *Ibid.*, p. 896.

Shastra and he supported the Hindu law to object the hostility to untouchables. Although Malaviya faced hostile reception by orthodox Hindus, encountered black flag, but he travelled widely to consult Hindu leader. Malaviya met Nehru and joined their hands on the constitutional advancement for untouchables.[77] So this effort showed how he regarded Gandhi's view heartedly for untouchables.

In 1934, opposite to Gandhi's wishes, the Nationalist Party was formed by Malaviya just like Swaraj Party. The objective of Nationalist Party was to fight against both communal award, and legislative interference in religious matters. Gandhi had no objection to Malaviya as Congressmen who were working for the same goal in different ways. But Malaviya was in dilemma that if he continued in Congress, he would lose their followers of *Sanatan Dharma* which was the main source of his strength; if he leaves Congress, he will be acknowledged as a rank communalist and lose Gandhi's esteem.[78]

During point to accept separate and joint electorates and seat reserved for minorities Jinnah was always aware of Malaviya's hold on the Hindus and was trying to establish similar hold himself on the Muslims. So he insisted Congress that Malaviya should be a party on this agreement. Malaviya opposed his view and preached the view that there should be no legislative interference in socio-religious matter. Malaviya and Jinnah both negotiated Gandhi for their purposes to satisfy their representative community goal, but their motives were different. Malaviya saw only Hindu people but Jinnah looked it in relation to Islam religion first then for the sake of Muslim community and lastly All India political party was established. But Jinnah did not agree to participate in All India political party. Jinnah published an article in the *Time and Tide*. He wrote

> Two thirds of its inhabitants professed Hinduism on one form or another as their religion, over 77 millions are followers of Islam, and the difference between the two is not only of religion in the stricter sense but also of

77. *Ibid.*
78. *Ibid.*, p. 927.

> law and culture. They may be said, indeed, to represent two distinct and separate civilizations. Hinduism is distinguished by the phenomenon of its caste, which is the basis of its religious and social system, and saves in very restricted field, remains unaffected by the contact with the philosophies of the West; the religion of Islam on the other hand based on the conception of equality of man.[79]

From this article the demand of two nations and the concept of Pakistan origin were recognized. Jinnah insists on division before freedom. But if critically evaluated Malaviya's view with Jinnah in political scenario, it concluded that Malaviya supported the welfare of Hindu, Hindi, and Hindustan. But his vision was not based on two nation theory. He told for the existence of two communities but never supported the partition of India. He always went in the conferences of communal unity, and expressed his views that communal unity was necessary for the purpose of freedom. He never told Gandhi against any Muslim leader. But time to time he appreciated them. But lastly the excessive concession that was proposed for Muslims could not but is abhorrent to the Hindu Mahasabha and to Malaviya.[80] So finally the future proposal depended either on acceptance of Pakistan or excessive concession to Muslims. Malaviya completely disagreed with this proposal. On the other hand, Jinnah said:

> We will fight for Pakistan and die for Pakistan.[81]

He again said that two months later

> We shall never accept any constitution on the basis of united India.[82]

But Malaviya never respond like that. So Gandhi and Malaviya views were same on partition issue of India.

---

79. *Ibid.*, p. 933.
80. *Ibid.*, p. 1055.
81. *Ibid.*, p. 1059.
82. *Ibid.*, also cited in Press Telegram, March 23, 1945.

During Crips Mission and Quit India (1942), Gandhi and Malaviya were again with each other. Malaviya declared his profound faith in Gandhi and said:

> If Gandhi is removed from our midst, our country and we shall perish.[83]

Malaviya personally did not like to approve some of the activity of Congress worker as wrecking of Railway trains, burning of post office, etc. He told to the students of Banaras Hindu University

> Avoid doing anything against Mahatma Gandhi's principles.[84]

Malaviya was loyal to Gandhi in Quit Movement. In 1943, Malaviya was too eager to get freedom. He made a fiery speech, asking the students to join the struggle for freedom. Malaviya said,

> What is the use of Studies when the country is in the clutches of slavery.[85]

In 1946, Malaviya made a journey to Delhi (April) to meet the British Cabinet Mission and to entreat Congress leaders not to agree with the partition of the country. Malaviya was too weak but his will did not allow him for rest. When Gandhi came to look after him before his visit to Shimla for cabinet mission in 1946, he said, by deep affection with him

> When you leave worrying.

Malaviya's reply was,

> When worry leaves me.

Gandhi says,

> Would you leave nothing for us to worry about? In that case I shall be younger still than I am. Leave all worries and transfer whatever burden you choose to me together with your power.

---

83. *Ibid.*, p. 1062.
84. *Ibid.*, p. 1043.
85. Dar, S.L. and Somaskandan, S., *History of the Banaras Hindu University*. Varanasi: Banaras Hindu University Press, 1966, p. 713.

Malaviya said that there is no power greater than *Nama Japa* (repetition of God's name).

Gandhi says,

> How can I attain the knowledge you derived from the Bhagvata and Mahabharata?

Malaviya said:

> The name of Ram is the essence of all Knowledge.[86]

So Gandhi always took spiritual strength from him.

In October 1946, when five thousand death and fifteen thousand causalities were done in Calcutta and Noakhali district of West Bengal. Mass killing of Hindus suffered Malaviya. He continued to issue message and exhorted people to organize them for the defense of the *Dharma*. On 11 November, Malaviya went in comma and peacefully breathed his last at 4.30 p.m. on Tuesday November 12, Margashirsh Krishna.[87] Gandhi was away touring the interior of the Noakhali district. He sent a long message in the form of his tribute which reflects how much he respected him:

> "Malaviya is immortal. Like the King of England whose death is proclaimed by the formula, the King is dead; long live the King", "It may be said of Malaviyaji from death has kindly delivered from physical pain, Malaviya the adored of Bharatversa is dead, long live Malaviya".

His unremitting toil from early youth to ripe old age has made him immortal.

> His internal life exemplified purity; his life was as clean as it was simple. He was a repository of kindness and gentleness. He had a marvellous memory. His knowledge of scripture was very great. A spirit of accommodation was part of his nature; at times it took the forms of weakness; only he was a powerful man and Gita says, no fault accrues to the mighty.

His multifarious activities were a necessary result of his being singled out for selfless service.

86. Gopal Das Nager in Jalkian, pp. 28-29.
87. Parmanand, *op. cit.*, p. 1071.

> His politics must leave alone. The Banaras Hindu University, his greatest achievement, must be judged not by the number but by the quality of its pupils. Is every pupil a representative of pure undefiled religion? If it is not so, it is nothing. His devotees should make the University a living example of true Hinduism.[88]

Thus, this massage of Gandhi reflected his bonding and regard for Malaviya as he regarded himself as a *Pujari* (Devotee) of Malaviya.

5.3.2 *Basic Differences and Similarities in Educational Philosophy of Gandhi and Malaviya*

From the above discussion, it is cleared that both visionaries highly committed and associated to each other on issues of political movement along with social conception of the welfare of the society. Malaviya and Gandhi were having similar views on educational objectives, characteristics of teacher and students, but differed on curriculum, teaching method, and medium of instruction, etc. which are discussed as.

By Education Gandhi did not mean only the training of literacy but he wanted harmonious development of all four aspects of the Human personality—body, heart, mind and spirit.[89] He took education not in a parochial sense of a classroom process, but consider it in broad sense. He wanted to develop three H's of students at primary stage that is Heart, Hand, and Head. Gandhi's education philosophy was based on four aspects that is free and compulsory primary education, education should be craft-centred, education should be self-supporting and self-sufficient, and instructed through mother tongue. Gandhi gave more importance to power of self-actualization and morality than literacy. He said:

> My experience has proved to my satisfaction that literary training by itself adds not an inch of moral height and character building is independent of literary training. I am firmly of opinion that the government schools have

88. *Ibid.*, p. 1075.
89. Sahu, B., *The New Educational Philosophy*. New Delhi: Sarup and Sons, 2002, p. 13.

> unnamed us, rendered us helpless and God less. They have filled us with discontent, and providing no remedy for discontent, have made us despondent. They have made us what we are intended to become clerk and interpret. And if it was wrong to co-operate with the government in keeping us slaves, we were bound to begin with those institution in which our association appeared to be the most voluntary. The youth of the nation are its hope. I hold that as soon as we discovered that the system of the government was wholly, or mainly evil, it became sinful for us to associate our children with it.[90]

While for Malaviya, education of modern science and technology, knowledge of English, formal education were necessary to understand the policy of Britishers. Both views were same on providing universal primary education and vocational education but in respect to higher education Malaviya views were differed from Gandhi as he favored the idea of machine, technology, industrial and scientific development for making India economically independent country.

Gandhi laid emphasis, "On the experimentation in education. In *Young India* (30/09/1926), he wrote that

> The field of education which holds the seeds of the future of the children of the soil requires absolute sincerity, fearlessness in the pursuit of truth and the boldest experiments, provided always that they are sound and based upon deep thought matured and sanctified by a life of concentration.[91]

Malaviya also gave importance to experimentation as he tried to establish well-equipped laboratory in Banaras Hindu University for experimentation. Both were experimentalist in his educational scheme. Gandhi experimented basic education policy in relation to primary education and gave a detailed plan. While Malaviya experimented modern Gurukul system in the

90. *The Leader*, September 22, 1920.
91. *Young India*, 30/09/1926.

form of Banaras Hindu University for the expansion of higher education.

Gandhi had evolved a philosophy of paedocentric education. In his philosophy of education the personality of the educand is of greater significance than the tool and subjects. Gandhi launched basic education scheme in 1937.[92] Through this educational scheme, he laid emphasis on the education of children from 7 to 14 year. In this scheme, educational process begins with parents and community. In second stage pre-basic education provide to children less than seven years. The third stage is the eight year programme of basic education for boys and girls between 7 to 15 years. Fourth stage is post-basic education of the adolescents. While basic education may be described as education for self-sufficiency, post-basic education should be planned as education through self-sufficiency. He said educational community at this stage should be residential possibly taking the form of a school village. Mostly basic education of Gandhi recognized as education produced skilled craftsmen. But in this scheme academic subjects are also taught through the medium of craft. If both the visionary compared from the curriculum point of view it analyzed that Malaviya basically decided the scheme for higher education not basic and secondary education. He favoured integrated curriculum for higher education. At the primary level he agreed with the Gandhi concept.

Gandhi aimed simplicity and not merely confined to the expensive buildings for educational purpose. Although Malaviya regarded all traditional rules of ancient India, but on the issue of infrastructure or building of Banaras Hindu University, he never compromised and had modern touch, as he made well-planned building, nice room having electricity and all facilities for teachers and students, along with fully equipped department and laboratory. He was answered frankly when Gandhi criticized him for the establishment of expensive buildings during his visit in university.

Malaviya and Gandhi were identical on the fact that there should be a close relationship between education and the

92. Mani, R.S., *Educational Ideas and Ideals of Gandhi and Tagore*, New Delhi: New Book Society of India, 1986, p. 82.

economic life of the people. So both gave importance to that educational scheme which makes self-reliant society. As Gandhi in his educational scheme focused on craft-centred education and wrote in *Harijan* (31-7-1937):

> The method adopted in the institutions in India I do not call education, i.e., drawing out the best in man, but a debauchery of mind. It informs the mind anyhow, whereas the method of training the mind through village handicrafts from the very beginning as the central fact would promote the real, disciplined development of the mind resulting in conservation of the intellectual energy and indirectly also the spiritual. I would, therefore, want to begin the child's education by teaching it a useful handicraft and enabling it to produce from the moment it begins its training. I am not writing this without some confidence, because it has the backing of experience.[93]

Gandhi's concept of self-financing was based on the idea of introducing spinning in every school. He focused on the fact that pupil worked six hours per day in school, and teacher provided them free education. So his idea provide self-supporting service to the school and learner by literary training as well as manufacture skill on spinning wheel.[94] So by making education craft centered Gandhi wanted to make education self-supporting. Malaviya also adopted vocational education in the form of industrial training to make pupils self-reliant and independent. So both were agreed on the fact that the cost of education could be minimized by providing the advantages, valuable, and skill-based education.

The Gandhian concept of Khadi was appreciated by Malaviya in Banaras Hindu University but his idea of craft education was broad. He wanted to associate this education with engineering department as he said in his speech of Higher education

> I believe in higher craft related education in University, but for achieving this goal it is important to provide

93. *Harijan*, 31/07/1937.
94. *Young India*, 2/02/1921.

> appropriate electricity and high class instrument and training as Japan engineering education provided last six years and from last two year students did all works there on behavioral practical knowledge. This college was associated with public work experience all the trainees related to industry, craft, and engineering came to same college and after finishing their education. They started their own vocation. So no doubt in deficiency of craft education, weaving, spinning skill and vocational education India will not lead to the higher status.[95]

Malaviya aimed to integrate industrial education in India. He had partial dissent from the report of the industrial commission. He said,

> Ruin condition of Indian industry, Britishers' policies were accountable. He cited Weber, a historian of Sanskrit literature, in support of the claim that Indians attained high skill in textile manufacture and the historian Pliny to the effect that Indian manufactures were extensively imported into the western world and earned for India the vast sums of money of the high quality steel was abundant proof : about iron pillar of Delhi, erected in fourth century.[96]

He described how the Britishers decline Indian manufacturer as they taxing cotton manufacturer at the rate of high 80% added value while raw cotton generally taxed at much lower rates. He expressed the gradual export to Britain and the growth of trade in the reverse direction which resulted in the impoverishment of the country. Thus, Malaviya advocated provision of agricultural, mechanical, and commercial education at all the level from primary to higher education.[97]

Gandhi was the supporter of *integrated education* to promote all-round development of the pupil. He wanted intellectual education would include knowledge of mathematics and the various sciences, literature added for recreation, which

95. Parmanand, *Madan Mohan Malaviya: An Historical Biography*. Varanasi: Malaviya Adhyan Sansthan, 1967, p. 291.
96. *Ibid*.
97. *Ibid*., p. 292.

give balance in his personality and the education of spinning, carpentry, and agriculture given to relate their comprehensive theoretical knowledge to the daily life experience.

So Gandhi wanted all-round education in which intellect, body, and spirit develop together into a natural, harmonious whole.[98] Like him Malaviya by integration of religion wanted to train soul, by addition of physical exercise and labour trained the body. Through education of different subject as discussed in later chapter he wanted to train mind of the pupil. So both of the visionaries wanted proper coordination of the three, i.e. mind, body, and soul.

Gandhi and Malaviya were regarded character building as the prime aim of education. Literary education have no value to him if it does not build sound character. In his opinion, character alone will effect on the masses. Therefore, he wanted students prove their credentials. In his speech delivered at the Pachaiyappa's college, Madras, to the students, he said,

> When your heart is not pure and you cannot master your passions, you cease to be an educated man. You have called your institution a premier institution; I want you to live up to the name of the premier institution which must produce boys who will occupy the front rank in character. And what is education without character and what is character without elementary personal purity.[99]

Therefore, education for Gandhi has not value without personal purity. In his view, character cannot be built with mortar and stone and from the pages of books but it comes from within not from the outside. According to him, it comes by providing the education of heart which cannot be imparted through the books learning but it can be achieved by the living touch of the teacher. Therefore, Gandhi wanted teachers must be themselves the men of faith and character who have received the training of the heart. So in Gandhi's view the prime need of all the nation of the world is nothing else but character building.

98. *Harijan*, 8/05/1937, cited in Towards New Education by M.K. Gandhi edited by Bharatan Kumarappa (1953), p. 48.
99. Mani, R.S., *Educational Ideas and Ideals of Gandhi and Tagore*. New Delhi: New Book Society of India, p. 129.

Like Gandhi Malaviya regarded character as most essential thing for human being and he mentioned character building as one of prime objective of the University. For character building he preferred Gita lectures and religious education.

Malaviya and Gandhi were different in higher educational pursuits. As Gandhi does not favor state running universities and in his opinion the higher education should be left purely to private enterprise. So Gandhi view on higher education reflected that he wanted to give more power to the universities and he desired that universities should vest entirely in the hands of private individuals and not the state.

Malaviya opinion was government provides adequate finance to the universities and a national body established by government to maintain the policy of higher education which in future manifested in the form of UGC. Yet Malaviya vision for higher education was modern but Gandhi view was also not much traditional as he said

> Under my scheme of higher education there will be more better libraries, more better laboratories and more better research institute. Under it we should have an army of chemists, engineers, and other experts who will real servant of the nation and all these experts will speak, not a foreign language but the language of the people. The knowledge gained by them will be common property of the people. There will be truly original work instead of mere imitation.[100]

Gandhi wanted pupils to be initiative, they act for themselves and thoroughly obedient and self-disciplined. Freedom that comes from the discipline and humanity cannot be denied. Malaviya also liked well-disciplined student and provided them freedom but under control. In relation to teacher and textbook Gandhi came to the conclusion that,

> Books are required more for the teachers than for the taught. It is the duty of the teacher to do justice with the learner by preparing his daily lesson from the material

---

100. *Towards New Education*, M.K. Gandhi, Navjivan Publication, 1953, p. 77.

> available to him. I have claimed to originality for the views and as in India the primary aim of education was the character formation of the pupils, thus for a teacher it needed not to lose his character and values.[101]

Malaviya also wanted to see high moral character and deep knowledge of the subject in teachers.

Gandhi preferred the establishment of National School where he wanted to propagate charkha, educating untouchables, and abolishing the curse of untouchables from the schools, bringing of Hindus-Musalman closer together. Malaviya also favored for the establishment of National School and for the attainment of complete *Swaraj*, but he was different from the Gandhian view, i.e. no financial help should be taken by the government for the development of school and colleges. Because he thought that this money was not paid by the British country but this was the right of Indians. Gandhi wanted that in schools spinning should be associated with science education and mode of instruction must be vernacular not replaced by English education. He said,

> No country can become a nation by producing a race of imitator. I do believe Chaitanya, Kabir, Nanak, Guru Govind Singh, Shivaji, and Pratap as a greater men than Raja Ram Mohan Rai and Tilak. I know the comparison are odious. All are equally great in their own way. But judge by the results, the effect of Raja Ram Mohan Rai and Tilak on the masses is not so permanent or far reaching as that of the others more frequently born.[102]

Therefore in Gandhian view India became poor and less able to defend herself and her children have less stamina. It is because of English education.[103] Thus, Gandhi as pleads for the use of vernacular language for primary and secondary education also he make strong plea for the same medium in higher education. While Malaviya preferred the use of vernacular and English both as a medium of instruction for higher education.

101. *Harijan*, 1/12/1933.
102. *Young India*, 27/04/1921.
103. *Ibid.*, 27/04/1921.

Gandhi and Malaviya both favored science education but their understanding was somewhat different. As Gandhi regarded science as a spirit, attitude not as a source of happiness and prosperity while Malaviya consider it as an equipment to overcome from the poverty and economic enhancement. But both were same on the balance expansion of scientific inventions. Gandhi wanted Master of Science not but slave. He was against the haphazard development of science, unrelated to the social and economic structure of India. His aim was to bring down Science from the so-called mountain tops where it was monopolized by the few, in interest of the few and reduce it to the term of masses. As he said in his speech at science institute, Bangalore,

> I tell you, you can devise a far greater wireless instrument which does not require external research but internal—and all the research will be useless, if it cannot link your hearts with those of the masses.[104]

Thus, Gandhi believed in scientific humanism Malaviya also appreciated science and research for human welfare and for economic strength of the society.

Both were idealist as they were focused on need of religious education for each individual. Both were wanted every child to be familiar with fundamental tenets of all faiths and have tolerant attitude for other religion. For both religion was the way of life therefore true religion was not divorced from any aspect of life. Both stressing on the importance of atmosphere in education. Both were preferring the Ashram education in Indian context. Both were pragmatic in their educational approach as both gave emphasis to give knowledge and skills necessary to deal the life situations. Both scheme of education is purposive, experimental, and activity centred. Both were pragmatic as gave emphasis on learning by doing and distrust mere bookishness and believes that child learn more from activity.

Both wanted to emancipate women from the various kinds of bondages in which they have been kept and the injustices

104. Mani, R.S., *Educational Ideas and Ideals of Gandhi and Tagore*. New Delhi: New Book Society of India, p. 141.

from which they were suffering. Both were keenly realized the truth that man and woman have their distinct contribution to make humanity and therefore they have their specific capacities and abilities as well as specific spheres in which they can distinguish themselves well. It was their conviction that unless courses of instruction were based on a discriminating ability fullest life of men and women could not be developed. But both visionaries were agreed on the fact that certain common subject shared equally by both men and women. Malaviya was not agreeing to provide co-education while Gandhi had not given any ultimate views on co-education. Both were against the Macaulay's education which manufactured the clerks, not patriots who love their motherland.

Thus, if Malaviya's views are analyzed, it is inferred that he was a social reformer for the primary education but educational philosopher for higher education vice-versa Gandhi was as deep thinker or educational philosopher for the primary education who made experiment for school level, but social reformer for higher education induced many of the rich, educated people to open National Universities in India.

5.4 Malaviya and Sir Syed Ahamed Khan

Malaviya and Sir Syed were the visionaries for higher education who established Banaras Hindu University and Aligarh Muslim University for the uplift of the society in 1916 and 1877, as Mohammedan Oriental College, and Aligarh Muslim University in 1920 respectively. Both were same on the view, i.e. interest of their belonging community. But country was dearer to them rather anything else. Sir Syed was a Muslim reformer of the 19th century, who was only the one men who tried to aware the Muslim community and country, and took them forward on modern lines. His supreme interest was intellectual development of the people through modern education. He was the first Indian Muslim who contributed for the intellectual enhancement and for institutional foundation for Muslims in Southern Asia.

Before establishing universities both visionaries had long history of educational activities like formation of schools, both left the job to fulfill their vision. Sir Syed was born twenty-four years before Malaviya on 17 October 1817 and he was the eye witness of first Indian Mutiny.[105] He saw a reputed position of Muslims and also read Muslim states before arrival of Britishers in India. His family belonged to Mughal administration culture. With an interest to write the books he started his career as Urdu writer at the age of 23 with religious tracts. In 1857, he wrote noteworthy book, *Asarus Sanadid* (book that provide a wealth of information on countries historical monuments in Delhi during eight hundred years long Muslim era).[106] Even more important was his pamphlet: "The causes of Indian Revolt" (Asbab-e-Baghwat-e-Hind). In this booklet, he fearlessly laid bare the weakness and errors of the British administration. The revolt of 1857 was one of the turning points of Sir Syed's life and for his historical writing. He won fellowship of the Royal Asiatic Society of Great Britain and Ireland. This was widely read by the British officials and had considerable influence on British policy. The supreme interest of Sir Syed was education; he never paid attention to anything else except education. He was titled as Sir by the British Government.

He remained honest in all the 45 years of his government job and he is best known for correcting things that included wrong religion concepts and writing to minimize the hate between Englishmen and Muslims. In spite of all suffering, Sir Syed was highly impressed by the culture and customs of Western society. He instituted scientific society in 1864 to create scientific temperament among the Muslims and to make Western knowledge available to Indians in their own language. He translated scientific works from English to Urdu. Yet he faced strong opposition by traditional Muslims but he brought out his ideas by publishing journals *Aligarh Institute Gazette*, *Tehzeeb-ul-Akhlaq* which was rightly named in English as

105. Qadir, A., Good Subject Sir Syed Ahmad Khan English and the Punjab University *Pakistan Journal of History and Culture*, Vol. xxx, No. 2, 2009 available at http://www.Foxitsoftware.com 13 Nov. 2013.

106. Ali, F., et al., The Legacy of Sir Syed Ahmad Khan in the field of education MCSER Mediterranean Center of Social and Educational Research Rome, Italy, 2011, www.mcser.org retrieved on 13 Nov. 2013.

Mohammedan Society reformer.[107] These journals succeeded in infusing a new desire amongst Muslims for acquiring modern knowledge.

Sir Syed successfully tried to awaken the Muslims towards the significance of modern education in order to stand on their own legs and lived a dignified life in accordance with Islamic thoughts. Similarly, Malaviya also tried to devote whole of his life for the welfare of Hindus, Hindu religion by delivering lectures on Gita, Upanishad, and Bhagavad. He tried to motivate Hindus to adopt Hindu *Sanatan* values in life which deteriorated in those days. Although he was much pained due to the deterioration of values in Hindu religion, but he also insisted Hindus to take interest in modern education to make themselves self-reliant.

Sir Syed was extremely unhappy about the position of Muslims in the subcontinent. Since the days after the Muslim period the social and economical status of Muslims had declined sharply and the role of Muslims in the war of Independence had left further decline as British took measures to ensure that their control was unchallenged. Most Muslims considered that British were just invaders and they had nothing to do with them. Sir Syed wanted Muslims had to accept the Britishers as their rulers and could obey them, developed a positive approach towards them. He suggested Muslims that if they needed socio-economic status in the society it had been necessary to accept the idea of Britishers and their education. Sir Syed wanted to see Muslims untied and prospering in their social, economical, and religious fortune.

Sir Syed was a man who was not only affected by environment generated by Britishers at the time of mutiny but guided by his inner will also. For the Muslim community Sir Syed was like the eye which weeps for the suffering of each and every part of the body. The suffering of the community worried him. While there were many reformists arose for the awakening of Hindu religion but Malaviya was only the visionary who

107. Sir Syed Ahmad Khan and books available at http://www.sirsyedtoday.org/books/default.aspx?cid=64 retrieved on 13 Nov. 2013.

worked for the higher education system based on modern need and traditional values along with religious creed.

Sir Syed had least interest in politics. On the other hand, Malaviya actively participated in politics through Indian National Congress session. Sir Syed advocated that Muslim should avoid getting involved in political issues until they achieved parity with the Hindu community in the field of education. He realized that the fundamental weakness responsible for the Muslim community backwardness was religious prejudices and traditional thinking, so he began to establish school for Muslims at Moradabad (1854), Ghazipur (1863). During his visit to England (1869-70),[108] he prepared a plan to establish Muslim Cambridge in India. After his retirement in 1876 Sir Syed devoted himself for the rapid progress of the college whose foundation stone was laid by the Viceroy in 1877. Muhammadan Anglo-Oriental College (1877) which was proposed and became the key of intellectual center for Indian Muslims.[109] The success of the college was due to his leadership and curriculum embodying both Western and Oriental studies. In 1886, Sir Syed organized all India conference, met annually at different places to promote education and to provide Muslim a common platform.[110] At the approx. same year in 1887, All Indian Congress session started. Both visionaries approximately have same dedication level for the completion of the respective university.

Malaviya and Sir Syed approach towards science and religion like Malaviya, Sir Syed's interest in religion was lifelong. He wrote on the life of Prophet Muhammad and devoted himself to write several volumes of a modernist commentary on the holy Quran.[111] He always made Muslims aware by saying:

---

108. Sir Syed Ahmad Khan A Joint Project of AMU and FAAA, USA available at http://www.sirsyedtoday.org/Default.aspx retrieved on 13 Nov. 2013.
109. Aligarh Muslim University: Home available at http://www.amu.ac.in retrieved on 13 Nov. 2013.
110. *Harijan*, 31/07/1937.
111. Sir Syed Ahmad Khan and books available at http://www.sirsyedtoday.org/books/default.aspx?cid=64 retrieved on 13 Nov. 2013.

> We will remain humiliated and rejected if we do not make progress in scientific field. Get rid of old and rituals hindering progress.

He told them to look forward, learn modern knowledge and do not waste time in the study of old subjects which have no value.[112] To understand the Muslims he cited example of young men and women of England that

> They are religiously engaged in hard work of industrial development of their country.[113]

His famous quote is that

> A True Muslim is one who must have holy Quran in one hand and science in the other.[114]

So all his sayings reflected his educational philosophy which act as force for uniting oriental learning with occidental learning. Malaviya's education philosophy was also based on the concept of the amalgamation of Oriental and Occidental learning. Both believed in scientific and technological adaptation for the development of their respective community. On one side where Sir Syed started the organization of All India Muslim Educational Conference[115] with motivate to open a number of educational institute in India to strengthen the Muslims, in the same way Malaviya laid the foundation of "Akhil Bharatiya Sanatan Dharma Mahasabha" with the noble objective, i.e. the enhancement of moral values and welfare of the Hindu Society. The Mahasabha's aim was to educate and propagate the high ideals of *Sanatan Dharma*, to establish Rishikul, Gurukul,

---

112. For a comprehensive analysis of the formation, early years and vision of the college, see David Lelyveld, Aligarh's First Generation: Muslim Solidarity in British India (Delhi: Oxford University Press, 1996).
113. Quadir, A. Good subject Sir Syed Ahmad Khan English and the Punjab University, *Pakistan Journal of History and Culture*, Vol. xxx, No. 2, 2009, available at http:// www.Foxitsoftware.com 13 Nov. 2013.
114. Barbara Daly Metcalf, Islamic Revival in British India: Deoband, 1860-1900, Karachi: Royal Book Company, 1989.
115. Josef, Progler, "Norms and Allegiance in Muslim Education", in Shirley R. Steinberg ed., *Multi/Intercultural Conversations,* New York: Peter Lang, 2001, pp. 565-89.

pathshallas, and school, publish books, periodicals, newspapers, and to train religious preachers, etc.[116] Malaviya through Mahasabha in 1928 repaired, renovated, several Ghats of the river Ganga laid foundation of Viswanath temple in March 1931, established Go Raksha Mandal. Under his president ship hundreds of conferences were organized by the *Sanatan Dharma* in all over India.[117] So the activities of both visionaries were approximately same in relation to community welfare.

But the difference in their approach was that Sir Syed struggled for Muslim to uplift and changed their traditional thinking into modern education system by first focusing on occidental learning. While Malaviya's first target was to expend oriental learning of *Sanatan Dharma* followed by the occidental learning. The objective of Sir Syed was to establish Aligarh Muslim University as like the British education system without compromising Islamic values. The aim of Sir Syed was not merely restricted to establishing a college at Aligarh but spreading a network of Muslim managed educational institutes, throughout the length and breadth of the country. Aligarh movement opens a number of educational institutes. It was the first of its kind of such Muslim NGO in India,[118] which awakened the Muslim people from their deep slumber and infused social and political sensibility into them.

Malaviya and Sir Syed were recognized by Father of Nation as Mahamana and Prophet of Education respectively.[119] These words reflected the similar labour of both persons not for their community but also for the nation. Both were analytical philosophers and their way of analysis was similar during organizing the facts. As reaction of Sir Syed's during Indian Mutiny and the response of Malaviya's during Jallianwala Bagh case was much same. Valuable recommendations were given by both of the visionaries in relation to incidents, keen observance, and way to express anything by law was common

116. Chaturvedi, S., *Madan Mohan Malaviya*. New Delhi: Publication Division Ministry of Information and Broadcasting Government of India, 1995, p. 40.
117. *Ibid.*, p. 41.
118. Josef, P., *op. cit.*, pp. 565-89.
119. *Ibid.*

in their response. Both visionaries influenced the Britishers by their opinion.

Both of the philosophers were same at the question of integration of religion in education and in matter of religious discussions. During writing of causes of Indian revolt Sir Syed wrote that English Government was the best on interfering with their religion and old established customs. He believed that government intended to force the Christian religion and foreign customs upon Hindu and Muslims. Likewise Malaviya also approached against the proselytizing by Christians and Muslim by force. Both were having the similar opinion on the oriental learning that is the study of Sanskrit and Arabic was ruined due to the British education system.

Malaviya and Sir Syed from their educational scheme wanted to preserve their own culture, tradition, and religion. So they initiated to establish universities according to their own thought. Both of the visionaries were better understood the motive of the British Government, i.e. to bring Indians to a pitch of ignorance, poverty and opposed the principle of Christian faith taught in missionary schools. Both were not extremist politician but moderate one, and they always made aware the ruling government to maintain friendly relation between the government and governed, neglect private relationship, love to all men.

Malaviya and Sir Syed's educational approach was same on the curriculum of higher education. Both wanted science education for Indian Youth to get rid of their poverty. Today Aligarh Muslim University is proudly Islamic and proudly Indian institution, a living symbol of composite culture of India and a bulwark of its secular principles. Malaviya and Sir Syed were same in terms of providing vocational education to youth and desired Hindu and Muslim youth to upgrade their education status and quality to get reputed place in administrative job in British Government. Both were favoured to English language as the medium of instruction for the understanding of British policies. They have understood that if Indian youths were capable academically, they could hold the British policy easily. So both delivered the same statement at the time of Non-Cooperation Movement during boycott of educational institute. Malaviya opposed the closing of University and Gandhi's view. Likewise Sir Syed appealed

> There are people who hold the opinion that our nation's cause will be promoted by discussing political affairs. I do not agree with that, but regard the spread of education to be the only means for the promotion of the National cause. In these days our nation should not strive for anything other than the spread of education. In our country, if education is sufficiently spread, we shall have sufficient means to arise from our backward position.[120]

This statement clarifies that the idea of Sir Syed and Malaviya was same on education.

In spite of the above similarities, Sir Syed and Malaviya views were different on the issue of nation and nationalist approach. Malaviya believed in one nation theory while Sir Syed's faith was in two nation theory. Actually, in 1867, Hindi-Urdu controversy was started. Hindus demanded Hindi to be official language but Muslim wanted Urdu to be official language. Just then Sir Syed supported the two nation theory and said that Muslim and Hindu were two separate kinds of people. He said that Urdu's place was in hearts of Muslims and was supported by them and could not be replaced by Hindi, which was the language of Hindu. Sir Syed realized that Hindu and Muslim could not work together. Malaviya view was different on this issue. He regarded India in the form of nation of diversity and welcomed equal freedom of each community.

Sir Syed understood that the political outlook of the two communities was different. He realized Britishers were mainstreaming all political evolution for the Hindus while the Muslims logged behind. Sir Syed thought that this difference was originated due to the difference in the mind set of Hindus and Muslims. Hindus regarded Britishers as cause of freedom

---

120. Gopal, R., *Writings and Speeches of Sir Syed Ahmad Khan*. Bombay: Nachiketa Publication Limited, 5 Kasturi Buildings, J. Tata Road.

from the miseries of Muslims rule, while Muslim regarded them as the bitterest foe who had usurped the political authority and several privileges that they had enjoyed so far. So Sir Syed's tried to agree Muslims to accept Britishers as rulers, and supporter. So in later age he attracted Muslims for separate electorate and representation in British policy.

On communal disturbance both visionaries' attempt was same as to achieve peace, but on the question of separate electorate Sir Syed agreed for the good of Muslims. Sir Syed was the father of Pakistan because of his belief in two Nation theory.[121] On the issue of Hindi-Urdu controversy, origin of Muslim league, Sir Syed approach was to wean Muslims away from the political agitation and focus their energy on education and economic uplift. As for example before 1939, faculties and students supported All-India nationalist movement, but after 1939 political sentiment shifted. They were inspired by the Muslim separatist movement. Students and faculty were mobilized behind Mohammad Ali Jinnah and Muslim League, gradually University became an epicentre of Pakistan movement. Although Sir Syed wanted to remain Muslims aloof from the politics, but event made Aligarh as the cockpit of politics.

However, it must be said that politics was not his cup of tea. Such persons were involved in policy making but not in politics. Sir Syed's political philosophy was characterized by five forces, namely fear, hope, appreciation, commitment, and pragmatism. His political thoughts were reflected during 1857, refutation of Hunter allegation against Wahhabi movement, his role in the viceroy legislative council, his participation in educational reform, his confrontation with the Indian National Congress. Malaviya himself was active in Indian politics but he never supported University as center of politics. While Sir Syed had difference with the Congress because he trusted Hindu backing behind Congress. Malaviya's attitude for Indian National Congress was positive, although in 1935 he formed

121. Ali, F., et al., The Legacy of Sir Syed Ahmad Khan in the field of education MCSER Mediterranean Center of Social and Educational Research Rome, Italy, 2011. www.mcser.org retrieved on 13 Nov. 2013.

the independent party to raise the voice against the government. Likewise yet he was unable to identify himself with Khilafat, but for the sake of nation, he supported Gandhi's view. This action of Malaviya reflected him as liberal Hindu.

Sir Syed realized that Muslim lagged behind the Hindus by half a century. He disliked the Western concept of democracy, and nationalism while Malaviya believed in both. For Malaviya education is the means of national dignity, so for him University and nationalism had a symbiotic relationship, and he said that I left 100 of Banaras Hindu University at the cost of nation. Thus, for him nation was first, religion was second and to fulfill his first and second priority he established University. Malaviya's vision of education was based on the ancient model including mainly *Dharma*, *Shastra*, Science, Psychology, Astronomy, and Medicine, etc. Malaviya had realized heartily decay of the Hindu community in terms of economic backwardness. He had deep understanding of every decennial census which discloses diminishing vitality, decreasing longevity and declining power of procreation among Hindus. So to overcome these problems, he proposed his noble idea of University, which was regarded as experiment of Hindu revivalism which merges traditional religion and modern institution of higher education.

On the other hand, Sir Syed believed in religious education and said that senses gave man immense power. He wanted Muslim youths gain excellence in different disciplines and at the same time practicing all virtues and attributes which Islam seeks to cultivate among its followers as large heartedness, broadmindedness, truthfulness, honesty, integrity, and universal brotherhood. Looking at the importance of education Sir Syed said:

> It was appeared to me that nothing could remove the obstacles to progress of Musalman but education and education, in its fullest sense, has been the object in furthering which I have spent the most earnest moments of my life, and employed the best energies that lay with in humble power.[122]

---

122. *Ibid.*

Both were humanist in their education philosophy. Sir Syed was considered by the people as "People of the book."[123] As true associates of Islam. Sir Syed although believed in two nation theory on the basis of controversy of Hindi and Urdu language, but basically his view was not devoted to establish Pakistan, but he wanted equal representation of electorate in political seats. On the case of Hindu-Muslim unity Malaviya and Sir Syed delivered same view which was quoted by Mahatma Gandhi in Rajghat on 24 March 1947, he said in the words of Sir Syed as Hindu and Muslim are like two eyes of the mother. India just as trouble in one eye affects the other too, similarly whole India will suffer when either Hindu or Musalman suffers.[124]

Sir Syed considered Indian Muslims as an integral part of the nation. He said:

> Over a century back, I have always said that our land of India is like a newly-wedded bride whose two beautiful and luscious eyes are the Hindus and the Musalmans; if the two exist in mutual concord the bride will remain forever resplendent and becoming, while if they make up their mind to see in different directions the bride is bound to become squinted and even partially blind.[125]

Sir Syed's analysis on the Muslim religion revealed that Islam in India is not unlike other religion, has been quite dynamic. It has been sensitive, and has incorporated the local cultural aspects in its practice and in doing so it has contributed to co-existence of religions, in the process of building the identity of the Indian nation. Like Sir Syed Malaviya was also believed in the co-existence of the individual. He made constant efforts to bring Hindus and Muslim closer to each other, emotionally and intellectually. The Muslim and Christian used to invite him to address their congregation. According to Malaviya, Hinduism was not only a matter of faith for personal devotion to God

---

123. Gopal, R., *Writings and Speeches of Sir Syed Ahmad Khan*. Bombay: Nachiketa Publication Limited, 5 Kasturi Buildings, J. Tata Road.
124. *Collected Works of Mahatma Gandhi*, Government of India, Vol. 18, Nov. 1997, p. 342.
125. Zachariah, R., Indian Muslim; where have they gone wrong. Bombay: Popular Prakashan, 2004, p. 258.

but a *Dharma* for his social and National behavior with others and thus, not against any other faith and regarded them as holy as Hinduism.

Sir Syed was somewhere different in his views from Malaviya, because he was affected by Wahabi ideology in which Hindus and Sikhs were considered as *Kafirs* and Muslim did *Jihad* for them. So he said that Wahabis were not anti-British, only anti-Sikh.[126] But at the cost of the religion both visionaries did not sake hand on any priority but they were the likeminded in relation to co-existence.

Sir Syed said,

> The human spirit is just like a mountain of marbles having several black spots on it, and unless the sculpture touches it, removes its dimness and roughness, turns into a model, polishes and shines it, it's beautiful nerves, charming colour and nice design remain hidden. Similar is the condition of human spirit. A human may be pious from the very core of heart, but unless he is subjected to education, his piety and other noble qualities lie hidden in him. They can bring into prominence only by the means of education.[127]

Like Sir Syed Malaviya's feeling, attitude, action, and relations were governed by natural spiritual law (Welfare of the Humanity). Malaviya always focused for the student to develop human value in them. Malaviya said:

> Speak the Truth, think the truth. Continue your studies throughout the life be just and fear none. Fear only to do that is ill or ignoble. Stand up for right. Love the mother land promote public weal. Do well where ever you got the chance for it. Love to give whatever you spare.[128]

---

126. Smith, 1946; 314, No. 9.
127. Ali, F., et al. The Legacy of Sir Syed Ahmad Khan in the field of education MCSER Mediterranean Center of Social and Educational Research Rome, Italy, 2011. www.mcser.org retrieved on 13 Nov. 2013.
128. Available at .a-tribute-to-the-heroes.blogspot.com/2009_07_01_archive.html retrieved on 13 Nov. 2013.

Thus, Malaviya's educo-religious philosophy was based on the tolerance, forgiveness, love, sacrifice, service, devotion to God, devotion to humanity, cooperation, fearlessness in following the truth, patriotism and the welfare of the society. So even both are not contemporary, but there are several common factors between them in relation to their activity for the welfare of the community. Their ideas synchronized in the culmination of two great institutions which originally came into shape by their own effort and British Government support. Philosophy of both visionaries were weaved by the fibers of humanism, character building and knowledge of oriental learning. Religion and science was the cornerstone in their education philosophy.

After critical evaluation of educational philosophy of Malaviya with other contemporary philosophers, it is detected that the education philosophy of Malaviya have all aspects such as social, political, economical, religious, and spiritual. His social messages incorporated three cardinal F's, viz. fearlessness, fraternity, and freedom.

Although he passed his life in poor economic conditions, but he could well understand his karmic circumstances and empowered himself to settle his karmic accounts in the best befitting ways to shape not only his future but also the future of the Indian society. His attempt to make rich society by educational reforms reflected him as educational thinker who believed in view that solution of each social problem exists in education. Other contemporary philosophers such as Gandhi, Tagore, Sir Syed also acted as social reformer did a lot for the society, but it was the only Malaviya who belong from the poor family and become a social reformist. He tried to overcome Indian poor people from their poverty by injecting proper education.

After analyzing Malaviya's educational philosophy from religious point of view, it can be concluded that all thoughts of Malaviya had central theme, i.e. love of *Sanatan Dharma*. He devoted his whole life for the holy purpose of Hindus and opposed Britishers for their hitting manner towards Hindu religious codes. The central deed of Malaviya reflected virtues such as be tolerant to other religion, be patriotic and truthful. So in his religious thoughts he was idealistic, and active in promoting conditions for moral, ethical, economic, social, and cultural development of the nation. Critically, it can be concluded that the behavior of Malaviya reflected him as orthodox religious thinker, but some time he looked like liberal Hindu also.

It is observed that early Malaviya was quite orthodox for Hinduism but later Malaviya was much liberal for Muslims, for Dalits, as well as for Britishers. Later Malaviya was much modern and accumulated the concept of English language, science and technology in education. He was not only accepted the modern view of education, but also did not agree on the views of Bhagwan Das and Annie Besant for the establishment of Theosophy department as integral part of Banaras Hindu University as well as formation of Kachha buildings in University. Later Malaviya was not typical follower of Hindu religion, but he was experimentalist and practical in his life action as he went to abroad in round table conference, although it was not allowed in Hindu religion. Later Malaviya's politics was based on the nationalist approach as he made a party that is nationalist party. Later Malaviya was social, but also individualistic in his ideas and action. As he denied the educational boycott of universities and welcome to Princes of Wales in Banaras Hindu University. When Malaviya's philosophy was critically compared with Tagore's educational idea's it is concluded that Malaviya was an idealistic, eclectic, and pragmatic philosopher while Tagore was naturalistic, experimentalist.

After critical comparison of Malaviya's educational thoughts with Gandhi's educational view, it is concluded that both philosophers are similar favouring all-round development of learner, character building. Both were the follower of *Satyamave jaytay*, fearlessness, religion, and physical development. It is detected that Gandhi gave more importance to Charkha, and vocational education by hand craft while Malaviya liked to defuse some high technology and machine in education system for vocational purposes. It is concluded Gandhi and Malaviya were acted as two poles for nation building. It detected that Gandhi's education philosophy originated for renovation of primary education in the form of basic education policy while he also awakened people for the establishment of national universities, without help of the British Government. While Malaviya's education philosophy was manifestation of the improvement in higher education system on the model of Indians needs. The education philosophy of both philosophers were based on Indian social values. It is concluded that like Tagore and Gandhi Malaviya also believed in rural upliftment but he did not believe on the foundation of pure customary approach for agriculture. He wanted some innovation and research in agriculture education, so further he proposed agriculture education in Banaras Hindu University. In their axiological thoughts both were same. Having higher moral values and favored idealistic teacher, good relationship between students and teachers.

After analyzing the views of Sir Syed and Malaviya in comparative setting it is concluded that both were the visionaries of higher education and same on the interest of welfare of their belonging communities. It is detected that Malaviya and Sir Syed's educo-religious philosophy was based on humanism, religion and science. Both the philosophers wanted to focus on integrated curriculum and appreciated education based on religion. In spite of many similarities there were some differences observed between these two. Sir Syed struggled for Muslim to uplift and changed their traditional thinking into modern through focusing their interest on occidental learning. While Malaviya made target to the oriental learning of *Sanatan Dharma* first than the occidental learning.

Therefore, it is found that for the sound foundation of Indian education system the credit goes to Tagore, Gandhi, Sir Syed, Malaviya who were formulated theory of education and implemented it in full as per their thinking. All visionaries helped the reformist movements in the field of education in India by their original scheme. Thus, all these visionaries did selfless duty for the welfare of nation. Gandhi said for Malaviya as, he is a prince amongst beggars who begged not for himself but a cause dear to him toiling with self-less devotion to translate words into deed. So all the visionaries not only in their respective institutions but in whole world acted as example, as a thought process which was discussed by intellectual giants for inspiring the students with their idealistic view and abounding knowledge. They were prepared students and teachers to drink deep and developed character and horizon. Therefore, visionaries of nineteenth century whether Malaviya, Gandhi, Tagore and Sir Syed all have the same fiber, i.e. love for nation, education, and humanity.

5.5 Limitations

Malaviya's educational philosophy lacks originality and systematic approach despite his vast knowledge and profound scholarship. He had not proposed any original philosophy in education. His work and education are inferior to Plato, John Locke, Herbert Spencer, John Dewey, etc. It is true that he had not written any education philosophy for the students of education rather he has considered the educational problems of a colonial society in general and of the common men in particular. He was the worshiper of *Sanatan Dharma* and the ideals of *Sanatan Dharma* were coded in his thinking. It is difficult to follow the religious lines in developing morality and character in secular India. The dilemma lies in the fact that the society is theocratic in nature where the state is secular in principle. In a multicultural and multi-religious society it is very difficult to run the educational institute on the prescription of religion.

He has described many important aims of higher education which must be inculcated in men. But failed to suggest a suitable method for development and integration. His emphasis on *Brahamcharya* which necessarily to be followed by the students of 18th century in the field of higher education may not be taken positively by many in modern times. His educational thoughts basically hovers around the basic idea of *Sanatan* Hindu methodology so mostly idealistic pattern followed by him. But if critically analyzed his educational ideas then it was observed that he has not rekindled any particular aspect of Indian Vedas and devoted his whole energy for the same. As Vivekananda not only proclaimed the glory of Vedanta in India but also rekindled the pride of Vedanta at international scenario. Tagore also took steps for the cultural advancement but no effort was done by Malaviya at international level for the expansion of *Sanatan Dharma*. Malaviya was much traditional metaphysical thinker in such reference. His idea on curriculum and methods of teaching reflected that he had applying little bit his own idea which inherited from his religious belief and some are borrowed from other society in which he live. So in his educational views his own thoughts are totally not interwoven but they are contributed by the others and situational practices. So mostly his ideas reflected eclecticism which not completely belongs to any particular school of thought but believe in the fact that modern life can be made richer and happier by drawing inspiration from all sides. In his schemes of education, educational psychology may find less place than the idealist and pragmatic views. In his teaching methods there is less focus on naturalistic approach. Malaviya's educational ideas were reflected his political and social emancipator image not as the emancipator of child. Basically, his ideas given for higher educational prospective but not paying attention on child education.

In amalgamation of the best of both the world East and West he has missed the point that both have different aims of life. Material ends cannot be pursuing by the spiritual men and vice versa. The integrating of materialism with spirituality in Malaviya's educational philosophy creates a confusion. The major outcomes of his educational philosophy are due to the situational compulsions of Indian society but after independence situation has changed even in Banaras Hindu University herself his educational philosophy is not being followed. Because religion have their own moral and intellectual limitations.

Crisis in modern society is being created by men who cleaned to be democrats, secular and humanist but Malaviya's educational philosophy does not provide any potent solution of the modern crisis. Without understanding the process of education and challenges before the modern men hardly any educational philosophy may be constructed in balanced way. Therefore, Malaviya appeared as educational leader rather the educationist.

6
Critique and Conclusions

The discussions in the preceding chapters reveal that the educational philosophy of Pt. Madan Mohan Malaviya is in some respects similar to contemporary visionaries who belonged to the Nation Oriented Educational Setup. As Malaviya's idea was developed during the freedom movement and in same socio-economic and political situation of dependent India which faced by the Mahatma Gandhi, Tagore and Sir Syed Ahmad Khan. So, this chapter including the summary of all chapters aims to develop a comparative study of Malviya's Philosophy with those of Gandhi, Tagore and Syed Ahmad Khan to understand overall assessment of his educational ideas. Chapter also focuses on the reflection of Malaviya's Educational Thought in Contemporary Higher Education in the light of Emerging NEP 2020.

6.1 Introduction

The freedom movement of India was the revolutionary phase that witnessed change in all spheres of national life. The colonial rule sparked many irreversible changes not only in India but also in the neighboring countries. With implementation of Macaulay's Minutes followed by various reformative initiatives like Charles Wood Dispatch, Hurtog's Committee, Sadler Commission, etc., the landscape of the Indian education system was completely changed. However, these changes were not initiated only by Britishers but many educational philosophers played significant roles in the development of the educational system. These educational philosophers not only influenced the country but the aura of their intellectual brilliance spread to western countries also. These efforts reestablished the *Vishwa Guru* image of India again. Madan Mohan Malaviya was one of the brightest and most precious gems of the group of these intellectuals. His ideas and visions about education, society, religion and nation played a significant role in shaping the educational development of India. His emphasis on using education as a tool to shape the character of individuals and transform the same into a productive workforce for the betterment of society and the nation as a whole. This illustrates his greatness and pragmatic approach. Banaras Hindu University is a glorious epitome of Malaviya's idealism and realism. Malaviya was a constructive idealist with a passionate love and vision for the country. He did not believe only in materialistic advancement but was more concerned with the problems arising in the metaphysical domain.

In the era of postmodernism, the issue of the survival of man is in question. Modern man does not believe in philosophies and speculations. He is unable to find the meaning and purpose in life. His actions are governed by immediate needs and impulses. It seems that the philosophies of values and peace are unable to meet the crisis and challenges of modern civilizations. Pursuit of virtues as prescribed in metaphysical traditions seems to be a solution of the aforesaid problems. In this context the educational philosophy of Madan Mohan Malaviya is relevant because it is a synthesis of the best of the both world material and spiritual.

6.2 The preceding discussion of previous chapters leads us to conclude the philosophical and educational thoughts of Madan Mohan Malaviya including critical evaluation of his Educational Philosophy with other contemporary Indian philosophers.

After analyzing Madan Mohan Malaviya's social, political, economical, and religious thoughts it can be concluded that Malaviya as a philosopher can be considered as an idealist, who believed in metaphysical tradition with a pragmatic view. He has faith in Vaishno cult of Sanatan Dharma.

6.2.1 His whole socio-economical, political and educational idea's hovers around a central theme Sanatan i.e., everlasting, unchangeable, ever fresh, perennial truth of life. In metaphysical tradition, philosophers believe in some eternity. Malaviya also belongs to this group of traditional philosophers. Like Plato he was in favor of cultivating virtues rather than adopting Values. He was a *Humanist* also, therefore his social thoughts meant for the whole mankind. He believed that the same spirit dwells in all living beings. Therefore, he not only identified himself with men, but also with all other living beings. He was a Naturalist also, as he believed in the worship of the natural power within, behind and beyond all the living beings, particularly the Sun, the *Ganga and Cow*. He was in favour of the natural environment as may be observed in the plan of Banaras Hindu University. He was a Pragmatist in his socio-economical and educational thoughts, as he blended the best of both Eastern and Western culture in his educational scheme. He was a *democrat* and strong believer in the ideals of equity, liberty, fraternity, justice and the scientific temperament. He adopted social service as the ultimate goal of his life which is reflected in his ideals and actions. His originality lies in the fact that he preferred the best of all the thinking of mankind, and never favoured a rigid sectarian view of life. As a *Nationalist* he always struggled against the poverty, slavery, and ignorance of the masses of his country. As a *Universalist and Humanist*, he considered the whole world as his extended family. He never opposed any idea only because it came from some other culture or country, but he preferred to choose the best out of everything. Thus, he was categorized as *Eclectic philosophers* also. His activity was not only confined to a specific field, but he was a versatile genius. His contributions in socio-economic, political, religious fields are as follows.

It was revealed that his s*ocial philosophy* never differed from his action, way of living and political movements. His social works were inspired by the concept of nationalism and religion. Malaviya's social work reflected the upliftment of untouchables, depressed class, women emancipation, favour of widow marriages, abolition of child marriages and animal sacrifices. Malaviya's social philosophy was based on understanding of social conditions and logic. During solving the problems of untouchables, he logically satisfied orthodox Brahmin Hindus, by citing the examples of the Hindu Rajas of ancient times, who gave shelter, food and love to such people. Along with this Malaviya knew the fact that the political importance of any community would correspond to its numbers in the population and the Hindus could retain their dominant majority only if the depressed classes remained attached to them. His social journey started from Allahabad. Seva (Service) from this way Malaviya tried to shape society, by establishing Seva Samiti. Although most of his social activities were considered for the sake of Hindu religion and Hindu community, he never liked the partition of the country into two nations, and favored inter communal and intra communal unity. Malaviya's cow-protection movement was not only due to his faith in religion, but it was logically explained by him from economic, agriculture, health point of view. Therefore, Malaviya wanted to promote such a social consciousness in which every individual binds himself with the higher ideals of service for the cause of social uplift.

His economic ideas were reflected in his speeches on financial bills, budget system, and commissions like industrial commission etc. According to him finance is not mere arithmetic; finance is a great policy. Without sound finance, no sound government is possible without sound Government, no sound finance is possible.

> Malaviya's economic philosophy was influenced by the nationalist views such as John Stuart Mill, Digby, Naroji, Ranade etc. were quoted by him in his speech. (Annual Proceeding of U.P. Legislative Council., Apr. 11, 1906, p. 62.)

His financial prepositions are not only of historical interest, but also relevant in modern context such as his ideas on revenue expenditure, land holdings, state bank, nationalization of Indian Railways, cooperative societies, adoption of modern methods of agriculture, etc. In the economic philosophy of Malaviya, welfare of the common man was supreme. So, he favored saving indigenous industries which were ruined and face the danger of extinction on account of foreign competition in those days. Malaviya's basic aim was to ensure that the state should promote Indian industries and should utilize Indian raw material, and be seen with Indian Capital by an Indian person and under Indian control.

Malaviya in his political philosophy showed attributes of progressive political leader, who contributed in shaping India as a modern progressive country from a dependent colonial economy. His ideas of liberty, democracy, equality, self defense, fraternity are in consonance with modern human rights. His political dreams were concerned with selfless politics devoted for the welfare of common men. The poverty of the masses, illiteracy, economic, mental, physical exploitation of Indians, suffering and sorrows of common men greatly perturbed him throughout his life. Malaviya in comparison to his contemporary leaders could be considered as a leader, who belonged to moderate school of political thoughts with nationalist touch. But he positively agreed with the thought that a country is not greater than humanity. After analyzing his speech on communal harmony delivered on the political stage, it was concluded that Malaviya was secular in his political approach, as he said

> India is the common motherland of all Hindus, Muslims, etc. (AAJ Apr. 12th 1924)

His political philosophy also reflects Ethico-religious thoughts because when he addressed on some political issues cited examples of norms discussed in Vedas and many other religious scriptures. For political freedom and for awakening the people, he understood the utility of a newspaper; therefore, in his view, the press needs lawful liberty. He believed in the constitutional methods to win any political, social problems of the nation. In the case of the Rowlatt Bill and Jallianwala Bagh tragedy, Chauri-Chaura Kand were won by him by applying his knowledge of law. He was a congressman with a difference. Later Malaviya formed an independent party that was named as Nationalist Party. Yet his all activities adopted a nationalist outlook, rather than becoming a prototype of the Muslim League. Malaviya was troubled on the issues of I.C.S. Service, defense or promotion of military, decentralization of power and utility of local self-government, which were mostly discussed by him in his political speeches. Therefore, it could be concluded from Malaviya's political philosophy that it was founded on social reforms, which was planned for the welfare of the Nation and promotes 3Ps as prosperity, progress, and peace.

The religious thoughts of Madan Mohan Malaviya were based on Sanatan Dharma which was understood by him as the eternal religion, the ancient law and Hindu view of life. Malaviya as a metaphysical traditional thinker, believed in the existence of an eternal being as tradition. He emphasized on virtues, which are essential characteristics of perennial truth or goodness as conceptualized by traditional metaphysical thinkers. Malaviya as a *karma yogi* believed in *Lord Krishna*. The axiology of his religious philosophy shows virtues like passionate love for humanity. Malaviya also presented a pragmatic theory of inquiry about religion. Malaviya viewed religion and science parallel to each other. For moral accountability and goodness Malaviya believed in God and always said if it is the objective of education to make a good citizen it is important to integrate religion in education. According to Malaviya no call is higher than that of Dharma i.e., right living. He believed in Cow (GO), Ganga and Gayatri which reflected his gratitude towards Nature. In one of his famous extempore speeches he once confessed, that it is one of the settled convictions of my life that religion is at the foundations of all greatness and goodness, and that without an abiding religious faith no affair of man can succeed. But he opposed those corruptions of religion which were codified as superstition. He abused all such rituals which enforce social discriminations. Thus, Malaviya's philosophical thoughts were much influenced by Sanatan Dharma and nationalist views and always centered on common man welfare.

6.2.2 The educational philosophy of Malaviya conceived education as the balanced training and development of the body, the intellect and the emotions of every individual. Accordingly, he made ample provision in Banaras Hindu University. He may be turned as the basic founder of the concept of holistic education not only in theory but in practice also. For holistic education he designed a grand scheme of education in the field of higher education, by taking inspirations from many sources like the Gurukul system of education, Greek system of education and Oxbridge and Redbrick model of education. He was utilitarian in formulating his educational thoughts.

The factors responsible for the genesis of educational thoughts of Malaviya were the poor condition of his family, high moral values of home environment, social events of his time, his understanding about the real need of society, and many contemporary problems like poverty, famine, draught, diseases, poor agriculture, economic and religious condition of the country etc. played positive role in genesis of Malaviya's educational thoughts. Dominance of western culture and religion on Indian civilization worried Malaviya to develop such an educational system by which Indian culture, religion and civilization could be saved.

Malaviya regarded university as a power-house needed to scatter the darkness of ignorance, poverty and cold misery which is hanging like a pall upon the country. Malaviya visualized that the students trained in higher education would be able to spread knowledge throughout the country and will develop the national spirit. At secondary level, he urged the establishment of technical schools and colleges for the support of indigenous arts and industries. Malaviya strongly recommended universal primary education.

Malaviya's purpose of education was to make India once again a super power. He considered education as a changing agent in the social sector, as a key for economic growth of the nation, as an instrument for political freedom and nationalism, for inculcation of tradition, culture, value and religious faith in human beings. He also emphasized on women›s education. In Banaras Hindu University, his center of attention was not to enhance community feeling, but he wanted to vanish communalism by promoting nationalism.

He framed realistic educational aims which arose out due to social and political experiences of his life. Therefore, his educational aims have social origin rather than to their metaphysics. The prime objective of his educational philosophy was Character Building. Another objective was to promote integrated education, to promote scientific, technical education. Malaviya said *ann chinta chamtkary, kateray kavita kuth*. Thus, he understood education as a process of self-reliance. His other educational objective was to promote productive, vocational and commercial education.

Malaviya's epistemology in relation to the curriculum reflected him as a realistic and pragmatic philosopher. In his view, illiteracy and ignorance laid at the root of every trouble. So, he dreamt of a new kind of curriculum taught by a new kind of school for a self reliant society. He provided tentative patterns of vocational studies in which cultivation of initiative and self help are dominant objectives. Seeing the economic condition of the country, Malaviya wanted to develop the scientific spirit in the Indians and less dependency on agriculture. He wanted to promote the Indian system of medicines and India to be dependent on skilled farming so that people earn more than their expenditure. Malaviya regarded physical health as an essential condition for physical happiness and soundness as the prerequisite for mental health. Malaviya appreciated the inter hostel/inter faculty competition of sports. Malaviya considered students should be provided military training side by side with cultural and vocational training. So Malaviya favored integrated curriculum.

Considering teaching methods, he preferred that knowledge could be obtained through one's senses, through own understanding, and by reasoning ability, so many times in the university, he motivated teachers to arrange group discussions on relevant topics. Malaviya focused on choosing that teaching method which motivates the desires, courage, wisdom and fearlessness in the learner.

In regard to teachers basically he focused on strong character, lofty knowledge of his subject, sweet communication, high moral values, discipline, economic sense in spending time, and caring like parents.

His thoughts were idealistic in relation to children. He wanted all round development of the child by providing all needful education and training. Malaviya told students

> Forget the world altogether or lay it wholly aside when engaged in study. (Parmanand, *Mahamana Madan Mohan Malaviya: An Historical Biography*, p. 486)

Along with this, he always facilitated students to follow Brahmacharya and narrated a slogan,

> Drink milk, exercise, repeat God's name every day; concentrate on your studies and your desires are sure to be fulfilled. (Parmanand, *Mahamana Madan Mohan Malaviya: An Historical Biography*)

It advocated a relationship between teacher and the student like the Gurukul System. As Malaviya started his childhood and early education in orthodox disciplined environment, but later he was admitted in the European disciplined school, then he although felt difficulty to manage orthodox religious and social prejudices and european discipline, but he was much disciplined in his orthodox practices, so he did not drink the water provided at school and had to come home to quench thirst. Likewise, his pledge of not taking food before, the target collection of funds during formulation of Banaras Hindu University, chanting of *Gayatri mantra*, all showed that he had firm determination for doing and achieving any goal. It was the result of his inner discipline. Thus, Malaviya favored self-discipline. Generally, he forgave students of the Banaras Hindu University on general issues, but mistakes related to character were intolerable.

Malaviya concept related to infrastructure of university/institutional buildings is realized in the buildings, hostels, play grounds, gardens, library and in the architectural plan of the Banaras Hindu University. Although he was mostly criticized by Gandhi, Bhagvan Das, Annie Besant, etc. for spending highly on the university building, his views were clear, modern and scientific. He desired university students to see the river Ganga in the morning and perform *Gayatri mantra* as mentioned in Rig Veda. So, he liked to provide a natural environment and religious culture in palatial buildings of Banaras Hindu University.

Thus, it is concluded that his educational philosophy is interwoven with idealist and pragmatic thoughts which originates from the social welfare concept. As an experimentalist, he experimented the concept of ancient gurukul system with blending of modern western science and technology in the form of Banaras Hindu University.

6.2.3 After critical analysis of Malaviya's educational thoughts with other Indian philosophers such as Tagore, Gandhi and Sir Syed Ahmad Khan, on the parameters namely originality, principles, aim, medium of learning, way of distribution of knowledge and harmonization of national views it was found that they had similarities and differences as mentioned below:

(a) *Malaviya and Tagore's Educational Thoughts*

Following similarities were found between Malaviya and Tagore's educational thoughts:

> It was founded that both advocated for higher education and established Banaras Hindu University and Shantiniketan in the same socio-political-educational condition of the country. Both were experimentalists in relation to higher education.

Both viewed education as the process of development of the whole man and not merely the intellectual development of the individual but focused on the development of the physical, moral, and spiritual aspects of the personality. Both were realist and humanist in their approaches towards education.

Following differences were found between Malaviya and Tagore's educational thoughts:

1. The inspiring factors responsible for the genesis of both visionaries were different. Basically Malaviya's educational philosophy was influenced by his family background, political activities, faith in Sanatan Dharma, etc. while in case of Tagore, factors responsible were the memory of his school days, interest in literary pursuits, poetic sense, love for art and music, love for Nature, faith in spiritual unity of all races, and practical realization of problems of rural people during his land lordship, all forced him to experiment with new models of education.
2. Malaviya was idealist, pragmatist whereas Tagore was naturalistic.
3. Malaviya was nationalist, while Tagore was recognized as an international face.

4. Both differed in molding of the Indian education system with influence of western culture and thought. Malaviya opposed the influence of western culture on the Indian education system while Tagore was a supporter of conglomerate culture. Tagore's vision of Visva Bharati was two folded. He wanted it to become the guiding center of Indian studies and at the same time a focal point of Asian studies while Banaras Hindu University was visualized by Malaviya as an epitome of Indian tradition, culture and values.
5. Both views differed on the medium of instruction. In the case of primary education, both preferred to use vernacular language as a medium of instruction. In higher education, especially in science subjects Malaviya agreed to use English as medium due to lack of vernacular literature in these subjects. While Tagore favored vernacular language in higher education also.
6. Their approaches were different on religion and its incorporation in education. Malaviya emphasized on the integration of religion in education for the character formation and a good citizenship while Tagore's ideas on religious education were based on the educational program, which emphasizes the harmony between Nature and man.
7. In Tagore's curriculum, Nature was the driving force and sort of laboratory where the conditions affecting life were to be tested.
8. Tagore was more artistic and naturalist while Malaviya was a realistic and utilitarian philosopher.

(b) *Malaviya and Gandhi's Educational Thoughts*

Following similarities were found between Malaviya's and Gandhi's educational thoughts:

1. It was revealed that both having similarity in their views on some issues, as removal of Untouchability, national language, provincial language, use of swadeshi goods (as Khaddar handmade cloth), development

of indigenous industries, communal unity, kisan, economic equality, education of health and hygiene, labor, women, political freedom from British slavery by non violence way, practice of truth in life, The Gita, love of Nation, etc.

2. Both of the visionaries wanted the proper coordination of the three i.e. mind, body and soul by education. Being a practical educationist, both conceived education not merely in terms of acquisition of knowledge or storing of facts but in terms of activity and experience.
3. Gandhi's educational philosophy was based on four aspects i.e. free and compulsory primary education, craft centered education, self-supporting and self-sufficient education imparted through mother tongue. Both were idealists and followers of truth. Self-actualization, self-sufficiency were the prime goals of their educational philosophy. Both agreed on the primary aim of education, i.e. the character formation of the pupils. Both said it is required from the teachers, not to lose their character and values.
4. Both did not favor Macaulay's views on education, which aimed at making Indians as clerks. Like Gandhi, Malaviya gave importance to universal primary education.
5. Gandhi's concept of self-financing was based on the idea of introducing spinning in every school. Under *Swaraj,* Malaviya also supported the same idea at secondary level, but he fully denied adopting it in the higher education system. He converted this idea in the form of Industrial vocational education in higher education pursuits.
6. Both wanted pupils as initiators, obedient and self-disciplined.
7. Gandhi preferred the establishment of national schools where he wanted to propagate Charkha, educate untouchables and bring Hindus and Muslims closer.

Malaviya also likes this for the attainment of complete Swaraj.

Despite of the similarities, they also differed on some issues

1. Factors accountable for the genesis of Gandhi's educational philosophy were the influence of Satyagraha in South Africa, experiences on the Tolstoy farm while Malaviya's educational philosophy was influenced by Indian culture, tradition, crisis, Sanatan Dharma and influence of western education.
2. Gandhi has evolved a philosophy of paedocentric education (Child centered education) while Malaviya's philosophy was *eclectic* in nature.
3. Malaviya was experimentalist in the field of higher education while Gandhi was in the field of child education.
4. At secondary level, Malaviya preferred vocational and technical education along with craft centered education. At higher education, his approach was quite different from Gandhi and he did not oppose the idea of machine and technology of western culture in the Indian education system.
5. On the issues of boycott of education and nationalization of universities, and motivating the university students in political movements, Malaviya differed from Gandhian view.
6. Both were differed on the view of imparting education through English. In Gandhi's view, by providing English education millions of the people will become slave. However Malaviya agreed to use English as a medium of instruction at a higher level for some subjects due to lack of vernacular literature.
7. On the issues of Nationalization of Aligarh Muslim University and Banaras Hindu University (meaning freeing them from Government control and their run entirely without Government's grants), Malaviya and Gandhi were not having same opinion.

8. Gandhi did not give more importance to higher education prospective, than the need of freedom. His dream was to prepare youth to fight against British rule. He agreed with the view to boycott the Government at all places and withdraw Indian youth from any educational institution which was governed by the British Government while Malaviya was different. He wanted to educate the youth first and make them eligible for acquiring the best post in civil services, military, etc. He wanted to make them skilled rather than make them illiterate leaders to fight for freedom.

Therefore, Malaviya was a social reformer for the primary education, but he was an educational philosopher in relation to higher education whereas Gandhi was as educational philosopher for the primary education, who made experiments at primary level by providing basic education policy but social reformer for higher education, induced many of the rich, educated people to open National Universities.

(c) *Malaviya and Sir Syed Ahmad Khan*

1. Both were the visionaries for higher education who established Banaras Hindu University and Aligarh Muslim University for the uplift of the society in 1916 and 1877, as Mohammadean Oriental College, and Aligarh Muslim University in 1920 respectively.
2. Both were same in their views i.e. interest of their belonging community. But the country was dearer to them rather than anything else.
3. Both were analytical philosophers and their analytical processes are many times the same.
4. Interest of both in religion was lifelong, which influenced their educational philosophy and they were expressed same view on integration of religion in education and on Hindu-Muslim unity. Their Educo-religious philosophy was based on Humanism.
5. Both of the visionaries wanted to preserve their own culture, tradition and religion so they initiated to

establish the respective universities, which are not based on the framework of the London University.

6. Both approaches were the same in regard to curriculum in higher education. Both focused on integrated curriculum and science education for the Indian youth to get rid of poverty.
7. Both were same in regard to providing vocational education and to upgrade their community youths in educational status and quality in order to get a reputed place in administrative jobs in the British Government.
8. Both were in favour of English language for the understanding of British policy, they understood if Indian youth were capable academically, they can hold the British policies.

Despite these similarities, following differences were observed between these two:

1. Sir Syed struggled for upliftment of the Muslims and favoured the view to change their traditional thinking by focusing on occidental learning. While Malaviya targeted for the oriental learning of Sanatan Dharma first, in comparison to the occidental learning.
2. Syed was highly impressed by the culture and customs of western society while Malaviya was influenced by Indian culture.
3. On the nation and nationalist approach they were different. Former believed in one nation theory while later believed in two nation theory. In the Malaviya view education and nationalism had a symbiotic relationship. Nation and religion were parallel for him; thus, he was nationalist in his educational approach. While Syed considered Islam dharma superior than the nation and he regarded India as only a place where Muslim resided for food, shelter, etc. in comparison to mother land concept. So, his first aim was to save the religion rather than the nation. Thus, he agreed easily on the concept of two nation theory, while Malaviya was not agreeing on the same. So even both were not

contemporary, but both were similar to the welfare of their community and their ideas were synchronized in the culmination of two great institutions which originally came into shape by their own effort and British Government's support.

So let us finally examine the philosophy of Malaviya ji then it is concluded that the product of his philosophy would be a man who possesses vitality, courage, sensitivity and Nation love including scientific realist ethical belief which help in social welfare. Although the major work of Mahamana reflects him as a moderate leader who worked continuously for the freedom of Nation and his educational qualification would support him as a lawyer not as a person who develop any school of educational philosophy in spite of this, he would be remembered in the history of education for many reasons. He would be remembered for his love of Nation and his comprehensive thoughts as he has pointed out the educational requirements for the scientific and technical education for Indians in Indian Industrial Commission (1918) including support of universalization of primary education during Gokhale Bill representation. His critical attitude towards British Education and administration opens new avenues for thought and broadens the Indians mental horizon for the use of Swadeshi products and National Education. Therefore, Malaviya has done his duty successfully. It is for this reason that he occupies an important place in the history of education.

6.3 Further the relevance of educational thoughts of Malaviya in the present educational social context was analyzed as,

- In relation to higher education, it is concluded that the 21st century has to face challenges like internationalization, privatization, quality assurance, Governance, fostering of research and innovation, competition for human and financial resources, etc. The Indian higher education system can't afford these changes. It is necessary to meet all the expectations and challenges of an increasingly globalizing world without endangering local culture and values. Banaras Hindu University is striving in the direction of proposing a model of higher education which would address the challenges of globalization without compromising on national priorities or Indian values. Parameters decided by Malaviya such as amalgamation of science and religion, character formation, expansion of Indigenous industrial education, vocational education are also relevant today.

- If Malaviya's indigenous economic philosophy based on swadeshi is followed in present contexts, the value of rupees will not come down as seen in the global market today. Indian policies depend much on foreign economy and market. Malaviya thoughts on Swadeshi i.e., the utilization of Indian raw material with Indian capital and by Indian personnel and under Indian control is followed by policy makers then half of the problems of the Indian youth will be solved.
- Malaviya's thoughts were relevant for practice of journalism, politics, culture, society, religion and nation. When corruption threatens to shake up the 74-year-old democracy, then it is important to revise the educational plan of the nation. However, our education system is innovative and based on e-technology but it lacks value sensitive citizenship education. As Malaviya stated,

  "Mere industrial advancement cannot restore India to the position which she once occupied among the civilized countries of the world. And even industrial prosperity cannot be attained amongst all concerned, and these can only prevail and endure amongst those who are fair in all their dealings, strict in the observance of good faith and steadfast in their loyalty to truth". (Maine, S.K. et.al., Visionary of India Madan Mohan Malaviya. P. 103)

  So it is concluded that the views of Malaviya in the present contexts of corruption ruled society are relevant.

- Indian society today talks about women empowerment, but in reality, women do not even feel safe. The question arises what type of education is needed for gender sensitization? Malaviya opposed the sentiments of men, who have converted women into a domestic drudge and instruments of their pleasure, instead of regarding them as their helpmate and better half; the result is a semi paralysis of our society.
- The vision of Malaviya ji was reflected in National Education Policy (2020) as the idea of integration of multidisciplinary, inter-intra disciplinary education along with establishment of MERU universities, all these initiatives were very well reflected in the BHU campus. It is in coherence with Para 11.1 of NEP (2020). "India has a long tradition of holistic and multidisciplinary learning in the 'liberal arts', from universities, such as Takshashila and Nalanda to the extensive literature of India combining subjects across fields. Ancient Indian literary works like Banabhatta's Kadambari described a good education as knowledge of the 64 Kalas or arts; and among these 64 'arts' were included subjects such as singing and painting, but also more 'scientific' fields, such as chemistry and mathematics, more 'vocational' fields, such as carpentry and clothes-making, more 'professional' fields, such as medicine and engineering, as well as 'soft skills', such as communication, discussion, and debate. NEP visualized to implement this idea in all higher education institutes where all the branches of creative human endeavor—including mathematics, science, vocational subjects, professional subjects, and soft skills—should be considered 'arts' indeed has distinctly Indian origins. This notion of 'knowledge of many arts'—what in modern times is called the 'liberal arts' (i.e., a liberal notion of the arts)—must be brought back to Indian education, as it is exactly the kind of education that will be required for the 21st century" The essence of the above cited text of NEP

2020 was reflected in the Mahamana speech during the 12th convocation of Banaras Hindu University he expressed his views as, "It was in October 1917 that the University started its work. In the twelve years that have elapsed much progress has been recorded. The ideal of the University was an institution which should revive the best traditions of the ancient gurukuls of India—like those of Takshashila and Nalanda, where Hindu sages taught and fed ten thousand students at a time and which should combine with them the best traditions of the modern Universities of the West where the highest instruction is imparted in Arts, Science and Technology." It is observed that in the same the BHU campus premises there are institutes of medical science including IIT, MMV, Malaviya Shishu Vihar to CHS and Dharm Vigyan Sansthan, Law, Commerce, FMS, Music, Sanskrit, etc. including various girls, boys hostel and teaching non-teaching staff enjoy the common residential campus, health, education and other facilities and share the common dialogue on social and educational issues outside the classroom. So, strong teacher-student relationships evolve in informal and formal discussions. There is a need to establish such a fully equipped residential campus of a Higher education institute in India because that model of education proposed by Malaviya Ji has been tested and verified for more than 100 years and their Alumens serve across the country and contribute a lot the cause, name and fame of Nation.

- The views of Pt. Madan Mohan Malaviya and other visionaries which discussed in this book are eloquently reflected in NEP 2020. As Human Resource Development Minister Dr. Ramesh Pokhriyal "Nishank," in his speech said that "As per the vision of new Mahamana Pt. Madan Mohan Malaviya, new education policy will be based on Vedic knowledge and modern science. It will come true to the expectations of Mahamana." No doubt it is true that India must regain the global leadership in higher education which may not happen merely by achieving place in top 100 in global ranking but can be attained by re-discovering, re-visiting, repurposing the basic doctrines, such as philosophy, values, purpose, pedagogy of Indian University System. Even today, while several national institutes and universities have been established, not a single University has reached even near the vision of Pandit Madan Mohan Malaviya or Gurudev Tagore in terms of holistic education in a multidisciplinary environment coupled with Indian ethos and pedagogy.

- So, looking at the reflection of Visionaries in NEP 2020 it is significant that academicians of Higher education will try to remodel and rebuild current universities according to the guidelines of NEP 2020. Consequently, higher education learners/institutions will be able to reflect the foundations of Indian knowledge systems and integrate advanced science, technology, social science, contemporary art and humanities together. For realization of this aim it is important that the Indian University system primarily free themselves from the colonist outlook, and recognize their own antiquity and splendid legacy. Secondly, they respect their own culture and indigenous values including languages without rambling the value of english to maintain global need. Thirdly, it is important to embrace technology-led innovation pedagogical imperatives in teaching-learning process, curriculum and assessment with integration of global and local coexistence for the attainment of quality higher education. The vision of Malaviya ji was so perfect and relevant as in contemporary education policy the idea of integration of multidisciplinary, inter-intra disciplinary education along with establishment of MERU university all reflects in the BHU campus.
- In NEP 2020, the proposed idea of re-imagining universities does not mean that Indian higher education now only glorifies the ancient values through discarding

western approach but policy focuses on the integration of Indian and western knowledge systems in education in the reflection of this point of view that there is need to know that these values should not be included in curriculum and practice blindly followed by dogmatic attitude. The above ideas which manifested in above text of NEP 2020 is the reflection of Malaviya's vision.

- The 21st century Indian education system entails a new model of progressive higher education system which is based on interdisciplinary approach and prepare academically intelligent, professional, skill based, self-reliant learner whose values are rooted in Indian culture who serve selflessly serve for the national development and for the cause of humanity. The same expectation was reflected in the speech of Malaviya ji who had wanted to make accountable to any higher education institute from global to local perspective as it reflects in his thought when he urged, "And the creator and Benefactor of the World, the universal soul moving in all, brought together his children of the East and the West, and induced their minds to that unanimity which meant good and right understanding and directed them to raise this Home of Universal Learning in the Capital Town of the Lord of Universe" (Printed in Copper Plate, 1916, BHU1). Again Malviya's pray was printed on founder stone and copper plate, 1916 "May saraswati, in earnate in the Shruti-Heart of wisdom, ever bloom and shine with worship from her human children, may they ever assiduously imbibe the Vital milk of knowledge flowing from her sweet breasts of science and Philosophy; may all hearts turn to acts of good alone; and may all hearts be filled with love of the supreme!" (Printed in copper plate, 1916).
- The present book may help in rising interest among the researchers and the learners about the visionaries and their visions, who were critically evaluated in this study. It may also suggest policy makers regarding

inculcation of Mahaman's thoughts in the curriculum of higher education.

- The book may be helpful for teachers, students and administrators in selecting the strategies to solve their concerning problem with the reflection of a visionary's point of view and it may facilitate wider sharing of ideas and experiences amongst all those who are interested and engaged in the area of value education.
- This book may also be helpful from the future perspective to deal with the problems of the education system by applying the Malaviya's views of education including researchers who are interested in philosophical research on Indian educational philosophers and their relevance in the present educational system. This book may suggest to the researcher to do the research on the role of Banaras Hindu University in national development especially when we all are celebrating this year Azadi ka Amrit Mahotsav as well as this book may also facilitate researcher to know the colonial hegemony through 'Science' in India as a critical discourse analysis as well as to realize the BHU as Scientific Institution in the light of protagonist Mahamana Pt. Madan Mohan Malaviya's views.

Bibliography

I. Speeches and Writings of Madan Mohan Malaviya

Address of Malaviya delivered Published University of Allahabad Minutes, 15 Dec. 1937.

Appeal Malaviyaji's Stirring Speech on Swadeshi Movement in All India Swadeshi Sangh with his correction facing page.

Banaras Hindu University Foundation Stone inscription.

Honourable Pandit Madan Mohan Malaviya: His Life and Speeches. Ganesh Co, Madras.

Madan Mohan Malaviya, Badrinath Temple Question of Transfer. Tara Printing Works Benares City, 15 January 1934.

Mahamana Malaviyaji Birth Centenary Commemoration Published by the Society all India Malaviyaji Centenary Celebration Committee BHU, Varanasi, 5, India, 25th Dec., 1961.

Malaviya Address at the Teachers Training College, BHU, 1935, Published in the Sanatan Dharma, November 24, 1935.

Malaviya Addressed in Court, Dec. 1929.

Malaviya Presidential Address to the Inaugural Session of the Hindi Sahitya Sammelan, Banaras, 1910.

Malaviya Speech at the Passing of the BHU Bill by the Legislative Council, 1 Oct. 1915.

Malaviya speech in Provincial Legislative Council Published in Leader, 23rd Oct. 1929.

Malaviya Speech in the Indian Legislative Assembly, February 23, 1928.

Malaviyaji's Note of Dissent on the Industrial Commission Report, 1918.

Pandit Madan Mohan Malaviya's Statement on Repression in India up to April 20, 1932.

Presidential Address of the Hon. Pt. Madan Mohan Malaviya at the 33rd Indian National Congress at Delhi on Dec. 26, 1918.

Presidential address to the Calcutta Session of Congress, December, 1917.

Report of the Allahabad Session of the Indian National Congress

Speech as pro Vice-chancellor in 1916.

Speech at installation of Rotary Press, the Leader, Oct. 23, 1929.

Speech of Malaviya on Foundation day of BHU in 1937 published by Aj, Feb. 22, 1937.

Speech of Sir Antony Macdonnel Published by the Government Press, Allahabad, p. 62.

Speech on the Abolition of Indentured Labour in Imperial Legislative Council.

The Maiden Speech of Malviya collected through from the Congress Report of 1886 by A.O. Hume.

II. Proceedings of the Legislative Council and Reports

Address to the BHU Court, Dec., 1921

AICC Papers

Congress Bulletin (1934-36) No. 1, Recording Proceedings of Meeting of AICC at Patana (May 18-19), May 25 1934

Congress Bulletin, 10 January 1935

Convocation address of Banaras Hindu University delivered by Mahamana Malaviya, 1929

Halifax Papers

Mahamana daily prayer written in own handwriting.

Mahamana Madan Mohan Malaviyaji ka Dharmopadesh. Printed by BHU, 1949.

Malaviya, M.M., A Criticism of Montagu-Chemsford proposal of Indian Constitutional Reforms. Printed by C.V. Chintamani at the Leader.

NAI Legislative Department Proceeding, April, 1916.

NAI, Legislative Deptt, B, Proceedings Nos. 64-65, April 1915.

Official report, NAI Home pole Secret 941-942, 1922.

Proceedings Legislative Depart. Govt. of India, Sept. 19, 1916.

Proceedings of the sessions of the Indian National Congress.

Proceedings of the U.P. Legislative Council for June 1900.

Proposed Hindu University plan dream of 1905.

Proceeding, General Department (U.P. Secretarial Records), October 1900.

Reading contemplated holding a round table conference and recommended it to the secretary of state, 1925.

Reading Papers

Reading: The First Marquis Reading II, 199.

Report dated 28th July, 1932 in N.A.I. Home poll. File No. 5/62, 1932.

Report of Indian Industrial Commission 1918 reprinted by D.B. Panday and S. Singh, *Industrial Growth and Development in India*, 2006.

Report of Indian Irrigation Commission, Visvesvaraya, M. Pandit Madan Mohan Malaviya, some personal reminiscences in 70th birth anniversary 20-commemoration volume of Malaviyaji, 1932.

Report of the Presidential Address, XXIV Indian National Congress, Lahore, Published by the leader office Allahabad, Dec., 1909.

The First BHU Prospectus "Why it is wanted and what it aims at".

The Statutory Commission Report by Pandits Madan Mohan Malaviya Published by Mr. Krisna Das Kohli at the Hindustan Times Press, Dec. 1927.

U.P. Government Proceedings, Municipal Department, November 1, 1903.

III. Newspapers and Journals

Abhyudaya

Pioneer

Pragya Journal, Vol. 21, 22 (1976, 1977)

Pragya Journal, Volume 56, Part 02 year 2010-2011

The Bombay Chronicle

The Hindu

The Hindustan Times

The Indian Review

The Leader

The Modern Review

IV. Books on Malaviya

Agarwal, V.S., *Malaviyajike Lekhaur Basan*. Varanasi: BHU Press, 1997.

Bakshi, S.R., *Madan Mohan Malaviya, The Man and his Ideology*. Varanasi: BHU, Press, 1991.

Besant, A. and Das., *Sanatan Dharma an Advanced Text Book of Hindu Religion and Ethics*. Chennai Adyar: The Theosophical Publishing House, 2000.

Bhatt, A., *Mahamana Malaviyaji*. Varanasi, 1950.

Bhatt, B.R., *Alok Purush Pt. Madan Mohan Malaviya*. Delhi: Rajesh Publication, 1990.

Chaturvedi, S., *Builders of Modern India*. New Delhi: Publication Division Ministry of Information and Broadcasting, Government of India, Patiala House, 1988.

Chaturvedi, S.R., *Mahamana Pandit Madan Mohan Malaviyaji ka Jivancharit*. Varanasi: Press publication and publicity cell BHU, 2009.

Chopra, D. *Patrakarita ke Yug Nirmata Madan Mohan Malaviya*. New Delhi: Prabhat Publication, 2008.

Dar, S.L. and Somaskandan, S., *History of Banaras Hindu University*. Varanasi: Publication cell BHU, 2007.

Dwivedi, S.K., *The Making of Malaviya*. Varanasi: Mahavir Press Behlupur, 2012.

Gahlot, S.M., *Nagari Malaviya Smriti Ank*. Varanasi: Banaras Hindu University Press, 1949.

Gajrani, S. & Ram, S., *Pandit Madan Mohan Malaviya*. New Delhi, 1922.

Gandhi, M.K., *Towards New Education*. ed. Bharatan Kumarappa, Ahmedabad: Navjivan Publishing House.

Girdhar, M., *Madan Mohan Malaviya ek Jivan Parichya*. Varanasi, 2007.

Gupta, S.L., *Pt. Madan Mohan Malaviya: A Socio-political Study*. Allahabad: Chug Publication, 1978.

Kaushik, A., *Madan Mohan Malaviya,* Delhi, 1999.

Lal, M.B., *Mahamana Madan Mohan Malaviya: Jivan aur Netritva,* Varanasi, 1978.

Maine, S.K., Panday, V. and Mauli, C.K., *Vision of Modern India Madan Mohan Malaviya*. New Delhi: Commonwealth Publication, 2012.

Mishra, J.P. *Madan Mohan Malaviya*. Delhi: Vidya Prakashan, 1987.

Panday, R., *The Making of Malaviya*. India: Kishor Vidya Niketan, 1956.

Panday, V., *Founder of Banaras Hindu Univrersity: Mahamana Pt. Madan Mohan Malaviya*. Varanasi: BHU Press, 2006.

Parmanand, *Mahamana Madan Mohan Malaviya: An Historical Biography*. Varanasi: Malaviya Adhyayan Sansthan Banaras Hindu University, 1991.

Pradhan, A., *Mahamana ke Vicharek Chayan*. Varanasi: Kabra Offset Printing Press, 2007.

Premchand, A., *Ek Mahan Siksha Sastri ke rup mai Madan Mohan Malaviya ke vicharo ka Adhyan,* Published thesis.

Rawat, P.L., *History of Education*. Bhopal: Ram Prasad & Sons, 1994.

Saran, V., *Mahamana Sri Pandit Madan Mohan Malaviyaji kay lekh aur bhasan*. Varanasi: BHU Press, 1962.

Shastri, S.K., *Mahamana Pt. Madan Mohan Malaviyaji ke do Vakavya*. Varanasi: Abhydaya Prakashan, 2000.

Shrivastav, Y.P., *Mahamana Malaviyaji*. Varanasi: Ashok Pushtak Mandir, Gyanwapi, 1961.

Shrivastav, H.C., *Campus Violence in Banaras Hindu University*. Varanasi, Allahabad: Indian International Publisher, 1974.

Sharma, C., *Mahamana Pt. Madan Mohan Malaviya*. New Delhi: Parmeshvari Prakashan, 2007.

Singh, R.P. and Shukla, R.P., *150 years of Mahamana's Service to Humanity*. New Delhi: Bharti Publication, 2012.

Singh, N.L., *Mahamana Malaviya Birth Centenary Commeration*. Varanasi: BHU Press, 1989.

Singh, Soran., *Madan Mohan Malaviya: Vyaktitva evam Krittiva*. New Delhi: Radha Publication, 1989.

Sundaram, Y.A., *Homage to Malaviyaji*, Banaras, 1949.

Sundaram, Y.A., *Mahamana Malaviyaji from the Torch Bearers*. Varanasi: Banaras Hindu University Press, 1948.

Tiwari, U.D., *Bharat Bhusan Mahamana Pt. Madan Mohan Malaviya Jivan evam Vyaktitva*. Varanasi: Banaras Hindu University Press, 1988.

Tiwari, V.N., *Mahaman Pt. Madan Mohan Malaviyaji ki Jivini*. Varanasi: Banaras Hindu University Press, 1989.

Tiwari, U.D., *A Short Biography of Mahamana Malaviya*. Varanasi: Mahamana Malaviya Foundation Varanasi, 2007.

Tiwari, U.D., *Mahamana Kay Prearakpresang: Sansmaran* Varanasi: Mahamana Malaviya Foundation, 1936.

Tiwari, U.D., *Inspiring Episode on Mahamana Pt. Madan Mohan Malaviya*. Varanasi: BHU Press, 2007.

Tripathi, R.N., *Pujaya Malaviyaji ke Saath Thees din*.

Verma, V., *Mahamana Chintan Alok*. Lucknow: Mahamana Malaviya Mission, 2001.

V. Books by other Authors

Altekar, A.S., *Education in Ancient India,* Varanasi: Manohar Prakashan, 1996.

Azad, A.K., *India Wins Freedom*, Bombay, 1959.

Banerjea, S., *A Nation in Making*, Delhi, 1963.

Besant, A., *How India Wrought for Freedom,* Adyar, 1915.

Bose, S.C., *The Indian Struggle, 1920-42*, Delhi, 1964.

Brubacher, J.S., *Modern Philosophies of Education.* New Delhi: Surjeet Publication, 1950.

Chaube, S.P., *Philosophical & Sociological Foundation of Education.* Agra: Vinod Pustak Mandir, 1999.

Chintamani, C.Y., *Indian Politics Since the Mutiny*, Waltair, 1937.

Desai, A.R., *Social Background of Indian Nationlism,* Bombay, 1954.

Ghose, S., *Rabindranath Tagore.* Delhi: Sahitya Academy, 1986.

Gopal, R., *Writings and Speeches of Sir Syed Ahmad Khan.* Bombay: Nachiketa Publication Limited.

Gordon, R., *The Hindu Mahasabha and the Indian National Congress.* United Kingdom: University of Oxford, 2005.

Indra Prakash, *A Review of the History work of the Hindu Mahasabha and the Hindu Sangathan Movement,* New Delhi, 1964.

Karmarkar, D.P., *Bal Gangadhar Tilak: A Study.* Bombay, 1956.

Kriplani, K.R., *Gandhi, Tagore and Nehru.* Bombay: Hind Kitab Limited, 1947.

Lovett, V., *A History of National Movement.* Landon, 1921.

Madan, T.N., *Modern Myths, Locked Minds (2nd ed.).* New Delhi: Oxford University Press, 2010.

Madan, T.N., *Religion in India.* USA: Oxford University Press, 2000.

Mani, R.S., *Educational Ideas & Ideals of Gandhi and Tagore*. New Delhi: New Book Society of India, 1964.

Mukherji, P., *Life of Tagore*. Translated by Sisirkumar Ghose, New Delhi: Indira Book, 1975.

Mukherji, R., *Great Speeches of Modern India*. New Delhi: Random House Publishers India Pvt. Ltd. 2007.

Naevinson, H.W., *The New Spirit in India,* Landon, 1908.

Naoroji, D., *Poverty and Unbritish Rule in India,* Delhi, 1962.

Nerhu, J. *An Autobiography*. New Delhi: Allied Publisher, 1962.

Pal, B.C., *Swadeshi and Swaraj,* Calcutta, 1954.

Panday, G. *The Construction of Communalism in Colonial North India*. New Delhi: Oxford University Press, 2006.

Rai, Lajpat, *Unhappy India*. Calcutta, 1928.

Rawat, P.L., *History of Indian Education*. Agra: Ram Prasad and Sons, 1994.

Renold, L., Hindu *Education: Early Years of Banaras Hindu University*. Oxford University Press, 2005.

Sahu, B., *The New Educational Philosophy*. New Delhi: Sarup & Sons, 2002.

Salkar, K.K., *Rabindranath Tagore his Impact on Indian Education*. New Delhi: Sterling Publisher Private Limited, 1990.

Sampurnananda, *Memories and Reflections,* Delhi, 1962.

Sharma, Y.K., *Doctrines of the Great Western Educators*. New Delhi: Kanishka Publication, 2003.

Singh, Y.K., *Sociological Foundation of Education*. New Delhi: APH Publication House, 2007.

Sinha, S., *Social Thinking of Rabindranath Tagore*. Bombay: Asia Publishing House, 1962.

Tagore, R., *My Reminiscences*. New York: The Macmillion Company, 1917.

Tagore, Rabindranath, My *School*, Viswa-Bharati, Pamphlet No. 1.

Taneja, V.R., *Educational Thought and Practice*. New Delhi: Sterling Publishers, 1983.

Tara, C., *History of Freedom Movement in India,* Vol. II, III & IV.

The Bhagavad Gita (English translation) Gorakhpur: Gita Press.

Wedderburn, William, Allan, Octatavian. *Hume: Father of Indian National Congress*, Landon, 1913.

Index